"*Better Capitalism* is an eloquent and articulate reminder of the importance of understanding economics in the context of our communities, country, and roles as business leaders. In explaining the profound connection between economics and theology, the authors have provided a strong case for the critical need for partnership between business leaders and communities to create a stronger and more robust economy that provides benefit to all."

—TONY REID
Senior vice president (retired), Marriott International

"This book plunges the reader right into the interface of theology (faith) and economics, exactly where thoughtful, responsible adults need to be situated in our crisis-marked world. Knowlton and Hedges pursue a simple paradigm of 'plantation vs. partnership.' 'Plantation' in their usage refers to a winner-take-all economics that exploits others for self-advantage. 'Partnership' concerns an economic practice of mutuality that contributes to the common good while attending to one's own interest. This simple either/or is explored in rich directions including finance, corporations, government, and culture. Along the way we get a healthy rereading of Adam Smith and Ayn Rand, away from a privatistic distortion. This book merits close, sustained attention as a compelling move beyond both careless thinking and easy ideology."

—WALTER BRUEGGEMANN
Professor, Columbia Theological Seminary

"American capitalism. We are all part of it; we all know there has to be a better way. Knowlton and Hedges reject complacency by confronting the problems with insight. They propose better ways ('Partnership Economics') with data, experience, and moral conviction; and they invite readers to tap the resources of imagination, dialogue, and courage. You may not agree with all their solutions, but this book will change how you think about your commitments and financial decisions—corporate, professional, and personal."

—R. ALAN CULPEPPER
Dean and professor emeritus, McAfee School of Theology, Mercer University

"I believe our country and world would be a better place if the principles of Partnership Economics were widely adopted. I will use this book in my personal life as I make choices about which companies I wish to support with my purchases and recommendations to family and friends."

—JULIE NYBAKKEN
Mathematics educator

"I applaud the authors' diligence and I look forward to seeing the influence on our culture that this excellent book produces. I find the work to be original and thought-provoking."

—DERIC MILLIGAN
Cofounder and CEO, Inheritance of Hope

"What an impressive, ambitious effort to tackle such weighty topics and identify and investigate a series of connective tissue between them all."

—STAN SEYMOUR
Attorney and associate pastor

"This is a great work, very timely and needed. The authors are to be commended for their efforts, ideas, and work."

—GARY SKEEN
President emeritus, CBF Church Benefits Board

"As a mid-level employee of a Fortune 500 company and a former seminarian, this was certainly relevant reading. Where a partnership approach is displayed, all kinds of growth follows!"

—AARON JARVINEN
Supply chain professional

"I was fascinated by this book and grateful that I read it. As a local church pastor, I found the topic and scope to be beyond my usual areas of interest and I might not have bought this book to add to my library. I would have missed out! The book is clearly written and accessible to those of us who do not regularly follow economics. Reading this compelling book was a good gift to my ministry."

—JAMES "DOCK"
Hollingsworth, senior pastor

Better Capitalism

Better Capitalism

Jesus, Adam Smith, Ayn Rand, and MLK Jr.
on Moving from Plantation to Partnership Economics

Paul E. Knowlton & Aaron E. Hedges

Foreword by David P. Gushee

CASCADE *Books* · Eugene, Oregon

BETTER CAPITALISM
Jesus, Adam Smith, Ayn Rand, and MLK Jr. on Moving from Plantation to Partnership Economics

Copyright © 2021 Paul E. Knowlton and Aaron E. Hedges. All rights reserved. Except for brief quotations in critical publications or reviews, no part of this book may be reproduced in any manner without prior written permission from the publisher. Write: Permissions, Wipf and Stock Publishers, 199 W. 8th Ave., Suite 3, Eugene, OR 97401.

Cascade Books
An Imprint of Wipf and Stock Publishers
199 W. 8th Ave., Suite 3
Eugene, OR 97401

www.wipfandstock.com

PAPERBACK ISBN: 978-1-7252-8093-9
HARDCOVER ISBN: 978-1-7252-8094-6
EBOOK ISBN: 978-1-7252-8095-3

Cataloguing-in-Publication data:

Names: Knowlton, Paul E., author. | Hedges, Aaron E., author. | Gushee, David P., foreword.

Title: Better capitalism : Jesus, Adam Smith, Ayn Rand, and MLK Jr. on moving from plantation to Partnership Economics / Paul E. Knowlton and Aaron E. Hedges; foreword David P. Gushee.

Description: Eugene, OR: Cascade Books, 2021 | Includes bibliographical references.

Identifiers: ISBN 978-1-7252-8093-9 (paperback) | ISBN 978-1-7252-8094-6 (hardcover) | ISBN 978-1-7252-8095-3 (ebook)

Subjects: LCSH: Capitalism, United States, Societies, etc. | Wealth—Religious aspects—Christianity. | Church work with the poor.

Classification: HB501 .B467 2021 (paperback) | HB501 (ebook)

05/11/21

To Rev. Dr. David P. Gushee—With abiding gratitude

Who as our professor taught us healing
through "transforming initiatives"

and now as our friend partners
in this transforming initiative.

Contents

Foreword by David P. Gushee | xi
Appreciations | xiii
Introduction and Warning | xv

Part 1: Problems on Our Plantations—*Re-Viewing* Economics | 1

Chapter 1: **Relentless—Vision, Rules, and Reality** | 3
    Something New Under the Sun | 3
    All Economic Exchanges Involve Frictional Costs | 7
    Exchanges That Merely Transfer/Extract Existing Value from One Party to Another Result in a Net Loss Once Frictional Costs are Considered | 8
    Exchanges That Create Value Beyond Frictional Costs for All Parties Involved Result in a Net Gain | 9
    As a Whole, We Receive the Average Net Result of all Exchanges | 11
    We Gain from Net-Positive Economic Exchanges and Lose from Net-Negative Economic Exchanges | 13
    Recap and Restatement of the Relentless Rules of Economics | 14
    Nothing is Certain but . . . | 14

Chapter 2: **Homo Economicus—Economic Human** | 17
    Not Walking Calculators | 17
    What God Has Joined, Let No One Separate | 18
    Ignorance is Bliss? | 20

Chapter 3: **Our Corporate Work Isn't Working** | 25
    It Smells Like Money to Me | 25
    The Responsibilities of Rights | 28
    Problem 1: All for One, but Not One for All | 30
    Problem 2: Too Big, Too Failed | 32

Problem 3: By Any Means Necessary | 34
   Three Modes of Moral Reasoning | 35
   A Merely Goal-Based Approach | 38
   FBUs: Of the Money, by the Money, and for the Money | 40
   Relentless Rules Reminder | 41

Chapter 4: **So What?** | 42
   Necessity is the Mother of Invention | 42
   Another Way is Possible | 43
   More to the Dream—Martin Luther King Jr. | 44
   A Clearer Vision | 46

Part 2: The Promise of Partnership—*Re-Thinking* Economics | 51

Chapter 5: **A Step Closer to an Old Dream** | 53
   An Edifice Which Produces Beggars Needs Restructuring | 54
   Finding the Highest Good Through Love | 55
   Homo Hermeneuticus—Interpreting Human | 56
   Relentless Rules Reminder | 57

Chapter 6: **In God We Trust** | 58
   Hebrew Bible | 58
   Re-Thinking Jesus Preview | 63
   Sermon on the Mount | 63
   From Above | 66
   From Below | 69
   Better Together | 73
   From God the Father to Another Father | 74
   Re-Thinking Jesus Recap | 75

Chapter 7: **The Father of Capitalism—Adam Smith** | 76
   Re-Thinking Adam Smith Preview | 76
   Moral Sentiments | 77
   Invisible Hand-Wringing | 77
   The Hand of the Impartial Spectator | 79
   Leave Laissez-Faire Alone | 82
   The Mutuality of Nations | 84
   Re-Thinking Adam Smith Recap | 87

Chapter 8: **The Mother of Capitalism—Ayn Rand** | 88
    Re-Thinking Ayn Rand Preview | 89
    The Utopia? | 90
    The Speech | 91
    The Power of a Conjunction | 94
    Re-Thinking Ayn Rand Recap | 97
    Where Do We Go from Here? | 98

Chapter 9: **The Partnership Economic Ethic** | 99
    God Provides and We Partner | 100
    To Partner is to Seek Mutual Benefit | 101
    Mutual Benefit is Created by Engaging in Exchanges That are Profitable for Our Self *and* the Other—Pursuing Our Economic Neighbor's Interest *and* Our Self-Interest | 102
    Corporately Our Purpose is to Sustain Profitability for All Stakeholders | 104
    Recap | 105

Chapter 10: **Our Corporate Work, Working!** | 107
    Practically Ideal | 108
    Improvement 1: All for One, and One for All | 111
    Improvement 2: More than Maximized | 113
    Improvement 3: Justified Ends *and* Means | 113
    Of the People, by the People, for the People | 120
    Relentless Rules and Partnership Economic Ethic Reminder | 122

Part 3: Putting Partnership into Practice—*Re-Living Economics* | 125

Chapter 11: **What the Powers of the Country Will Kill You For** | 127
    Homo Agens—Acting Human | 127
    Caveat Lector—Let the Reader Beware | 128
    Caveat Emptor—Let the Buyer Beware—New Normals | 130

Chapter 12: **The Rubber Meets the Road—Companies** | 135
    Building to Last | 135
    What is Enough? | 138
    The Devil is in the Details | 142
    Partnership Has a Price | 145

Above Board | 148
Pensions—We Should Reap What We Sow | 152
Educational Companies | 156
Arbitrary Arbitration | 161
A Reader's Response | 166

Chapter 13: **The Rubber Meets the Road—Government** | 169
Short and Sweet or Less is More | 169
Not-Special Interests | 172
Partnership Rules Apply to Rule-Makers, Too | 177
Clear, Consistent, Broad Fiduciary Standard | 180
Predatory Lending—When Medicine Becomes Poison | 182
Tax Modifications | 185
We Have Antitrust Laws—Enforce Them! | 189
Public-Private "Partnerships"—Field of Schemes | 197

Chapter 14: **The Rubber Meets the Road—Professions** | 201
Classical Professions | 201
Financial Professions—Truly Mutual Funds | 204
Trusted Trustees? Beginning the World Anew | 207
Meet the Press | 210

Chapter 15: **The Rubber Meets the Road—Culture** | 214
Eating Strategy for Breakfast | 214
We Are They! | 217
Enough—the Household Version | 219
False Idols and False Rewards | 224
Too Easily Satisfied vs Transformational | 227
Comparative Advantage vs Community Advantage | 230
No Such Thing as Passive Partners | 232

Chapter 16: **So What? Where Do We Go from Here?** | 235
Relentless Rules and Partnership Economic Ethic Reminder | 235
Simple but Not Easy | 236
Not Easy but Worthwhile | 238
How Does the Story End? | 240

Recommended Further Reading | 243

Bibliography | 245

Foreword

David P. Gushee[1]
Past President, American Academy of Religion
Past President, Society of Christian Ethics

BETTER CAPITALISM IS AN extraordinary creative achievement, without parallel in the literature of economic and business ethics, Christian or otherwise. Paul Knowlton, JD, MDiv, and Aaron Hedges, MBA, MDiv, here engage pretty much the entire landscape of modern economic life with a realistic but values-rich challenge to move beyond what they call *plantation economics* and instead move to what they call *Partnership Economics*.

In three sections, Paul and Aaron review the state of our economic life, rethink its values and practices, and then propose practical initiatives to "relive" pretty much every substantial sector of personal, corporate, and governmental economic affairs.

When Aaron and Paul first approached me about helping to support the development of this project through the Mercer Center for Theology and Public Life, I had no idea that it would grow into the magnificent work that it has finally become.

I first knew these men as seminary students whom I had the privilege to teach at Mercer University here in Atlanta.

Aaron came to graduate school with extensive nonprofit and business experience. He also arrived equipped with a tremendous mind for moral theory, further evidenced by his graduating top of the class in both the MDiv and MBA programs. He has lived the organizational life from first paid employee of an entrepreneurial start-up to chief operating officer as the organization has grown to serve families from forty-five states. Aaron has consulted for small businesses and served in multicultural ministries

---

1. Rev. Dr. David P. Gushee is the Distinguished University Professor of Christian Ethics; Director, Center for Theology & Public Life, Mercer University.

ranging from sports camps for urban youth to church planting in Andean Bolivia.

Paul arrived with an unusually broad and diverse background, beginning with his start as a first generation Cuban-American and some years as a foster child. His engineering undergraduate degree equipped him with the ability to imagine and build physically, as well as opportunities to advance rapidly through his chosen corporate career. Paul's legal training and experience has gifted him with analytical skills to deconstruct and reconstruct. To his foundations of engineering, law, and business he has added insights from his seminary training, for a truly interdisciplinary approach to every question.

Both possess a piercing curiosity and practical intellect that made the very most of every educational opportunity I could help offer to them. Since seminary days, these friends have continued their respective trajectories, advancing professionally while seeking both greater understanding of and better possibilities for our society. Now they have brought their research and real-world experience together to produce this extraordinary manifesto about economic life.

One of the things I like most about *Better Capitalism* is the way it shoots the gap between our current cultural extremes: it is by no means a defense of laissez-faire capitalism but neither is it a socialist manifesto. It applies biblical values to economic life but not in any kind of pie-in-the-sky way. The book is chock full of fresh and deep research, and this data then informs the book's realistic, concrete reform proposals that corporate executives, government officials, and everyday people can implement.

One of the greatest joys of being a scholar occurs when you see your students absorb, engage, critique, and then transform your best ideas into their better ideas. I know that my dear friend Glen Stassen, who died in 2014, would be more than thrilled to see this book, because it builds on key insights that he and I developed in our work *Kingdom Ethics*. I love to be able to reveal here the fact that the "three modes of moral reasoning" model in chapter 3 was developed by Aaron as a creative refinement of a more primitive paradigm that Glen Stassen and I offered in our first edition of *Kingdom Ethics*. As well, the treatment of Matthew 6:19–34 by Aaron and Paul in chapter 6 is in my view an advance on what Stassen and I were able to do in our own treatment of this text in *Kingdom Ethics*. And so on. What a thrill to see this!

I commend this work to you as a breakthrough contribution by important new voices in the field of economic ethics. To have played a part in helping make this work possible is a proud achievement.

Appreciations

Indeed, it takes a village.

Starting with our initial village at the Atlanta, Georgia campus of Mercer University, we are grateful to Rev. Dr. Jeff Willetts. You struck the match that lit our flame for re-envisioning and transforming capitalism. To Rev. Dr. David Gushee, we are grateful that you protected and fanned that flame. And to Kelli Appel, Esq., Nancy Merphad, and Greg DeLoach, we are grateful for the incubator space to innovate and write.

To Al Perreca, we are grateful for your early and tangible encouragement. To Stephen Reeves we are grateful for your early and quick support of our writing through your willingness to share your own. To Stu Rees, we are proud to include your illustrations and appreciate your easy collaboration.

To our advance readers Joe Coleman, Russell and Dana Hedges, James "Dock" Hollingsworth, Aaron Jarvinen, Deric Milligan, Julie Nybakken, Marylee and Bob Putnam, Stan Seymour, Gary Skeen, Marta Knowlton, and Lance Wallace: thank you for your thoughtful and thorough feedback to help us improve the book's substance and style. We are humbled by and deeply grateful for your time, care, and candor reviewing our work. Thank you for the significant ways, as well as many small yet meaningful ones, that you have made this book as well as our ongoing work better. Numerous strengths of the book are thanks to you; its shortcomings are entirely our own.

To our respective wives, Amy and Allison, you are partners *par excellence*. We are indebted to you for your patience with us throughout this project and throughout our lives. We love you.

To Aaron's young kids, my joyful appreciation to Estella, Theodore, and Jack, without whose great affection and encouragement this book would have been completed much faster.

To the Cascade team, we are grateful for the care and attention of Michael Thomson, Rodney Clapp, Shannon Carter, Ian Creeger, James Stock, and others behind the scenes.

Introduction and Warning

"In my lifetime I have freed thousands of slaves, and I would have freed thousands more if they only knew they were slaves."
—source uncertain, but sometimes attributed to Harriet Tubman

PAUL FIRST HEARD THE phrase "the truth will make you free" in his public school fourth grade history class. The teacher was patiently introducing Dr. Martin Luther King Jr., and the civil rights movement he helped launch and lead. Perhaps because her voice quivered as she repeated the phrase and Paul paid more attention for a moment, those words have since indelibly rung in his ears if not, too, in his spirit.

Fast forward a couple of eventful decades to law school, where in a First Amendment and individual liberties lecture the constitutional law professor was explaining the most likely origin of that phrase for Dr. King was the Bible's Gospel of John. That made sense; Dr. King was a seminary-trained Christian minister and he used biblical references and imagery as source material for his writing and speeches.

The challenge of rehearing and considering that familiar phrase through the crosshairs of new legal training, however, was that it now felt incomplete. Paul could not set aside a pressing sense of urgency to determine, there and then, why it was now lacking. He mentally lost much of that lecture contemplating myriad lessons and attendant scars around pursuits of truth and freedom.

Finally, a memory of a woman's TV voice fought its way through to emerge with a gift: "The truth may set you free, but first it will piss you off." Paul wryly smiled and nodded to himself as he connected that voice and sentiment to Gloria Steinem, who is usually credited with originating that quip. Indeed, being jarred or ticked when confronted with an unexpected truth is frequently the lived experience, because if we're willing to engage the truth the next step is toward growth, and growth involves pain. We suspect it was Dr. King's and Ms. Steinem's lived experiences as well, especially when engaging capitalism and economics.

Economics affect virtually every aspect of our society, from cradle to grave and beyond. Cradles are not free, after all, and those of higher quality tend to cost more. Economic considerations persist even beyond death, as either economic blessing or debt is left for the survivors. Nor are economics constrained to individual lives. Every collective entity—from a dating couple to the United Nations—must navigate economic realities. This universality calls to mind another time an economic truth tried to set Paul free.

A law firm where he was an associate was hosting an annual meeting and all the attorneys were in attendance. During a breakout session with the managing partner, whom we designate here simply as Mr. X, the conversation turned to the executive committee's decision to raise attorney salaries. The raises were, of course, accompanied by a mandatory increase in the associate billing requirements to cover those raises and increase profits for the partners. Stressed associates began peppering Mr. X with questions about how they were to achieve work-life balance, an emerging concern in the legal industry. Mr. X appeared increasingly frustrated as he responded to questions.

Paul did not expect that conversation to resolve anything, so he stole a glance at his newly acquired Rolex to see how much time was left before lunch. He was still admiring his trophy when Mr. X landed his short and fateful defense. "Look," he exhaled to the group, "the practice of law is a plantation system, and you're all very well paid."

The conversation was over then and there, and the phrase "plantation system" immortalized in Paul's memory, if not too his spirit, by the image of him simultaneously admiring his Rolex and realizing it was the very evidence of Mr. X's defense. Paul had just been sucker-punched by a truth that ticked him off. His usual response to this kind of situation is to explore and understand, so over the next several weeks he gave Mr. X's words serious thought.

There was no evidence or reason to understand Mr. X's plantation system revelation as race-based or limited to the American slavery experience. Paul knew Mr. X as a student of history and as someone too intelligent and sophisticated not to intend a significant meaning. No, his comment was more far-reaching. This may be a difficult position for some not present during that comment to accept, especially in light of America's painful race relations, so we'll share why it carries a different weight.

Introduction and Warning

Plantation systems in the western hemisphere began with Spain, which wasted no time introducing and establishing plantation mentality and systems—asset exploitation, domination, and accumulation—in the Caribbean islands right after Christopher Columbus's 1492 voyage. The Spaniards' first exploitation was of the enslaved Indigenous people. Spain and her investors were benefiting from the raw goods harvested and minerals mined, but the forced labor supply was quickly dwindling.

Historians suggest the likely reason King Charles I changed policy in August 1518 and authorized Spain to ship enslaved Africans directly to the Caribbean was because the enslaved Indigenous peoples were dying from European diseases and colonial violence.[2] The Spaniards needed to exploit lots of laborers in order to exploit the newly found other half of the creation, and their labor market was primarily Africans turned into slaves. Once firmly established in the Caribbean islands, this exploitative method of capital and asset accumulation spread south, west, and north. By the eighteenth century plantation systems operated on every continent, exploiting natural resources and people of every skin color. Despite the abolition of chattel slavery, plantation systems continue around the world to this day in endless variations, as we'll explore in Part 1.

Mr. X's plantation statement meant something beyond race both because of that larger historical context and the immediate setting. While a small handful of attorneys at that retreat could claim a minority racial status, such as Paul with his first-generation Spanish-Cuban heritage, as a whole they were lily White. Paul needed to continue wrestling with Mr. X's plantation system revelation until he found the significant meaning.

He began to piece together the meaning, or at least uncover the primary clues that would lead him to understanding the truth behind the sucker punch. First, Mr. X was a corporate attorney—a practice of law wherein you fight for and protect every advantage possible for the corporate client, typically a favorite kind of client because it timely pays its invoices. Second, Paul recalled from his corporations law course being introduced, like legions of lawyers before him, to the axiom: "The primary responsibility of the corporation is to maximize shareholder value." Third, while the business forms of law firms vary, the larger ones typically function very much like corporations. Taken together Paul found the significant meaning—the gateway to a painful truth for those associates: they were working in a corporate setting, and they were not shareholders.

Now he understood. Although more than a little embarrassed that it took him so long, Paul connected his head knowledge (he knew who he was

---

2. Little, "Details," para. 3.

and his function) and situational awareness (he knew where he worked and how he earned his money) to the reality of his lived experience—all those associates were just plainly told to work harder to make wealthy people wealthier, no matter the personal cost or collateral damage. Those personal costs and collateral damages were noticeably accelerating through attorney ranks in firms across the country, starting with the toll on physical and mental health, and increasingly expanding to include divorce and suicide.

Now Paul *really* understood: the plantation system model was the playbook of virtually every corporation across our country. His Rolex was losing its luster as a hidden-in-plain-sight economic truth was trying to set him free. How did he not see the plantation system earlier? He had spent all of his career to that point in a corporate setting. He felt as foolish as a fish that when asked, "How's the water?" ignorantly responds, "What's water?" Once he realized that he was fully immersed, if not baptized and drowned, in a plantation system—no matter his role or compensation, his work was exploited and controlled by others—he asked himself whether he was curious enough to unflinchingly seek an accurate understanding of how America's version of capitalism evolved and is currently practiced.

Paul sensed that if he responded wholeheartedly in the affirmative, instead of accepting the status quo, he would have to go foundationally deep and systematically broad with intellectual honesty. Deep, broad, and honest not merely to comprehend, as if he had the luxury to pour himself into a purely theoretical pursuit, but to discover, develop, and articulate practical and effective correctives. It is not enough to be pissed; that energy must be purposefully harnessed and directed to thinking and acting that offer tangible solutions. Otherwise, the truth never gets the legs and lungs it needs to carry us through the journey to freedom.

Who are You?

"Who are you? Who, who, who, who?"
—Pete Townshend

You care, and you are open-minded. You care about something that matters to many people's lives: perhaps commerce, or work, or money, or morality, or religion, or spirituality. And while you care deeply about at least one of these things, you are open-minded about the others and how they matter to many people's lives. Whether your greater interest is business or faith, or you have great interest in both, as someone with a stake in our society,

Introduction and Warning

you care enough to keep an open mind about both realms and how they intersect.

Unfortunately, these realms have not been intersecting very often, at least not on good terms, in our current experience of capitalism. Business leaders and faith leaders often have a gap, if not a gulf, between them. This is a failure we all suffer from. Each camp can benefit from better interaction with the other, and together we can better benefit society as a whole.

What might an effective bridge between the business and faith camps look like? We find a helpful analogy in what engineers call a bascule bridge (from the French work "level" and illustrated below).[3] The rest of us call this a drawbridge.

Most simply stated, each leaf (side or half) of a bascule bridge is pivotally connected at one end and rotated as needed to be raised or lowered. When the leaves are raised, as illustrated here, the deck or roadway is disconnected and passage is impossible between the sides. Interestingly, when standing on a lowered leaf and looking at the other leaf fully raised, the raised leaf resembles an impenetrable barricade not unlike the drawbridges of medieval times lifted to barricade a castle under attack. When both leaves are fully lowered they connect; a contiguous bridge is created and passage between the sides is possible. You can see where the analogy is going.

Professionally and personally, you have experienced a drawbridge scenario. At times you have been a leaf lowered, trying to connect with the other leaf to form a bridge for mutual benefit. At times you have been a leaf raised—intentionally or unintentionally, you've been unable to connect with another leaf. Through our training and experience, your authors each stand with one foot squarely in the world of business and the other squarely

---

3 "Draw Bridge" by buldg216 is licensed with CC BY-ND 2.0.; https://search.creativecommons.org/photos/cf904b03-97f8-4c28-bc0c-1175ed205b4d.

in the world of faith, and with that posture we find that these two communities can be bridged for the immense benefit of both. This posture has greatly benefited us and those we have led in our interdisciplinary roles of entrepreneur, business owner, minister, director, partner, COO, and CEO, as well as in our biggest roles of husband and dad.

If you understand or may even be motivated by the analogy of the drawbridge, this book is for you. What would it look like for you to lower your leaf and connect with others for mutual benefit? What would it feel like to walk across lowered leaves and share insights with the other side? What might result from you and others collaborating in new ways, ways that were not possible with either leaf raised? What might be the second- and third-degree effects, and who might be the multitudes benefited through your new collaborations? How excited might you get by learning that sophisticated drawbridges have multiple leaves that extend in different directions, not unlike people, providing even greater opportunity for connections that open possibilities to even more collaboration and benefit?

If these are adventures that resonate with you, then you, our friend, should read on.

What's in it for You?

With apologies to Winston Churchill—"Capitalism is the worst form of economics, except for all those other forms that have been tried from time to time . . ."

At some point in your business life you have looked up from the task or person in front of you, paused before your head explodes, and thought to yourself, "There's got to be a better way!"[4] We've been there, too. Perhaps one of those times was a plantation system moment of discontent trying to point you to a truth. Perhaps one of those times was a truth trying to set you free.

So what are the benefits of this book to you? This book offers you that better way. Whether you are in school preparing for the world of work or have experienced multiple careers, whether you make decisions that affect others or are affected by others' decisions as their employee or customer, whether you are part of a multinational corporation or a small business or a ministry or a government, we submit that you are directly

---

4. Ever called a company and been put on a "brief" hold, or offered the perfect solution during a staff meeting only to be told "that's not the way we do it here"?

Introduction and Warning

or indirectly affected by plantation systems. We offer you the more profitable—beneficial—viewing, thinking, and living of capitalism through what we term "Partnership Economics." This book adds value for you across the full landscape of capitalism and the bridged worlds of business and faith.

In Part 1 we introduce and survey the contours of the plantation system perspective that Mr. X referenced. This is a ***re-viewing*** of our economics, specifically present American corporate economics. "Corporate" in our context is not limited to mean the legal status of a business entity, but more broadly includes every multi-person organization. From the insights of behavioral economics, we offer awareness of our situation and see it as it truly is, in order to realize the need for change. The truth begins to make us free only if the truth is known. And the intersecting economic and theological truth is that corporate plantation systems are deeply flawed and destructive for all involved—including Mr. X.

Not all is doom and gloom, though. Hardly. We end Part 1 with the question, "What might it look like if business leaders like Mr. X were true to their title of 'partner' and willing to do business in a better way?" Not only is change possible, but because capitalism reinvents itself every few decades, the timing is right to begin guiding it into its next better version.

In Part 2 we develop a profitable (in the fullest sense of the word) better version—an alternative to plantation economics, which is Partnership Economics. This is a ***re-thinking*** of economics. Beyond mere awareness that there is a problem, interpretation and understanding of this awareness are needed. The truth further moves to make us free when the truth is known *and* understood. Floods of economic (mis)information require a sound interpretive framework to yield understanding of better economic possibilities. We find partnership[5] to be the key to such a framework and trace the thread of partnership in economics from Jesus to Adam Smith and more recently to Ayn Rand and Martin Luther King Jr., with strong support from John Bogle.

You do not have to be an expert on economics, law, ethics, or theology to join this journey—you just need to care about and be open to the possibility of a better way of life. Experts are welcome, too, of course. However you arrive, the challenge is to be "curious enough to unflinchingly seek an accurate understanding of how America's version of capitalism evolved and is currently practiced." This part also contains our constructive proposal for an economic ethic centered on partnership. Partnership Economics are

---

5. We use and intend the word *partnership* throughout this book to mean a relational sense of mutuality and mutual benefit. We do not use or intend the word *partnership* in the legal sense of meaning a particular type of entity status (e.g., LLP), unless we clearly make that distinction.

more profitable for more people for more time, more morally sturdy, and more life-giving than the current destructive, dehumanizing norm.

Part 3 is where the rubber meets the road. This is a ***re-living*** of economics. For awareness and understanding to be valuable, they must result in action. The truth fully makes us free only when the truth is known, understood, *and* enacted. This admittedly is the most difficult section—the hard work is in the details, the details of how an ethic is put into practice. This also is the most important section, precisely because it dares to provide specific, actionable[6] guidance. We explain and provide concrete examples of how to implement the better way of Partnership Economics, and we strive to make our proposals clear and actionable. They may prove hard, however, simply because they will require courage. Partnership Economics guidance is centered on corporations but extends from individuals (who, paradoxically, must take personal responsibility to partner with others in corporate forms) to governments and culture (which influence and are influenced by corporations). Join us in doing battle to heal.

The Invitation, the Warning

"Fight for the things that you care about, but do it in a way that will lead others to join you."

—Ruth Bader Ginsburg

Really—join us! We invite your collaboration, critiques, questions, comments, ideas, etc. at info@partnershipeconomics.com. We look forward to hearing from you and moving the conversation and action forward together.

As corporations drive not only American economics but, increasingly, American society, we are all stakeholders in the present and future of capitalism. Shifting from plantation systems to Partnership Economics, in thinking and acting, will be deeply challenging—but ultimately worthwhile.

---

6. We use and intend the word *actionable* throughout this book in the business sense of meaning information that enables a decision to be made or action to be taken. We refer to suggestions and recommendations as "actionable" because they are capable of being put into practice. We do not use or intend the word *actionable* in the legal sense of meaning "giving rise to or cause for legal action."

More than worthwhile, we contend this shift is necessary if we all are to truly grow, economically, and ethically.[7]

The economic story is neither finished nor predetermined. We have the choice, the opportunity, and the necessity to grow beyond plantation systems corporately, as partners. Will the economic truth make you, all of us, free? We invite you to be curious enough to partner with us in finding out. Fair warning, though—parts may anger or piss you off.

---

7. We wrote these words before the COVID-19 pandemic and the related global economic slowdown and further exposure of so many flaws in our current form of capitalism. Since then the urgency for a better capitalism has only increased.

Part 1

Problems on Our Plantations —*Re-Viewing* Economics

"To understand the hidden secret of the modern industrial world in which I find myself, I have to return to another world. The world is at once wartime Nice[8] and the plantation—the sugar isles on which Europe's prosperity was built."

—J. M. G. Le Clezio

PLANTATION ECONOMICS IS ONE person or group destructively exploiting or wielding control over another and/or resources.

A plantation system is any human construct that creates and/or permits inequities in support of plantation economics.

In this Part 1 we introduce and survey the contours of the corporate plantation system perspective illustrated in the Introduction. This is a *re-viewing* of our economics, specifically present American corporate economics. From the insights of behavioral economics, we gain awareness of our situation, see it as it truly is, in order to realize the need and advantage for change. At the intersection of economic and theological understanding is the truth that our present corporate plantation systems are deeply flawed and destructive for all involved, including those at the very top. The need for change becomes unmistakable.

The first step is admitting we have a problem.

---

8. The Italian beachfront city where the Resistance launched a surprise attack and liberated it from Nazi occupation.

Chapter 1

Relentless—Vision, Rules, and Reality

"For a while he trampled with impunity on laws human and divine; but, as he was obsessed with the delusion that two and two make five, he fell, at last, a victim to the relentless rules of humble arithmetic."

—Louis Brandeis

Something New Under the Sun

IN 1951, TWENTY-ONE-YEAR-OLD PRINCETON economics student John Bogle wrote a thesis on something he had never heard of before—the fledgling mutual fund industry. His two premises were that mutual funds do not generate returns higher than market averages and that the fees and expenses of mutual funds were too high. He concluded, "Future growth can be maximized by concentration on a reduction of sales loads and management fees."[9]

Bogle's work drew the attention of the founder of the Wellington Fund, who hired him. By 1965 he was executive vice president of Wellington Management Company. By 1966 he was CEO. By 1974, he was . . . fired. The bear markets of 1973–1974 and resulting poor funds performance led to disputes and Bogle's ouster.

---

9. Burton, "Opinion," para. 9.

In Bogle's words, he was "fired with enthusiasm." "Our challenge at the time was to build, out of the ashes of major corporate conflict, a new and better way of running a mutual fund complex."[10] In 1975 Bogle launched not just a new company but a new kind of company. This was to be a mutual *company*—it would operate "mutual" funds with true mutuality, keeping costs low so fund investors would benefit along with fund managers. This new vision was named Vanguard.

In 1976, Bogle led Vanguard to launch the first index fund, a new kind of investment that tracked the returns of a full index of market stocks, and did so at the lowest possible costs. Industry veterans greeted the innovation as "Bogle's Folly," "un-American," and "a sure path to mediocrity." Bogle was relentless and pressed on with the expectation of opening his index fund with $150M in assets. Investors greeted the opportunity with just $11M.

Bogle still was convinced his new vision was right. "What I'm battling for—building our nation's financial system anew, in order to give our citizen/investors a fair shake—is right. Mathematically right. Philosophically right. Ethically right."[11]

And right it was. "Bogle's Folly" has been relentlessly gaining steam for more than forty years and is now the largest issuer of mutual funds in the world. It has more than $5 *trillion* under management. If only we could all be so foolish.

Not only have millions of Vanguard customers benefited immensely from its thoroughly mutual nature, but its once-radical, low-cost, passively managed index funds have been mimicked throughout the fund industry. Broadly diversified funds with low costs that deliver fair, market-level returns have made compounding wealth dramatically more accessible for people around the world—and the fund companies have done just fine, too. Bogle had a "foolish" vision, put it into practice with a company, and transformed an entire industry and millions upon millions of lives.[12] He changed the world. If only our world had more such foolishness.

Bogle innovated in both theory and practice from the mutual fund to the mutual company—Vanguard is owned by its funds, which are owned by their shareholders, so Vanguard effectively is owned by its customers. Whatever benefits the company benefits the customers and vice versa. The main way this plays out at Vanguard is that the company charges low fees (only the costs involved in running the company), and increasingly many

10. Buckley, "Life of Vanguard's Founder," para. 6.
11. Buckley, "Life of Vanguard's Founder," para. 20.
12. In 1979, the median cost to purchase a fund was 8.5% (https://www.sec.gov/news/studies/feestudy.htm#item10). If you've ever paid less than that to invest in a fund, with any brokerage, you have John Bogle to thank.

customer-owners invest there because of those low fees. The customer-owners get their fair share of market returns, and the company gets a growing number of pleased customer-owners. This is an outstanding and now time-tested example of partnership.

We are innovating in both theory and practice for a mutual *economy*—not just a fund, not "just" a company (even one as successful and influential as Vanguard), not "just" an industry, but an entire economy and culture of mutuality and mutual benefit. This is no small undertaking, we realize, but it is a worthwhile one, and regardless of the odds, we have to start somewhere. Bogle himself urged, "Our ownership society is gone and will not return. Our agency society has failed to serve its principals, as corporate managers and fund managers alike have placed their own interests above the interests of their beneficiaries and owners. It is time to begin the world anew, and build a fiduciary society in which stewardship is our talisman."[13]

Expanding Bogle's "stewardship" in finance to a broader economic vision, we say "partnership." It is time to "begin the world anew," with partnership as the foundational principle. To that end we are also guided by the wisdom of the inventor and futurist Buckminster Fuller, a contemporary of Bogle's, who wrote, "You never change things by fighting the existing reality. To change something, build a new model that makes the existing model obsolete."[14] Our intention here is not merely to critique existing modes and ethics of capitalism but to constructively present theory and practice (together a disruptive technology) for an approach that is more profitable in the fullest sense.

Bogle is also instructive in the difficult realities involved with implementing such vision. His concepts and company were initially derided as foolish, guarantees of mediocrity, even un-American. Reflecting on the many criticisms, Bogle offered great perspective: "So it's also clear that it is a disruptive technology. And it works, but any time you try to introduce a new idea, first it's it'll never work. Then, it'll work but only for a short time. Then, the guy's really lucky. And finally, you know, he's right."[15]

The early difficulties and derision did make that full progression to achievement and acclaim. Revered economist Paul Samuelson put it this way in 2005: "I rank this Bogle invention along with the invention of the wheel, the alphabet, Gutenberg printing, and wine and cheese: a mutual fund that never made Bogle rich but elevated the long-term returns of the mutual-fund owners. Something new under the sun." (For clarity,

---

13. Bogle, *Don't Count On It*, 96.
14. Fuller as quoted at https://www.goodreads.com/quotes/13119.
15. Gardner, "Jack Bogle," para. 13.

Samuelson's reference to "never made Bogle rich" must be taken as relative to other financial industry titans. In Bogle's own words in his book *Enough*, his wealth was "just this side of astonishing."[16])

Part of Bogle's genius was the ability to boil down the essence of his entire approach to Brandeis-inspired "relentless rules of humble arithmetic"—short and sweet, factual statements about the fundamental realities of investment math. This is a formulation that is substantive enough to create conviction that lasts through hard times (and has been proven quite right over and over) while also being brief. Relentless rules can be conveyed quickly and convincingly. They put ideals into a form with immense practical value for both communication and implementation.

Relentless rules cut through ideology; they are not opinions but rules that simply "are." Even those who may not share certain ideals have to reckon with the logic of "the relentless rules of humble [investment] arithmetic." They cut through large and potentially complex matters as well as long-held misconceptions to make sense of it all in a way that is broadly understandable and actionably helpful. With brevity, they create shared understanding of ideas and, the opportunity at least, for shared actions based on those understandings.

Bogle's death, as this book was being written, is a deep loss. However, we can honor him and even expand upon his impact by bringing his "common sense" and mutual approach more into being. A fitting place to start is with our observation of the *relentless rules* of economics.

1. All economic exchanges involve frictional costs.
2. Exchanges that merely transfer/extract existing value from one party to another result in a net loss once frictional costs are considered.
3. Exchanges that create value beyond frictional costs for all parties involved result in a net gain.
4. As a whole, we receive the average net result of all exchanges.
5. We gain from net-positive economic exchanges and lose from net-negative economic exchanges.

---

16. Batnick, "Bogle's Big Mistake," para. 20.

All Economic Exchanges Involve Frictional Costs

Frictional costs simply mean the costs of the time, energy, money, and/or other resources that are needed to perform the exchange. No exchange "just happens"; there is always some cost involved.

A purchaser of a good or service not only spends money on their purchase—they also spend time on it. Purchasing an item for $10 after an hour of comparison-shopping time and energy is more costly than purchasing the same item for $10 with only a minute of shopping time and effort. Try as we might to reduce the time and effort needed to make a purchase, they are never completely eliminated. No transaction, not even online impulse shopping, happens outside the flow of time and completely without effort to make the purchase, so no transaction happens without those frictional costs.

If the purchaser goes somewhere to make their purchase, they incur a transportation cost. If the purchaser has their purchase shipped to them instead, the transportation cost is still there in the form of shipping, which must be paid by either the buyer or the seller.

The company that produces that good or service exchanges compensation for work by its employees, but the employees' commuting involves costs that are either not compensated for the employee, or paid for but not productive for the employer. Telecommuting requires connectivity over networks that are not free with devices that have shipping costs on top of the actual product costs. Both devices and the networks connecting them require ongoing maintenance.

The old line says that the only certainties are death and taxes. Taxes are a frictional cost. Taxes (on income, sales, property, capital gains, etc.) and transactional fees (on financial transactions, credit card purchases, bank accounts that hold our cash, etc.) are pervasive frictional costs that aren't likely to disappear. Even if we could theoretically remove these human-made transactional costs, other frictional costs from the physical realities of time and energy needed to enact transactions remain.

As long as we live in space and time, frictional costs *are* as certain as death. Space requires energy to navigate each exchange, and time waits for no one and no exchange. Just as surely as all physical movements involve some loss of energy due to physical friction, all economic exchanges involve some loss of value due to frictional costs.

Exchanges That Merely Transfer/Extract Existing Value from One Party to Another Result in a Net Loss Once Frictional Costs are Considered

The notion of a "zero-sum game" is often used to describe exchanges in which value is transferred from one party to another. "Zero-sum" indicates that the total value involved did not change—one side gained and one side lost, without total value increasing or decreasing.

Unfortunately, this is not true. Because every exchange has frictional costs, transferring value from one party to another has frictional costs, so the value is decreased when it is transferred. The exchange does not have simply a winner and a loser; one side loses value in the exchange, the other side gains—*and both* sides suffer frictional costs.

If $10 is exchanged from Person A to Person B over the course of five minutes, the total value involved is no longer just $10, it is $10 minus a combined ten minutes. What superficially appears to be a zero-sum game is in fact a negative-sum game. Even the "winner," Person B, lost five minutes, a cost that diminishes the value of what he or she won.

If exchanges were truly zero-sum games, then they could be done back and forth with the sum of the value remaining unchanged. Continuing the example, the $10 could be exchanged back from Person B to Person A after another five minutes. Would this mean everything was reset, and both Person A and Person B would be exactly as they had started? No. They both have the same number of dollars that they started with, but they both have spent (lost) ten minutes.

In real life, no two (sane) people would spend an entire day passing $10 back and forth and pretend that this was a zero-sum activity. The loss of the time and energy would be obvious. We must also dismiss the insanity of pretending that any exchange that merely transfers value from one person to another is zero-sum.

Viewing transfers of value as zero-sum games, while ignoring frictional costs, is like carrying a rock up a hill and saying it's still the same rock. Of course it's the same rock, but the act of transferring it takes a toll. Transfers of existing value involve a loss of value once frictional costs are considered.

Exchanges That Create Value Beyond Frictional Costs for All Parties Involved Result in A Net Gain

Economic exchanges are not limited to mere transfers of existing value. Exchanges can create value for all parties involved. These are called "positive-sum games" because the value involved changes positively.

For instance, suppose that eating exactly one apple and one orange a day keeps the doctor away, and that those fruits spoil after a week. Then there is value in someone having up to seven apples and seven oranges at any given time. If Person A has eight apples and six oranges and Person B has six apples and eight oranges, they both have a piece of fruit that is effectively valueless (because it will spoil before they can benefit from it). By exchanging an apple from Person A for an orange from Person B, both people are trading away something that has no value for them and receiving something that does have value for them.

"One man's trash is another man's treasure" is economic truth. Spoiling pieces of fruit are trash, but to those who can use them before they spoil, they are literally fruitful. There is such a thing as a "win-win"—exchanges in which both sides gain value. These positive-sum exchanges create more value than existed before the exchange, for all parties involved.

The concept is the same with services and intangibles as with physical goods. A person with medical knowledge in need of smartphone repair and a person skilled in repairing phones who needs medical help could exchange their knowledge or service and both gain value. People who have more goods or knowledge than time, energy, or interest for a labor-intensive task can exchange their goods or knowledge for the labor of people who have more time, energy, or interest in that task.

Even when value is created for all parties involved, relentless rule number one still holds: frictional costs take their toll. If those frictional costs are greater than the value created, the exchange as a whole produces a net loss—it is not truly positive-sum.

Back to our apples and oranges example. Suppose each piece of fruit is worth $1, and it takes $3 worth of combined time and energy to find a trading partner and perform the exchange of an apple from Person A for an orange from Person B. They each began with $13 in value from their useful fruits. (Recall that the value is in consuming exactly one apple and one orange per day, and that the fruit spoils after seven days. So one of Person A's eight apples has no value when stockpiled—it will spoil before it can be valuably used. When holding eight apples and six oranges, there is value in only seven apples and six oranges. In the same way, Person B's holding of six apples and eight oranges means one of the oranges has no value. The value of their fruit, when hoarded and not exchanged with a partner, is $13 from seven [of eight] apples and six oranges for Person A, and for Person B $13 from six apples and seven [of eight] oranges.)

They each traded away a fruit that had no value for themselves because it would have spoiled and in exchange received a fruit worth $1. Afterward they both have $14 worth of useful fruit—seven apples and seven oranges each. So their combined value before the exchange was $26, and their combined value afterward is $28. But if they lose a combined $3 worth of time and energy finding each other and making their trade, once frictional costs are considered their combined value after the exchange is only $25—less than their starting value. They would have been better off letting their extra fruit spoil than expending so much time and effort to generate so little return.

In our modern economy, direct exchanges of goods or services for other goods or services are rare—most of our exchanges involve money. A benefit of using money is that it lowers frictional costs. Money, unlike physical products or human-delivered services, doesn't have a shelf life or expiration date. It doesn't have limited business hours or a closing time or seasonal availability. It requires little expense or time to store and to transport and to exchange. It doesn't require that people find exchange partners having exactly the goods or services they need *and* who value exactly the goods or services they can offer.

These benefits are truer of paper money than of metal coins, and they are especially true of electronic money, toward which currency is making a large-scale shift. Money that is transacted via credit and debit accounts, bank transfers, and electronic payments have especially low frictional costs. Money does not eliminate fundamental frictional costs, and those managing money, including electronic money, tend to add human-made frictional costs, but using money does reduce frictional costs. This makes it easier to overcome frictional costs so exchanges can provide a true net value creation.

Using money, Person A, who has an extra apple and needs an orange, doesn't have to search high and low for the perfect Person B who has an orange *and* needs an apple. Person A can exchange their apple for money with *anyone* who needs an apple, any time before it spoils. Then Person A can use that money to buy an orange from *anyone* who has one. Person B can do the same—exchange their orange for money with *anyone* and then buy an apple from *anyone*. If each fruit-for-money exchange costs ten cents, then both Person A and Person B begin with their $13 worth of useful fruit, spend ten cents each to sell their excess apple or orange, respectively, and spend another ten cents each to buy their desired orange or apple, respectively. They have each turned their $13 worth of useful fruit into $14 worth, increasing their combined fruit value from $26 to $28. Since their frictional costs now total only forty cents, their total value after these exchanges is $27.60—these exchanges have created true value, all participants have benefitted.

An exchange many will find familiar is the garage sale (or its digital-era counterpart, person-to-person online marketplaces). The seller of, say, an extra chair, seeks value in place of this item they never use. The buyer of the chair seeks value in the form of something good to sit on. If the chair sells for $5, the seller turned something they had no use for into $5 they can use, and the buyer turned $5 they couldn't physically sit on into a chair they can use for that purpose. Both have gained value in the exchange. As long as they kept frictional costs below $5, this simple transaction results in a true net gain.

Whether exchanges involve physical goods, intangibles, knowledge, services or labor, and whether they are direct trades or use money, a true net gain is achieved only when, for all parties involved, value is created and that created value exceeds frictional costs.

As a Whole, We Receive the Average Net Result of all Exchanges

Economic exchanges are far-reaching and inescapably interconnected. We wake up each morning in beds in which each component (mattress, box springs, pillows, sheets, etc.) was acquired via economic exchange. Before they were acquired, each of those components was manufactured via economic exchange between the manufacturing companies and their employees. Before those components were manufactured, their raw materials were transported via economic exchange. Before the raw materials could be transported, they had to be procured, also an economic exchange.

All of that economic web is in play just for our sleep. The web expands as you consider the similar ripples of economic exchange involved in the buildings in which we all live, work, and play (their many physical materials, plumbing, heating and cooling systems, electrical infrastructure, furnishings, etc.), our means of transportation to and from those buildings (planes, trains, automobiles, boats, and their thousands of component parts, plus the airports, roads, railways, and waterways), the clothes we wear, the devices and appliances we use, the food we eat, the tools for preparing food, chemicals for maintaining and cleaning all these things, and on and on, ad nauseam.

Beyond the pervasive physical products and their underlying economic exchanges, we must also recognize intangible economic exchanges.

All of the physical products were developed with research, refined with expertise, and delivered with paid service. Professional services (medical, legal, financial, religious, etc.) and knowledge workers of all sorts make our daily lives livable—further multiplying the interconnectedness of economic exchanges.

Simply put, there is no such thing as an isolated economic exchange. Every individual, at every moment of their existence, is directly or indirectly involved in numerous, interconnected exchanges. As you read this, you participate in exchanges that have provided this book to you, kept you fed and hydrated and healthy enough to read, put a roof over your head or provided means of traveling somewhere outdoors, and educated you in the ability to read, just to name a few.

John Donne may not have been writing about economics in 1624, but his poetic lines hold true economically: "No man is an island, entire of itself; every man is a piece of the continent, a part of the main; if a clod be washed away by the sea, Europe is the less, as well as if a promontory were, as well as if a manor of thy friend's or of thine own were; any man's death diminishes me, because I am involved in mankind, and therefore never send to know for whom the bell tolls; it tolls for thee."[17]

No person is an economic island, and no exchange between persons is isolated. There is no exchange that affects only "them"—some other person or people, in some other place. Every exchange has ripple effects throughout the highly interconnected economic web, so whatever affects "them" affects "us." Economically speaking, there is no "us" and "them"—*we* are interconnected. "We" is all of us; "they" are all of us. "We" *are* "they."

Given this interconnectedness, humble arithmetic, as Bogle liked to phrase it, by definition requires that the average result of interconnected economic participants equals the total result of their exchanges divided by the total number of participants. Just as Bogle recognizes the rule that investors as a whole get average market returns because investors as a whole *are* the market, we must recognize the rule that people as a whole get average economic returns because people as a whole *are* the economy.

In an economy that hypothetically has only two people, if their exchanges produce a total net result of $100/day, those interconnected people would receive an average gain of $50/day. If their exchanges produce a total net result of negative $100/day, they would receive an average loss of $50/day each. In real-world scenarios that have many more people, the math still works exactly the same: the total net result of economic exchanges, divided

---

17. Donne quoted at https://www.goodreads.com/work/quotes/6791114.

by the number of people in the economy, equals the average result received by those interconnected people.

Unlike Garrison Keillor's Lake Wobegon, "where all the children are above average," relentless rules allow no tongue-in-cheek exemptions to mathematical definitions. Some economic participants will be above average and others below, but by definition, we—altogether—receive the average net result of our interconnected economic exchanges.

We Gain from Net-Positive Economic Exchanges and Lose from Net-Negative Economic Exchanges

Pulling all of the above relentless rules together, we arrive at the logically inescapable conclusion: we, altogether, gain when the interconnected web of economic exchanges produces net gains, even after frictional costs are considered, and we, as a whole, lose when the interconnected web of economic exchanges produces net losses.

Economic exchanges that are net-positive, even after frictional costs, increase average value to all economic participants—all of us. Exchanges that are net-negative decrease that average value for everyone.

If Person/Group A takes value from Person/Group B, that transfer of value minus the relentless frictional costs is a net-negative in the interconnected economic web. Writ large, such taking of value makes us all losers after frictional costs. Even if Person/Group A seems to "win" the exchange in an isolated sense, they have contributed a net-negative impact to the interconnected economic web, which lowers the total value of overall economic activity, which lowers the average economic value for all participants—including Person/Group A.

Using simple numbers, suppose Person A takes a value of $10 from Person B, with a frictional cost of $1. Also suppose their economy has ten people and a total value of $1,000 before this exchange. After the exchange the total value of their interconnected economic web is reduced to $999. So this exchange has reduced the average value for each participant in this economy from $100 to $99.90. Only from a very limited perspective does Person A appear to come out ahead by gaining $10 at Person B's expense, because Person A's total economy has lost value. All participants in this economy, including Person A, now have one less dollar available for overall economic activity.

The notion of some gaining at others' expense is like saying, "Your side of the boat is sinking!" We are in the same economic boat—if it's sinking, it's sinking for all of us. When someone loses value, through non-value-generating exchange and/or frictional costs, we all lose.

We each win, in the only economically comprehensive and lasting sense, when we all win—when the average value of our interconnected economic exchanges is increased by fully net-positive exchanges. I truly win in an economic sense when my exchange partner also wins—when we create value that exceeds frictional costs. Writ large, this excess value creation makes all the interconnected economic partners more valuable, for themselves and for each other.

In the expansive, highly interconnected economic web, "I" win when "we" win—and "we" win when we all win.

Recap and Restatement of the Relentless Rules of Economics

1. Frictional costs are in every economic exchange.
2. Therefore merely transferring existing value is a losing proposition.
3. Therefore exchanges must create value greater than frictional costs to produce a true net gain.
4. We are they, and we, altogether, are average.
5. I gain/lose when we gain/lose, and we gain/lose when we all gain/lose.

Our recognition of these relentless rules underlies our approach to economics, so they will be referenced throughout. These rules simply are what they are; we cannot choose to change them. Our choice is to recognize, think, and act in beneficial ways in light of them, or continue to be caught on the wrong side of their relentlessness to our detriment. Partnership Economics is the structure by which to recognize, think, and act beneficially in light of the relentless rules of economics—the way to create more net-positive economic exchanges and therefore increase the average benefit for all economic participants.

Nothing is Certain but . . .

"Death is very likely the single best invention of life."
—Steve Jobs

... death and taxes. We discuss taxes later. For now we feel the responsibility to point to the reality of the relatively short lives we're all given, and the continual motivation that should provide to all of us. We are not pessimists; we are pragmatists.

Economics is part of the larger fabric of human society, our public life together, and as such is subject to even greater rules and realities. The most significant of these was poignantly expressed in a 1973 M*A*S*H episode. After a young soldier dies despite surgeon Hawkeye's best efforts, Colonel Henry Blake tells the distraught Hawkeye there are two rules about war—"Rule number one is: 'Young men die.' Rule number two is: 'Doctors can't change rule number one.'"

All rules, including the relentless rules of economics, are in the shadow of the relentless reality of death. The reality of death is not popular to attend to, but it attends to us. Our approach to life, including economics, will therefore be better if done in intentional awareness of the relentless reality of death.

We don't have to be so cynical in light of this relentless reality of death that we fail to make efforts to help people while death is lurking; neither should we give ourselves over to a detached idealism that pretends death can be avoided. Neither cynical nor "pie-in-the-sky" idealistic, we can be purposeful and practical in living as well as possible and pursuing public health/well-being in the fullest sense, including economic, fully aware that death lurks.

Awareness of death need not result in denial or in panic, both of which are harmful to life. Denial about death results in an apathy, ennui, lethargy, depression, complacency to "pass time" or even, tragically, "kill time" frivolously—wasting the precious and limited resource of time. Panic about death results in paralysis, anxiety, fear, inability and/or unwillingness to truly live despite being technically alive—also wasting the precious and limited resource of time. We hope this sounds obvious, especially given the relentless rules of economics: it is harmful for people/the economy/public society to waste precious and limited resources.

We can and should live, really *live*, in light of the relentless reality of death—whether death from crises like pandemic, war, acute illness, natural disaster, or death from the less sensational but every bit as relentless ways it asserts itself, at the personal level as well as the public level. Awareness of death can sharpen our sense of the need to live well and focus our intentionality on how to make the most of the limited resource of life we in fact have—rather than the unlimited life we presume in "normal" times or the "shock" of inevitably realizing that life isn't unlimited.

Paradoxically, death ends earthly life yet acknowledging death enriches life. Between the extremes of denial about death and panic about death—which are common even though extreme—lies an expanse of life-enriching awareness of death. When you know death is lurking—which it is—you don't waste the life that you have but make the most of every opportunity. For public life, and particularly how Partnership Economics is part of and benefits public life, we should reduce wasted life and make the most of every opportunity that we have.

We don't benefit from denial about death, nor do we benefit from panic about it; in the face of death Partnership Economics helps us all live as well as possible with the limited time and resources available. The specter of death need not cause us to abandon economics nor do it poorly but can motivate us to do economics in increasingly life-giving ways, as partners.

Chapter 2

Homo Economicus—Economic Human

> *"I can calculate the motion of heavenly bodies,
> but not the madness of people."*
>
> —Sir Isaac Newton after he infamously lost
> his wealth investing in the South Sea Bubble

BECAUSE ECONOMICS INFLUENCES ALL of human life, it is important to pay attention to how human life also influences economics. This is a two-way street. People are not only subject to economic realities—we also are creatures whose decisions and behavior impact economic realities.

As you read and reflect on these human and economic realities, we invite your collaboration, critiques, questions, comments, ideas, etc. at info@partnershipeconomics.com. We look forward to hearing from you and moving the conversation and action forward together.

Not Walking Calculators

Our decisions and behaviors have many variables. Humans are not walking calculators who automatically take the "ideal" course of economic action as it may be calculated theoretically according to the mathematical models of classical economics. Behavioral economics takes human psychology into account for economic decisions and behaviors. This is good. It is helpful to consider how we, as human creatures rather than mathematical machines, actually behave economically. This also is unflattering. In the real world of behavioral economics, we very often do not make ideal economic decisions. The truth will set you free . . . but first we have to face some realities.

So how do we humans actually behave economically? Three major factors shaping our real-life economic decisions and behaviors are ignorance, uncertainty, and confusion. We warned that this is not flattering. Ignorance simply means we are unaware of economic matters. For example, do you know the size of the national debt? Most of us know it is big, really big, but how big?[18] Uncertainty means that, when we do have some awareness of economic facts, we are uncertain about what those facts mean, uncertain of how to interpret and make sense of the facts. Continuing the example, what does it mean that the national debt is that big? What does the national debt consist of? What effects does it have? How does the national debt relate to other economic measures, such as gross domestic product? Confusion means that when we have some awareness of economic facts and also some understanding of their meaning, we are confused about how to put that understanding into practice—we aren't sure what to *do*. Continuing the national debt example, aware of the size of the debt and understanding all it involves and how it relates to other economic measures, what can or should we do about it?

Classical economics assumes that people have all the relevant information, understand all of that information, and are willing and able to act on that understanding. Behavioral economics, helpfully but unflatteringly, shows that those assumptions are exactly that—hopeful assumptions at best and not realities. The reality of behavioral economics is that we don't have all the relevant economic information—we are affected by ignorance. We don't fully understand the economic information we do have—we are affected by uncertainty. We don't fully know how to act on the understanding we do have—we are confused about what to do economically.

What God Has Joined, Let No One Separate

Beyond psychology, human handling of economic matters is also influenced by theology and morality. If speaking of theology is unappealing to you, it is important to recognize that everyone has an embedded sense of theology. It is like personality—everyone has one, whether or not you analyze it or are even aware of it. It simply is there, part of who we are. Indeed, to deny a theological perspective is to make a theological claim and stake one's

---

18. Amadeo and Boyle, "The U.S. Debt and How It Got So Big." (Over $26 trillion as of July 2020.)

ground on the basis of beliefs framed as what they aren't. Because theology affects us—whether consciously or unconsciously, whether stated as what one does believe or what one doesn't believe—it is better to develop awareness of it than to have economic behavior subject to ignorance.

If you love theology but are uncomfortable mixing it with economics, well, that is a "norm" that needs to change. Better to develop understanding of how theology and economics intersect than to have economic behavior subject to uncertainty, and better to develop practices from the overlapping insights of theology and economics than to have economic behavior subject to confusion.

Too often economics and theology are treated as unrelated, or even harmful to each other. If you find yourself in the why-does-theology-need-to-get-involved-with-economics camp or the economics-is-better-off-without-theology camp, we encourage you to read on. We happen to love both theology and economics and find that they are best together and that both are diminished when kept separate. Failure to consider how economics and theology combine only worsens the behavioral economic problems of ignorance, uncertainty, and confusion.

Because we as human creatures are ignorant, uncertain, and confused both about economic facts and what to do with them, we rely on convention and make sub-optimal economic choices. We tend to do what is considered normal and/or conventional and/or convenient, going with the flow of pre-made defaults (even when the default "norms" are destructive) rather than making intentional, helpful economic choices. We tend to underestimate costs and risks and overestimate benefits and potential, a dangerous combination.

For instance, credit card debt that is not paid off within the initial statement period will cost interest in a range of 12 percent or higher, and the most generous credit card rewards programs offer only 5–6 percent cash back (or the supposed equivalent in points or airline miles), yet Americans have over $1 *trillion* in credit card debt.[19] The math of benefiting at best 5–6 percent while costing at least 12 percent is obviously a losing proposition, yet using credit cards in this way is "normal." We, collectively, carry credit card debt averaging $8,400 for every American household because it is convenient and conventional, not because it is an intentional calculation of the ideal course of action. We get excited about the benefits ("I got a free such-and-such!") and downplay the costs ("just a little interest"), quite apart from their mathematical realities. Using credit cards this way reeks

---

19. $1.08 trillion as of Q3 2019.

of ignorance, uncertainty, and confusion . . . and it's the reality of how we behave economically.

As unflattering as behavioral economics is, it provides clarity. Its truths can set us free. Acknowledging that there are such powerful human behavioral aspects to economics makes economics relatable to anyone who has some familiarity with human behavior, which is all of us humans. You don't need a PhD to engage economics any more than you need to be a botanist to shop for fruit. Anyone who knows people can (and should) deal with economics intentionally and beneficially. Our intention is that this book helps each reader move away from economic ignorance toward awareness, away from economic uncertainty toward understanding, and away from confusion toward confident action. This will benefit each reader individually and those with whom they interact, which is the gateway to Partnership Economics.

Ignorance is Bliss?

The first step to better economics is overcoming ignorance, re-viewing "norms" and getting facts in perspective. This is a move from ignorance to awareness: awareness that current economics, particularly corporate economics, are deeply flawed for all involved, and awareness that economics matter to God.

The philosopher and Harvard professor Michael J. Sandel is no stranger to addressing the moral and civic questions of our time. In a 2012 article he wrote for *The Atlantic* titled "What Isn't for Sale?"[20] he neatly gives an overview of America's shift in the past four decades from a market *economy* to a market *society*. This shift, we contend, is as damaging as it is seismically dramatic. We also suspect a market society mentality has always been a hidden cornerstone of plantation system economics.

What's the distinction between a market economy and a market society?

> A market economy is a tool—a valuable and effective tool—for organizing productive activity. In contrast, a market society is a way of life in which market values seep into every aspect of human endeavor. It's a place where social relationships are made over in the image of the market. . . . Do we want a market economy, or a market society?

---

20. Sandel, "What Isn't For Sale?" The following paragraphs draw on this article.

We reference and briefly discuss Sandel's article here because it provides a good contextual overview by which to further understand what Mr. X, in the Introduction, called a plantation system.

Beginning in the early 1980s, America's President Ronald Reagan and Great Britain's Prime Minister Margaret Thatcher began to strongly proclaim the conviction that free markets and government deregulation were the pathways to prosperity and freedom. As the Cold War ended in the early 1990s and President Bill Clinton and Prime Minister Tony Blair continued the work of their respective predecessors, free market thinking and economics grew to dominate politics and policy. While countries around the globe began embracing market mechanisms in the thinking of their politics and operations of their economies, a blind faith developed that espoused markets as the primary means for achieving the public good. This is especially true in capitalist and emerging capitalist countries. Like the hostages of a Trojan horse incursion or malware attack, however, the blindly faithful were ignorant to the reality that market values had been invited to creep in, permeate, and implicate every corner of social life.

Sandel explains how market values implicate social life by creating a marketplace society that allocates a dollar value to humankind's relationship with each other and Creation. The result is a price-permitted upending of our relationships with each other and Creation. Just a sampling of the new relationships now justified through market values thinking, and the price in 2012 of those relations, includes: hunters buying the right to hunt and kill an endangered black rhino in South Africa for $250,000; corporations in the European Union buying the right to pollute carbon dioxide into the atmosphere for $10.50/metric ton; buying the right to immigrate to the United States, with the potential for permanent residency, for $500,000; and renting a surrogate mother's womb in India for $8,000, less than one-third the price in the United States.

Today, as Sandel observes and these examples attest, that blind faith in the markets as the primary means for achieving the public good is now in question. The Great Recession did more than expose weaknesses in the abilities of markets to efficiently allocate risks, much less achieve the public good. "It also prompted a widespread sense that markets have become detached from morals, and that we need to somehow reconnect the two." Sandel agrees that greed played a part in the 2008 financial crisis and its lingering aftermath, but that is hardly the complete answer. "The most fateful change that unfolded during the past three decades was not an increase in greed. It was the reach of markets, and of market values, into spheres of life traditionally governed by nonmarket norms."

Consider the now ubiquitous examples of for-profit higher education, for-profit hospitals and related healthcare providers, and for-profit prisons. Likewise, the use of private military contractors to fight in Iraq and Afghanistan, the blurring of boundaries between advertising and journalism, corporate naming rights of parks and civic spaces, and campaign finance in the United States that all but permits the outright buying and selling of elections.

The use of markets to allocate and deliver—if not grip and control—social goods and services was almost unknown before the Reagan era. Most probably, as every U.S.-trained law school student learns by the end of first year contracts and torts classes, because in America's early history the free market and privatization efforts for public services failed spectacularly. Services like road paving, fire hydrant supply lines, and public safety failed so frequently that local and state governments were forced to take over responsibility for these errantly privatized services—simply to ensure reliable delivery to all citizens. While those lessons appear to have been remembered, honored, and properly applied by previous generations, those lessons have been all but lost on us today. To the modern person the notion of daily life being guided by market values is largely taken for granted, which is unfortunate because that perspective sets the stage for the repeating of painful lessons.

We ask, "Within the marketplace and within our society, must every interaction be a transaction and every need be coupled to a (frequently increasing) price tag?" Sandel offers two reasons we should be concerned that market values have permeated social life to create a market society: inequality and corrosion.

Regarding inequality, life is harder for those with modest income and means. Inequity is always apparent when viewed from below, but less painful when considering life's luxuries. A person of modest means might like to experience daily champagne and a Bentley but can be content without those luxuries. On the other hand, as money increasingly buys or is required to buy life's necessities, like unpolluted water and air, or freedom, the starker and more painful the consequences of inequity in the lived experience become. The joy of life risks being reduced to simply how much of it we can each afford to purchase.

We haven't been trained to think of markets as having a corrosive aspect, but corrosion is as much a threat to society as is inequity. While inequity is easier to quantify and measure, corrosion is arguably more damaging because it is more subtle and less obvious, and more directly shapes our values and morals. Placing a price on something doesn't just allocate goods or experiences, it expresses and promotes attitudes about those goods or experiences and those attitudes can easily become corroded.

Consider the example of paying underachieving students to read books, as is done in some school systems and possibly in many homes. While the monetary incentive might get the students started, it can just as easily soon create the attitude that reading is work for which to demand payment. The foreseeable results include some students stopping reading when the payments stop, and some students demanding more money for reading more or more difficult books. Either way, most students will not learn to appreciate reading for its inherent benefits. What might be the corrosive effect on patriotism if we were permitted to sell our citizenship to a foreigner who wants to skip the immigration process? What might be the corrosive effect on the family if we were permitted to sell our children to a desiring couple who wants to skip the adoption process? To build on Sandel's original question, Do we want a market economy, or a *corroded* market society?

One reason we've collectively arrived at a market society is that after decades of insisting people leave their ethics and values at the door when they enter the workplace, we've created a moral vacuum in the marketplace. Nature indeed abhors a vacuum, which has since been filling with everything-has-a-price market values.

"Questions are the engines of thought," is a favorite phrase of ours. Do you increasingly see financial and wealth inequality in our society? Do you increasingly see the corrosion of civility and interpersonal relations in our society? Do you increasingly see the damage we collectively have done to our environment? Can you begin to see how we created the very structure that results in this kind of damage to ourselves, our societies, and our environments?

Sandel observes, "[E]conomists often assume that markets are inert, that they do not affect the goods being exchanged. But this is untrue. Markets leave their mark. Sometimes, market values crowd out nonmarket values worth caring about." Sandel immediately follows that observation with an example that circles us back to Mr. X's plantation system revelation.

> When we decide that certain goods may be bought and sold, we decide, at least implicitly, that it is appropriate to treat them as commodities, *as instruments of profit and use* (emphasis added). But not all goods are properly valued in this way. The most obvious example is human beings. Slavery was appalling because it treated human beings as a commodity, to be bought and sold at auction. Such treatment fails to value human beings as persons,

worthy of dignity and respect; it sees them *as instruments of gain and objects of use* (emphasis added).

You will remember the story of Mr. X explaining that all the law firm associates were being given raises but were required to work longer hours to both earn those raises and generate the increased profits the partners wanted. None of those associates could legally claim to be a slave, because they were each free to quit and try to find a law firm that doesn't operate under the same business model. (Good luck with that.) Each of them would, however, reasonably agree they were being manipulated *as instruments of profit and use*. They weren't offered a choice; the increased work expectations were imposed on them. In fact, when some pushed back, they were plainly and directly told that they're in a plantation system.

We now appreciate that Mr. X spit out his pithy, visceral revelation. Being angry at that truth has kept it real for us as we search for a better understanding. It also gives us context for understanding what one calls a plantation system another calls a market society. By whatever names we call our treatments of each other, it's well past time to re-view the norm of plantation systems and market societies.

CHAPTER 3

Our Corporate Work Isn't Working

> "The changes . . . compare the evolving 'corporate system'
> with the feudal system."
> —Justice Louis Brandeis (1933)

It Smells Like Money to Me

MILTON FRIEDMAN'S "THE SOCIAL Responsibility of Business Is to Increase Its Profits" ran in the *New York Times Magazine* on September 13, 1970 ("Friedman's article").[21] It's not hyperbole for us to assert it's among the most influential business pieces written in the past fifty years.[22]

Even if you're not familiar with the article itself, you've likely heard and lived its title. Like a Molotov cocktail flung into a dry California valley, the influence of Friedman's article exploded to scorch every crevice of America's economic and cultural landscape. Upon close inspection it doesn't carry enough factual support or logic to account for its influence. Rather, it relies on bald statements buttressed by fear-mongering. Here we turn to discuss just its last paragraph:

> I have called ["social responsibility"] a "fundamentally subversive doctrine" in a free society, and have said that in such a

---

21. Friedman, "Social Responsibility."
22. Denning, "Pernicious Nonsense." See also Bower and Paine, "The Error at the Heart."

society, "there is one and only one social responsibility of business—to use its resources and engage in activities designed to increase its profits *so long as it stays within the rules of the game, which is to say, engages in open and free competition without deception or fraud.*" (Emphasis ours.)

If you're a business person or investor, isn't Friedman's ethic of simply counting profits a clearly defined and measurable goal? Doesn't that clarity make it attractive? Doesn't that clarity make it easy to get behind and support? Yep, that was the trap, and we completely fell for it.

And what do we make of that caveat, "so long as it stays within the rules of the game, which is to say, engages in open and free competition without deception or fraud"? That is an interesting, if not laughable, disclaimer. If increasing profit is the exclusive responsibility of business and social responsibility is a fundamentally subversive doctrine, where does that really leave "the rules of the game"? When profit is viewed as a singular pursuit, the obviously foreseeable motivations are to change the rules of the game, limit competition, and even engage in deception or fraud. Not unlike regular events over the past fifty years in corporate America.

Hypothetically speaking, even if we all accept and agree with Friedman's business ethic of profits *above* all else, still that should not be deemed the *one and only* social responsibility. Rather, that ethic should be paired with the acknowledgment that honoring the rules of the game (society's laws) is also a social responsibility. Why would we expect businesses pursuing the "one and only" responsibility of increasing profit to want laws that enable Friedman's stated standard of "open and free competition"? In reality the playbook is to shape rules and laws to the business's own advantage through financing relentless lobbying and political campaign contributions. Making self-serving rules is not the same as staying within the rules intended to benefit society as a whole!

For just one example of how Friedman's ethic provides for rules that support plantation economics, let's consider the economic concept of externality. Externality is generally defined as a cost or benefit that affects people other than those involved in the economic activity that produced it, and that is not reflected in costs or prices, such as pollution and other negative externalities.

Externality is a simple enough concept, yet a false one in light of Relentless Rules 4 and 5 (RR4&5). Externality truly became a dangerous weapon when, in support of Friedman's profit ethic, economists chose to frame and offer it as a valid business option. In other words, to shift part of the cost of doing business to others without their agreement and even to their detriment was a valid business decision offered by economists (if and for however long you could pull it off, of course). A brief story illustrates the profit-above-all ethic and supporting rule of externality.

In the early 1990s Paul was a forensic engineer at a consumer products conglomerate. He loved that work, his manager, and the company (at least most days most of the time, which is a satisfactory benchmark). His responsibilities took him nationwide, and one matter required that he visit the massive plywood mill that manufactured the structural panels at issue in a potential claim. During that visit and while touring the oldest section of the mill, the shift supervisor turned to explain the crew installing new pollution controls at the far end of the building, an enlightening backstory.

The shift supervisor explained that the mill had been allowed to operate for decades without meaningful pollution control equipment. This led to manufacturing "by-products"—air pollution vented into the atmosphere and waste dumped into the adjacent stream. If you've ever experienced the smell of sulphuric acid (remember that rotten egg smell experiment in grammar school science?) or sloshed through a sewer overflow, then you have a sense of the air pollution and waste this mill generated.

Local citizens living near the mill began to complain to the plant manager about the awful smell and chemicals in the stream generated by the plant. The plant manager's practiced response was soon familiar to everyone. He'd pause, point his nose upward, and inhale deeply for emphasis before proclaiming, "It smells like money to me." His point was clear: his only responsibility was to make a profit, and his way of delivering that point suggested that he didn't have to care about much else. When not at the job site, the plant manager lived comfortably several towns away where he and his family weren't inflicted with the "smell of money."

This story from the shift supervisor unintentionally teaches the economic concept of negative externalities. In the view of that plant manager, he wasn't polluting. In his view he was *externalizing* that part of the cost of manufacturing and therefore it was a no-brainer to reduce expenses. If there wasn't a law that prohibited him from polluting, he was "within the rules of the game" and was convinced that it wasn't his responsibility that the plant under his direction was causing problems for the community. And even if there were a law in place, then he and the company lawyers and lobbyists were allowed to try to get that law abolished or changed. He was "just doing his job" of making money for the company. In fact, we shouldn't be surprised to learn he deeply believed he was doing exemplary work saving money by not installing pollution control measures that weren't required by law.

The object lesson and truth trying to set us free is clear. The Friedman fiction that the one and only social responsibility of business is to increase profit leads to bending and breaking the rules of the game while using the very wealth gained in the abuse to insulate the abuser from the negative effects.

Examples of negative externalizing abound in today's marketplace and culture. In addition to environmental pollution like that described above, common examples include inhaling second-hand smoke from cigarettes, pedestrians and drivers hit and killed by vehicles operated under the influence of alcohol or narcotics, and massive fires started by electrical utilities whose equipment fails because maintenance costs were postponed in favor of paying dividends to shareholders.

What are the limits of externality? How much cost shifting in support of this profit-first-and-only ethic are we willing to burden? How much further are we willing to abuse our environments and each other in support of Friedman's fiction that business's sole social responsibility is to increase profits? There are no limits and there is no end as long as this profit-above-all fiction continues as the primary marketplace ethic.

The Responsibilities of Rights

We're obliged to take further issue with Friedman and his singular corporate ethic. Friedman contends that corporate executives are agents of the owners (shareholders) and are bound only to act according to their desires. He has no place for larger social considerations—yet he says even corporate executives are bound by laws and ethical customs. Friedman's stance is muddied by this mixed message. Are executives bound only to the shareholders, or do they in fact have obligations to the larger society, which creates laws and ethical customs?

Friedman, in the article he pens, goes on to argue that acting in the social interest is at odds with the owners' interest. This view is narrow and short-sighted; are not shareholders part of society? Friedman makes the worthy point that actions of corporate social responsibility are often used to generate positive publicity for the purpose of offsetting the perceived negativity of profit-seeking. He is right that profit should not be criticized in and of itself and seen as competing with social action. He is wrong, though, in saying profit should be praised in and of itself and that it can be pursued apart from any social interest. (Contradicting himself, as noted, with the caveat that "laws and ethical customs" must be considered.) Our Partnership Economics approach recognizes the value of profit *and* social interest. It is unnecessary, unhelpful, and ultimately unrealistic to pit corporations and society against each other. Remember the relentless rules: "we are they" and "we" gain when we all gain (RR4&5). Partnership shows how shareholders and society can and should be complementary.

One aspect of Friedman's argument deserves special attention in our time. He contends, "Only people can have responsibilities. A corporation is an artificial person and in this sense may have artificial responsibilities, but 'business' as a whole cannot be said to have responsibilities, even in this vague sense."[23] In 2010, however, the Supreme Court, in *Citizens United v. Federal Election Commission,* ruled 5–4 that corporate entities have the same right to free speech under the First Amendment as individuals. Even Justice John Paul Stevens, author of the dissenting opinion in the case, acknowledged that "we have long since held that corporations are covered by the First Amendment."[24] Contrary to Friedman's emphasis on the artificial nature of corporate "personhood," recent legal interpretation has afforded corporate "persons" rights that are not at all artificial but very real, and expansive. And no one could seriously claim that corporations have only artificial impact. To grant corporations the rights of individuals and not-at-all-artificial powers but relieve them of responsibilities is clearly inconsistent. This legal precedent surely implies that certain responsibilities are incumbent upon the corporate members of our society. By acknowledging mutual responsibilities, we can better partner for mutual benefit as well.

Friedman's message is provocative and has been widely influential, despite the critiques above. If we allow a broad and generous understanding of his stipulation that "laws and ethical customs" are to be respected by corporations, then we could agree with him. As long as they operate within the legal and ethical context society deems appropriate for corporations, their purpose is to create profit within and for their society. This is technically true—and unfortunately irrelevant as of this writing. Because of the expansive power increasingly afforded to corporate "persons" and the way they wield that power through lobbying of lawmakers and mass messaging of society, we cannot honestly say that corporations operate within the legal and ethical context society establishes for them. The defense that a corporation is "playing by the rules," such as paying little to no tax because tax law allows it, rings hollow when the corporation influenced the tax law. Making the rules isn't the same as following them.

We will have more to say, and more importantly more to do, on this topic in Part 3. For now suffice it to say that corporations can be a valuable

23. Friedman, "Social Responsibility."
24. Liptak, "Justices," para. 19.

part of society, but they must partner as truly *part* of society rather than bend society to serve the corporations' narrower interests. Corporations are created by society—society should not be created by corporations. Corporations can and should benefit society—not the other way around.

Currently, however, corporations following the ethic championed by Friedman suffer from three fatal flaws, damaging to both the corporations and broader society.

Problem 1: All for One, but Not One for All

I'm looking for people who share my goal of making me gobs of money.

Words matter. In that light, let's distinguish between the words *shareholder* and *stakeholder* because they're frequently confused, and we use them often.

A shareholder can be defined as one who owns a share or shares of a company or investment fund. Sufficient for our present purposes, a shareholder is understood as an owner-entity that simply seeks a financial reward for its financial investment in a corporation (or in a fund that holds ownership in multiple corporations). A stakeholder is a broader concept and can be defined as one who has a share or an *interest*, as in an enterprise. Sufficient for our present purposes, a stakeholder is an entity of any kind that has an *interest* in the activity of the corporation. A stakeholder can be a shareholder of course, but not necessarily and frequently is not.

Shareholders are included among stakeholders, along with all others who also have an interest—a stake—in an enterprise.

In our story of the consumer products conglomerate mill, the tens of thousands of people across the country who owned the conglomerate's stock at that time but with no other interest in what was happening at that mill are fairly characterized as shareholders. Stakeholders include all the players in the story (seen and unseen) who may or may not have a financial investment but do have an interest in what the corporation does. Those stakeholders range from the residents living near the mill forced to breathe the mill's polluted air, to the externalizing plant manager, to later employees who risk being mischaracterized as not caring for the environment because of events decades earlier. Whether or not employees' retirement savings are tied to the conglomerate's stock, which would make them shareholders, they are stakeholders because of the influence and impact of the conglomerate on their life as employees. With that distinction made, let's move toward exploring corporate influence and developing a Partnership Ethic.

The influence of corporations in contemporary American society is hard to overstate. As a snapshot of corporate heft, in 2008, 5.8 million corporations filed income tax returns with the Internal Revenue Service; these corporations controlled $76.8 trillion of assets and generated $28.6 trillion in revenue.[25] To put these numbers in perspective, consider that the population of the United States in 2008 was 304 million.[26] This means that for every person in the U.S. in 2008 corporations controlled assets of $253,000 dollars. Also recognize that the 2008 Gross Domestic Product for the U.S. in 2008 was $14.2 trillion[27]—half the amount of corporate revenue. Despite the 2008 downturn, the values of corporations' revenues and assets have risen significantly and consistently over the two previous decades. Corporations have tremendous economic clout in the U.S., and they continue to grow.

The vast economic size of corporations has several implications. One is that corporations affect far more than just their shareholders. They also have many millions of employees working with their massive assets and many millions of customers delivering the huge revenue stream. Because U.S. corporations paid $698 billion in taxes in 2008,[28] they both influence and are influenced by government policies. Finally, much of corporations' $76.8 trillion of assets consists of natural resources, meaning that corporations have significant influence over earth's life-sustaining environment.

25. Census, "Table 753."
26. Census, "Statistical Abstract of the United States."
27. Bureau, "Gross Domestic Product."
28. Census, "Table 753."

This all reveals the first major problem with the current corporate ethic of prioritizing profit maximization for shareholders. Shareholders simply are not the only party with something at stake in corporations. Every corporate employee, every corporate customer, everyone under government's influence, and everyone living in the environment—all people, present and future—are impacted by corporations. A corporate economic ethic must consider all stakeholders, not merely shareholders.

The "too big to fail" false dilemma that led to government bailouts in the 2008 economic crisis, as just one example, should serve as a cogent reminder that corporate influence (or malfeasance) does not stop at shareholders. Indeed, the losses that the shareholders of banks and other financial institutions in 2008 should have accepted and borne as their risk of being proud capitalists, were instead shifted and forced upon American taxpayer stakeholders in the form of additional debt added to the federal deficit. Like a page from the Dr. Jekyll / Mr. Hyde playbook the current corporate ethic is a duplicity, myopic in sharing benefits and profits yet virtually unfettered in shifting risk and consequences. True capitalists accept the benefit and risk; true plantationists accept the benefit and externalize risk.

And therein lies an irony our predecessors were forced to learn in the Great Depression (1929), we were forced to relearn in the Great Recession (2008), and we are presently being taught again by the COVID-19 pandemic and related economic fallout: we have an illusory construct that capitalism involves competing, without connecting the reality that inherent in all competing are the interdependence and mutual responsibilities that are the very foundation of that competition. The theologian Luke Bretherton revealed our illusory construct nicely when he wrote, "If one part of the body suffers, or if only the interests of the few are attended to, eventually all suffer as the system collapses"[29] (RR5).

Problem 2: Too Big, Too Failed

The second problem with the profit maximization ethic is its utter ambiguity regarding time. Profit maximization for today is not the same as for next year, much less the next decade, much less the next generation. Shareholders would reap the maximum profit today if a corporation liquidated all its assets, yet most companies see the need to invest in future operations. Lack of clarity on timing is not merely a semantics problem, though; it also reveals short-term thinking and greed. It may also reveal a laziness in thinking and planning because it's mentally easier, although perhaps more

29. Bretherton, "Neither Borrower nor Lender," 33.

damaging in every other way, to focus on corporate performance for just a fiscal quarter. Moreover, let's be honest with each other. Is it not likely that over the decades we've been lured and trapped into focusing on maximizing shareholder value simply because it's the simplest metric to measure, track, gauge, and by which to manipulate executive compensation?

Although corporations are legally granted indefinite lifespans, their average actual lifespan is considerably less than that of humans, ranging between twenty and fifty years. Only 25 percent of the original S&P 500 companies (circa 1957)—the largest and presumably most stable corporations in America—survived forty-six years to be studied in 2003.[30] Clearly something in the current system is flawed, and it is not benefiting shareholders any more than other stakeholders. As Jesus observes in Matthew 6:25–34, God's provision has been feeding birds, clothing fields, and nourishing humans for millennia. Corporations, on the other hand, operating under the current corporate "maximization" ethic, are lucky to provide anything for even fifty years.

The problem of companies' inability to provide value, much less maximize it, for even a portion of the human lifespan is further highlighted by reviewing the famous *Built to Last*. It's the product of six years of research at the Stanford University Graduate School of Business by Jerry Porras and Jim Collins. This is a well-researched study by highly respected business thinkers that has been acclaimed by many business leaders. Published in 1994, it identified eighteen "truly exceptional," "enduringly great," "*more* than enduring," "best of the best" companies and a blueprint "for building organizations that will prosper long into the twenty-first century and beyond."[31]

However, twenty-five years later (as of January 1, 2019; hardly long into the twenty-first century much less beyond), eight of those eighteen companies (Citi, Ford, GE, HP, Merck, Motorola, Nordstrom, Sony) have since underperformed the general stock market (S&P 500 index), while others have shrunk in market capitalization, and at least two (Motorola, Philip Morris) have been forced into major restructurings, divestments, or buyouts. Other companies (Hello, Boeing) faced real questions about their continued viability. The authors of *Built to Last* make a point to say part of the enduring greatness of these companies is "more than profits"—they have an outsized and lasting impact on the world. This factor is hard to measure with precise numbers, but most readers will agree that the impact and cachet of more than a few companies on this list have waned.

---

30. Richards, "Unbelievably Solid Companies," para. 5.
31. Collins and Porras, *Built to Last*, back cover copy.

Cue the quip attributed to Yogi Berra, "Prediction is hard, especially of the future." Even among companies rigorously selected specifically on the basis of enduring greatness and being "built to last," there is an inconsistent ability to deliver on the claim of maximizing shareholder value. A coin toss would have been as effective at identifying companies that could deliver shareholder value above the general market, and at least three out of the eighteen lost shareholder value over a twenty-five year period while the S&P 500 delivered gains of over 500 percent.

Building to last is a wonderful aspiration, and we applaud the desire and effort to better understand how companies can deliver sustained value. Indeed, we are fans of *Built to Last*, having been trained with it as a text in our graduate programs and used as a strategic planning tool in our professional roles. (We speak to it further in Part 3, chapter 12). Companies change constantly, and it is possible that some of the eighteen companies identified changed in unhelpful ways following that book's publication.[32] The characteristics advocated by *Built to Last* may be valuable in principle, but that value is of limited practical help if the characteristics cannot be counted on to endure.

Profit maximization for shareholders implies benefit for *current* shareholders, who seek to maximize profits for themselves. How much thought is given to value for *future* shareholders? This mentality results in inflating corporate values in the short term and then bailing. The familiar strategy of "pump and dump" springs from this mentality. Again, the 2008 crisis, and its Orwellian designation of "too big to fail" for big companies that quite obviously failed, make all too clear the consequences of this ethic. Profit maximization for current shareholders simply is not sustainable; it leads to inevitable failures and crashes that damage all stakeholders (including shareholders) and jeopardize—or end—the corporation's very existence. A sound corporate ethic would seek sustainable profitability. The current ethic is simply too shortsighted.

Problem 3: By Any Means Necessary

The third problem with the current corporate ethic is that it is entirely end-oriented. This is the-end-justifies-the-means approach that carries the danger of ignoring any sense of right and wrong in pursuit of the goal. If the only purpose or goal is profit maximization, then that purpose justifies far too many means. Even with rules and laws in place, the myopic goal of profit maximization is a powerful temptation to bend or ignore those rules

---

32. That is, they were built to last but did not continue *building* to last.

and laws, and the damage is done before outsiders ever become aware. A purely end-oriented ethic will always carry the "by any means necessary" risk and is the only ethic needed to support plantation system economics. A Partnership Ethic on the other hand is well-rounded and balanced, adding considerations of means and character to the (sustainable) profit purpose. We turn now to explain and put structure to a Partnership Ethic.

Three Modes of Moral Reasoning

Ethical reasoning considers the ways or modes in which moral norms function, in addition to their form. Done well, ethical reasoning comprises three modes, formally called teleological, deontological, and characterological. In this section we draw extensively from the work of Christian ethicists David P. Gushee and Glenn H. Stassen, notably their book *Kingdom Ethics*,[33] to define these three modes and illustrate their forms. Further drawing on this part of the work of Gushee and Stassen, we show how, done well, ethical reasoning integrates and uses all three modes to form a unified ethic for decision-making. Here we begin a demonstration of the concepts with an example from recent headlines, then in Part 2, chapter 10 we continue the example and show that applying a unified approach to economic ethics yields the transforming initiative that is a Partnership Ethic.

The word *teleological* comes from the Greek word *telos* for "end," "goal," or "purpose." In this goal-based mode, actions are right or wrong depending simply upon whether or not they advance the desired goal. From this perspective actions are evaluated not in and of themselves but on the basis of their results; the goal justifies the means. An interesting example of a purely goal-based mode appears in John 11:50–53, where Caiaphas argues that "it is expedient for you that one man should die for the people, and that the whole nation should not perish" (RSV).

Deontological emerges from the Greek word *deon*, which means "obligatory" or "binding." A deontological approach is obligated to refrain from using wrong means to achieve results and is bound to justice and fairness in acting. From this perspective actions have a moral component, actions are inherently right or wrong. Accordingly, this rules-based mode cares about achieving good ends *if just rules or principles are obeyed*. For example, a principle of justice and fairness says it is wrong to discriminate against a Hispanic person for access to health care. Once that principle is respected, then we should also pay attention to the goal of offering health care. So a continued effort to discriminate against Hispanics by cutting funding

33. Gushee and Stassen, *Kingdom Ethics*, 77–81.

for health care and denying everyone access, under the pretense of treating everyone equally, would also be immoral and unjust. Again, the rules-based mode cares about achieving good ends using just rules or principles.

Characterological is a term used by Gushee and Stassen to point to our character—that part of our inner selves that holds our virtues, who we are as people. Our virtues do not operate in a vacuum but work with the rules and principles that guide us in how we act. This character-based mode can develop virtues from virtually any source, from the dangerously evil to the rightly holy. In the ultimate sense, the character-based mode springs from one's understanding of God's character. We all derive virtues from how we perceive ultimate reality.

For those of us who seek to develop a character that supports righteousness, and particularly for those of us who call ourselves followers of Christ, the virtues expected of us are summarized in Jesus's Beatitudes and also found in the writings of the Apostle Paul. Once we understand the virtues Jesus names and the Apostle Paul expounds, we see these are the characteristics critical to enabling us to be people who embody the prayer "thy kingdom come, thy will be done, on earth as it is in heaven."

Here we illustrate the Beatitudes and how these parallel the writings of the Apostle Paul.[34] We do not imply that this is an exhaustive list of Christian virtues nor are these an arbitrary selection; they are the heart of biblical virtues. We present this table for the clear guidance it offers and as an easy reference.

Jesus's Beatitudes	Paul's Virtues
humility and meekness[35]	humility and gentleness
righteousness	righteousness
mercy	kindness, compassion, love, forgiveness

---

34. Gushee and Stassen, *Kingdom Ethics*, 37.

35. Words like *humility* and *gentleness* and especially *meekness* are wholly misunderstood today and therefore disdained. In the context of Christian virtues these and similar descriptors should never be misunderstood and misassociated with concepts like "mousy" or "weakness." Rather, properly understood, these describe the hard spiritual discipline and characteristic of seeking and following the Spirit's direction rather than one's own. Think of perhaps the world's greatest and most courageous leader (Moses) and those who follow in his example (e.g., Jesus, St. Teresa of Avila, Lincoln, Gandhi, MLK Jr., Saint Teresa of Calcutta, Mandela, etc.). "Now the man Moses was very humble, more so than anyone else on the face of the earth" (Numbers 12:3 NRSV), and God entrusted Moses "with all my house" (Numbers 12:7). Indeed, we should all be willing to be so humble.

purity of heart	purity or goodness
peacemaking	peace, tolerance, unity, patience
suffering persecution for justice and Jesus's sake	endurance
(blessed are you)	joy

To summarize, "The deontological [rules-based] mode is about what we *should* do; the teleological [goal-based] is about what we *could* do; and the characterological [character-based] is about what *we* would do."[36] Integrating these three modes results in well-rounded decision-making, as charted in the Unified Ethical Decision-Making Diagram immediately below.

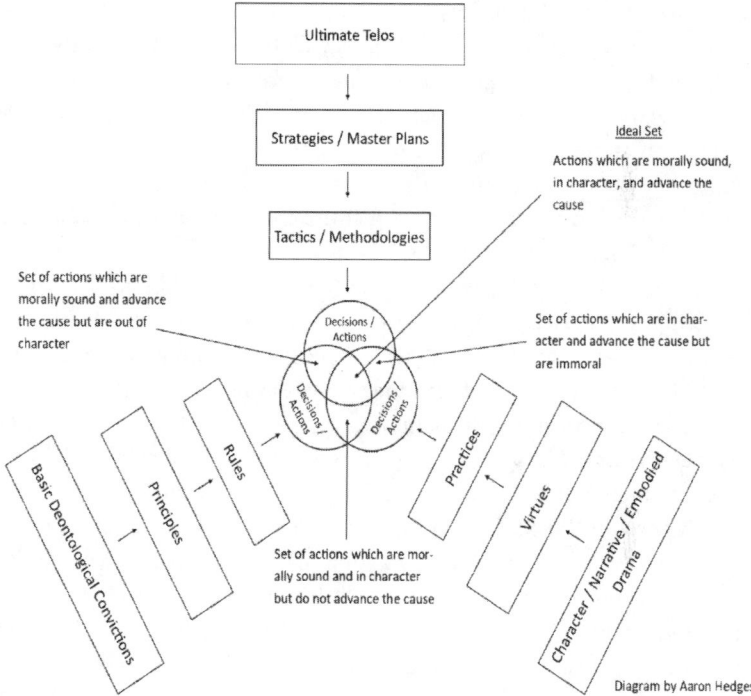

Unified Ethical Decision-Making Diagram, or Unified Ethical Modes

---

36. Gushee and Stassen, *Kingdom Ethics*, 79.

A Merely Goal-Based Approach

What happens when a corporation takes a solely (and soulless) goal-based approach to maximizing shareholder profit? The California utility Pacific Gas and Electric Company (PG&E) (NYSE:PCG) unexpectedly provided us an exemplary and timely answer. As we write this section, we read in our news feed the announcement that yesterday PG&E pled guilty to one count of unlawfully starting the 2018 blaze named "Camp Fire" (so-called because it originated along Camp Creek Road) and eighty-four counts of involuntary manslaughter. The Camp Fire is the deadliest blaze to date in California's fire-riddled history.

For our readers who will benefit from a brief update on this part of PG&E's relevant history, the corporation's faulty equipment was found responsible for starting at least thirteen separate wildfires that devastated northern California beginning in early October 2017. Apparently, those equipment failures and subsequent fires were not sufficient notice for PG&E's leadership or shareholders. The Camp Fire, ignited by faulty PG&E equipment, started the morning of November 8, 2018, in Butte County, California, eventually burned a total of 154,336 acres, destroyed 18,804 structures (including decimating the entire town of Paradise, California), and resulted in eighty-four deaths.

Forensic investigations concluded that PG&E's failure to inspect and maintain its electrical distribution towers led to equipment failure that started the Camp Fire. According to reports, the equipment that failed should have been inspected and maintained at least every five years, but no records of inspections or maintenance could be found for the previous seventeen years.[37] Most if not everyone would acknowledge PG&E's breach of duty to maintain its equipment rises to the level of gross negligence.

Reportedly, PG&E had "been criticized in recent years for the role its equipment was found to have played in a series of catastrophic fires across the state, including the Camp Fire."[38] A little more than a year later, and after independent investigations confirmed PG&E's grossly ill-maintained equipment was responsible for igniting the Camp Fire, PG&E issued a perfunctory apology for "the role our equipment had in this tragedy" (note PG&E's blame on the role of its ethics-absent equipment, rather than any blame on the role of its ethics-absent leadership). The following month, unsurprisingly, PG&E filed for bankruptcy protection from the billions in claims tied to the Camp Fire.

---

37. Hanna and Moon, "PG&E's Failure."
38. Hanna and Moon, "PG&E's Failure."

What was the PCG (the stock ticker symbol for PG&E) share price movement during the prior seventeen years when PG&E inspections and maintenance appeared to be absent? Around November 8, 2002 (sixteen years before the start of the Camp Fire blaze), PCG traded at $10.68/share. For the hypothetical shareholders who purchased PCG shares at $10.68/share, held for the next fifteen years, and perfectly timed a complete selloff around September 8, 2017, when PCG traded at a peak of $70.64, they realized a return of 561 percent. For attentive and active shareholders closely following PG&E, they may have limited losses by selling the following month, around October 13, 2017, after suspicions of PG&E's role in the October 2017 northern California firestorms began to surface and PCG share value fell to $57.72/share. For a great many passive PCG shareholders, their losses continued when on November 9, 2018, the day after the Camp Fire and renewed suspicions were ignited, PCG share value fell further to $39.92/share.

A few months later, around January 18, 2019, within the required fifteen-day waiting period required under California law before filing for Chapter 11 bankruptcy, PCG traded at $7.23/share; a 32 percent decrease from the November 2002 price. No doubt financial advisors will soon be recommending PCG to their clients, or anyone who might read their social media, pumping PCG up as a stock that one day will reach its previous highs. No doubt those financial advisors' disclaimers will not include the phrase or admission "plantation economics."

Any hypothetical PG&E *shareholders* who perfectly rode the PCG run up may have realized *gains* of well over 500 percent without giving thought to lapsed safety inspections or grossly negligent maintenance practices and the inevitable disasters to follow. Meanwhile, those very factors inflicted *losses* on thousands of PG&E *stakeholders*, including their lifetime possessions, homes, businesses, livestock, pets, children, parents, and their own lives. A "maximize shareholder value" goal-based mode without rules-based or character-based considerations is an ethic that supports plantation economics, and plantation economics yields the kind of damage PG&E shareholders and stakeholders alike suffered. In Part 2, Chapter 10, we rethink the example of PG&E from a Partnership Economics perspective.

FBUs: Of the Money, by the Money, and for the Money

> *"How come when I ask for a pair of hands,*
> *I get a human being as well?"*
>
> —Henry Ford

Earlier we asserted that our nation has shifted from a market economy to a market society. Here we put a sharper point on that assertion by observing and naming our nation's conversion from a capitalist economy-democratic society to a capitalist economy-capitalist society. This conversion is stark, significant, and increasingly damaging.

For at least the last few decades virtually everyone from business and law schools, to corporations and shareholders, to media and the courts have espoused a corporate ethic of "maximize shareholder value." As a society we should not be shocked that this ethic has mutated from our corporate lives and interactions—where many if not most of us spend most of our time—to exert its choke-hold on our personal lives and interactions.

A shining hallmark of our capitalist economy-capitalist society is the dehumanizing of the interconnected relationships in which we engage, relationships that support both a healthy capitalism and a healthy society. On one level, we dehumanize our personal interactions. Such as when one person insists on paying another for a kindness, so as to mitigate any obligation to the person performing the kindness. In this way personal interactions become impersonal transactions. On another level, we dehumanize the actual people with whom we have our personal interactions. Such as when a leader dismisses the reasonable concerns or needs of those within her organization because they interfere with her organizational agenda. In this way she dehumanizes her people, especially if it's within her power to address those concerns or needs. We illustrate dehumanizing with a lived example.

"FBU" is not a term taught in law school. Rather, we learned it while observing a law firm implode. This firm had an excellent reputation, in part because it recruited well and took the time to develop its recruits into excellent lawyers. The crisis this law firm faced during a rapidly expanding bull market was that it was beginning to quickly lose junior attorneys, lured away by substantial salary increases and signing bonuses.

After one emergency meeting of the partners, as reported by a junior partner permitted to attend, solutions to stem the loss of junior attorneys were hotly debated. He shared with a group of junior attorneys that during that meeting one of the firm's more influential equity partners argued strongly against increasing junior attorney salaries as a way to neutralize the monetary incentive to leave. Reasonable minds could differ on that view, but not after it was revealed that the equity partner argued that the junior attorneys were merely "FBUs," meaning fungible billing units. Such dehumanized FBUs could be replaced without increasing the salary expenses to him and the other equity partners.[39]

Given the optics of the equity partner's influence coupled with the apparent lack of rebuttal by the rest of the partnership, the stampede to the exit by junior attorneys (even those not previously inclined to leave but now alarmed by the FBU perspective) was swift and the firm's demise almost as swift. Ultimately, the unchecked dehumanizing of the junior attorneys as FBUs cost every stakeholder in that firm—from the highest-ranked partners to every attorney, employee, related family member, and client.

What are your stories of FBUs or experiences like "it smells like money to me"? How have you seen the destruction and dehumanization of plantation economics? Painful as they are, we welcome your stories at info@partnershipeconomics.com so together we can do battle to heal. We look forward to hearing from you and moving the conversation and action forward together.

Relentless Rules Reminder

1. Frictional costs are in every economic exchange.
2. Therefore merely transferring existing value is a losing proposition.
3. Therefore exchanges must create value greater than frictional costs to produce a true net gain.
4. We are they, and we, altogether, are average.
5. I gain/lose when we gain/lose, and we gain/lose when we all gain/lose.

---

39. A footnote for now because of lack of space but a point we expect to return to in future work: understand that FBU is a race- and gender-neutral term. Once a person in power has placed the value of money ahead of the value of people, and once people have been dehumanized by labels like FBU, issues like workplace inclusion and diversity are thoroughly dismissed and buried. That's when fighting for workplace inclusion and equality becomes futile, because that's not the real fight in the minds of those holding power. The real, upstream fight is over money and control or power.

CHAPTER 4

So What?

"To change the world, we must bring new things into being. But how do we go about creating the unmade future? I believe that all we can do is foster the optimal conditions in which it—whatever 'it' is—can emerge and flourish. This is where real confidence comes in. Not the confidence that we know exactly what to do at all times but the confidence that, together, we will figure it out."

—Ed Catmull

Necessity is the Mother of Invention

WE MUST NOTE THAT the problems with the "profit maximization for shareholders" ethic are not diminishing. As corporations grow, so does their influence on all stakeholders—all humanity, government, and environment, present and future. Short-term greed and the strictly goal-based pursuit of profit have led to crashes and crises on a recurring, cyclical basis. In recent history, the bursting of the tech bubble and numerous accounting frauds shook all stakeholders in 2001. Only seven years later the housing bubble and mortgage financing schemes crashed, harming the entire global economy. Just a decade after the "Great Recession," the COVID-19 pandemic again exposed the damaging and extensive ripple effects of many corporations' inability to provide durable value to their various stakeholders. There can be no doubt about the scope of corporations' influence. Not only are all stakeholders harmed by these cycles, corporations also fail their shareholders when they falter, rendering the current corporate ethic self-defeating.

You have heard it said that corporations should maximize profits for shareholders. But we say that the resulting vicious cycle must be recognized for what it is. In response, what initiative might be transforming?

Another Way is Possible

We recognize that the language of plantation evokes America's painful race-relations history and that race relations in America remain sorely in need of a partnership approach. As we write in 2020, this pain is renewed and on display in events across our country. From peaceful protests to violent riots to racially tinged immigration policies to Native American neglect to heated #BlackLivesMatter debates to race-based COVID-19 fearmongering, the giant soul of our nation is stirring. In our view, the pain we all experience in regard to race is tied to the economic disparity of plantation systems—not just literal plantations in the early American South but also far more widespread and still ongoing practices of exploiting rather than partnering. Until the related issue of economic exploitation is substantially addressed, our nation will not be able to overcome the racial infighting we're all watching play out from sea to shining sea. As we focus in this book on economic matters, we do so with the hopeful expectation that value is also added to interrelated areas of need, including race relations.

In his book *No Future Without Forgiveness,* Archbishop Desmond Tutu shares his insights from the fight to overthrow apartheid in South Africa (the epitome of plantation system economics) and his work on the Truth and Reconciliation Commission. In the last chapter he makes an abrupt observation about the fragility of reconciliation. We point to his insight because it's critically informative about how America must adapt if we are to reconcile our race relations. Tutu writes:

> In South Africa the whole process of reconciliation has been placed in very considerable jeopardy by the enormous disparities between the rich, mainly the whites, and the poor, mainly the blacks. The huge gap between the haves and the have-nots, which was largely created and maintained by racism and apartheid, poses the greatest threat to reconciliation and stability in our country. The rich provided the class from which the perpetrators and the beneficiaries of apartheid came and the poor

produced the bulk of the victims. This is why I have exhorted whites to support transformation taking place in the lot of blacks.

For unless houses replace the hovels and shacks in which most blacks live, unless blacks gain access to clean water, electricity, affordable health care, decent education, good jobs, and a safe environment—things which the vast majority of whites have taken for granted for so long—we can just as well kiss reconciliation goodbye.[40]

Archbishop Tutu plainly and pointedly speaks to better economics as a necessary precondition of successful reconciliation, which we seek to address with a constructive Partnership Economic Ethic.

Race relations are also valuable to keep in view as we consider Partnership Economics because they provide examples of positive change being possible even in the face of powerful, seemingly impossible opposition. As with race, simply wanting things to be better economically doesn't make them better. A better way must be conceptualized and implemented. Tutu's work in South Africa, and in the United States that of Martin Luther King Jr., have demonstrated that even deeply entrenched social problems can be changed for the better. And part of the change that King envisioned, or famously had "a dream" for, was economic. That dream remains collectively ours to materialize!

More to the Dream—Martin Luther King Jr.

The Reverend Dr. Martin Luther King Jr.'s first great dream for America was for her to eradicate her sin of racial inequality. His daring leadership during America's civil rights efforts of the 1950s–1960s gifted us with significant accomplishments toward that continuing dream. His second great dream for America, the next mountain to climb but for which he was only able to cast the vision and sketch the plan, was to eradicate her sin of economic inequality.

Dr. King was born and raised in America's segregated South during the Jim Crow era. Beginning with the view from the porch of his childhood home, he saw the detrimental effects of economic exploitation and inequity on the Black community. As he grew and his view widened, his lived experience confirmed in him the need for correction. Fortunately, his religious conviction, intellect, and education gifted him with the thoughts and words to begin moving toward that correction.

---

40. Tutu, *No Future Without Forgiveness*, 273–74.

King saw the devastating effects of the segregated South and, by extension, the segregated nation. Those who established the segregated society, he observed, "segregated southern money from the poor whites; they segregated southern mores from the rich whites; they segregated southern churches from Christianity; they segregated southern minds from honest thinking, and they segregated the Negro from everything."[41]

Segregation at its heart, Dr. King argued, is a travesty of justice perpetrated upon the American mind. At its core this travesty of justice, this crushing injustice, sprang from an ingrained theological ignorance buttressed by the cruelest of man-made laws.

The theological ignorance was rooted in prideful, zero-sum cultural fallacies including rugged individualism and absolute self-determination, at least for Whites. Raising awareness about the interrelatedness of Americans—indeed all humans, White and Black, rich and poor, Dr. King spoke of us all as "caught in an inescapable network of mutuality."[42] Despite our cultural fallacies, we all come into a ready-made world where we must rely on each other and none of us could survive alone. Using the example of the ubiquitous nature of globalization (even in the 1960s), he noted, "[T]his is the way our universe is structured, this is its interrelated quality. We aren't going to have peace on earth until we recognize this basic fact of the interrelated structure of all reality."[43] (RR4)

Turning to the legal constructs that facilitated the theological ignorance, Dr. King noted, "There are two types of laws: there are *just* and there are *unjust* laws. . . . A just law is a man-made code that squares with the moral law or the law of God.[44] An unjust law is a code that is out of harmony with the moral law. . . . Any law that uplifts human personality is just.[45] Any law that degrades human personality is unjust."[46] Dr. King was not speaking to simply the patently unjust Jim Crow-era laws on the books that physically and socially separated Blacks and Whites. He was also speaking to the kind of capitalism that exploited people.

Dr. King insightfully and incisively re-viewed the problematic nature of America's plantation economics. But he was not one to merely state problems. He was also gifted at rethinking constructive, promising solutions, an

---

41. Washington, ed., *Martin Luther King Jr.*, 122.
42. Oates, *Let The Trumpet Sound*, 452.
43. Oates, *Let The Trumpet Sound*, 452.
44. Deontology (rules-based) and characterology (character-based).
45. Teleology (goal-based).
46. Washington, ed., *Martin Luther King Jr.*, 89.

essential step that we follow in Part 2. To see some of the more beneficial ways forward, we all will need to be open to new perspectives.

A Clearer Vision

Many of us have a carefully cultivated perspective with which we navigate the complexities and nuances of life. We know a civil engineer, for example, who in his college program was taught to read and extract only the information he needed in order to (with an eye on the design budget) efficiently work and solve the physical problem in front of him. He was a good student and learned that method well. But that training and experience—those myopic lenses through which he then operated—tended to cloud his way of seeing and thinking. Well into his career, it is difficult for him to see a perspective or different solution than the one he's already settled on, although he can see other points of view when he is willing to do so.

Others of us have cultivated the ability to see and hold multiple perspectives simultaneously. Lawyers, by way of just one example, are trained to look for and try to see as many perspectives around a particular issue as possible. The potential client walking into the law office might be the pedestrian injured in a big-rig wreck who has to sue the trucking company in order to cover her medical expenses, or the owner of the trucking company that needs whatever defenses are available for the same big-rig wreck. No matter the role, the good lawyer wants as clear a vision into that wreck as possible and should want it from every angle possible.

Usually all one needs is a receptive posture and to relax a little in order to achieve clearer vision. Those moments of clearer vision are like piercing an optical illusion. For example, looking for the first time at the illustration below,[47] our engineer friend immediately saw the left-side facial profile of an old woman. After being assured there was another woman in the drawing and allowing himself not to concentrate on the image of the old woman, the image of a young woman looking away eventually emerged for him. In little time he could then alternatively see either old woman–young woman image as he shifted his perspective. When shown this same illusion, an attorney friend said she had no difficulty seeing both faces immediately, and in little time she could see and hold both faces (in what she said feels like) simultaneously.

---

47. The Illusions Index, https://www.illusionsindex.org/i/young-woman-or-old-woman.

So What?

Is it possible to go even deeper, to get even clearer vision from even more perspectives? Yes!

Stereograms, commonly known as 3D images, are created by artists using a computer program to encode a three-dimensional gray-scale image within a complicated two-dimensional pattern. Viewing a stereogram requires depth perception and can be easy if the viewer does not strain to force an image, or does not refuse to see the image that lies just below the surface. One simply rests their eyes on the stereogram and allows the image to emerge from within the pattern. Most people can see the image within a stereogram by allowing their eyes to focus at a point in the center of the stereogram and just behind the paper's surface. An example is the pattern immediately below, and adjacent is the knight-dragon image that is within and emerges from this stereogram.[48]

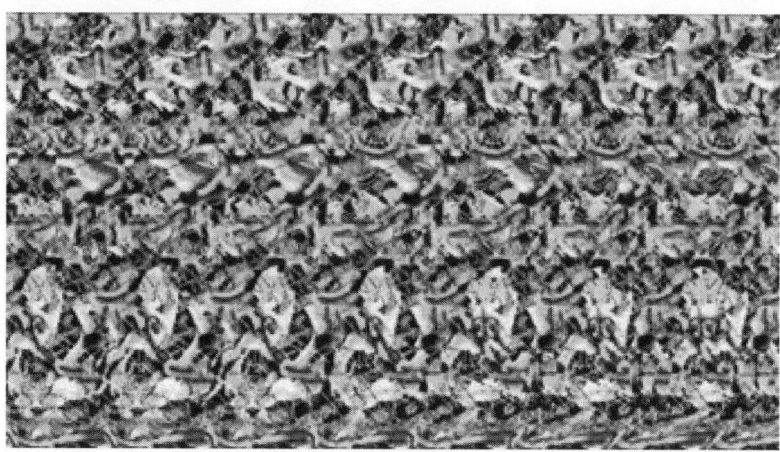

---

48. http://www.magiceye.com/gallery/081111h.html. We are fans of the work of Tom Baccei, Cheri Smith, and Bob Salitsky, and their art form known as Magic Eye®.

We want you to look into that stereogram and see this knight-dragon image for yourself, don't just take our word for it. If at first you don't succeed in seeing any image, we encourage you to relax your vision. You don't have to search for this image, just allow it to emerge and it will.[49] We're not asking you to disconnect your brain or thinking, but to relax and be receptive to gaining clearer visions into what at first looks like complexity. Stick with it until you, too, see the knight-dragon image within the stereogram.

Now we turn toward Part 2 of this book. There we explore the writings of Scriptures, Adam Smith, and Ayn Rand from perspectives that may be new to you. That likelihood of newness is the reason to show you, in these visual and memorable ways, how clearer vision into perspectives that you were not looking for and might otherwise miss is not only possible but relatively easy.

You may be like our engineer friend, practiced with one-dimensional perspectives about Scriptures, economics, and capitalism. This may make some of Part 2 difficult to perceive at first blush, especially as we challenge misconceptions about what Jesus, Smith, and Rand said or wrote. Or, you may be like our lawyer friend, more practiced with multi-dimensional perspectives. In any case, we invite you to remain caring and open-minded enough to wrestle with what we claim until the equivalent of the knight-dragon image emerges for you.

> "Clearer vision into perspectives that you were not looking for and might otherwise miss is not only possible but relatively easy."

49. Learn more about Magic Eye® at https://www.magiceye.com/faq/ and access the company's recommendations of how to view their art at https://www.magiceye.com/avada_faq/help-how-do-i-see-in-3d/.

So What?

We look forward to you meeting us on the other side of Part 2 with clearer vision from more perspectives regarding Jesus, Smith, Rand, and the pictures they actually painted for us. Clearer vision from more perspectives opens the doors to *re-thinking*.

Part 2

The Promise of Partnership —*Re-Thinking* Economics

"Hope is not only, as Kierkegaard thought, the 'passion for the possible.' Hope reaches out further over against historical possibilities and can even be characterized as a 'passion for the impossible,' the not yet possible."

—Jürgen Moltmann

"Not yet possible! There speaks the truly committed planner . . . Far-sighted people will take it into account, so that 'hope' will be differentiated by 'planning' only in degree."

—Oliver O'Donovan

IN PART 2 WE develop a more profitable alternative to plantation economics, which we term "Partnership Economics." This is a *re-thinking* of economics. Beyond mere awareness that there is a problem, interpretation and understanding of this awareness are needed. The truth further moves to make us free when the truth is known *and* understood. Floods of economic (mis)information require a sound interpretive framework to yield understanding of better economic possibilities. We find partnership to be the key to such a framework and trace the thread of partnership in economics from

Scriptures to Adam Smith, Ayn Rand, and Martin Luther King Jr., with frequent reference to John Bogle. With more room we would draw from more voices in support of Partnership Economics, and look forward to doing so in the future.

Chapter 5

A Step Closer to an Old Dream

"Along the way of life, someone must have sense enough and morality enough to cut off the chain of hate. This can only be done by projecting the ethic of love to the center of our lives."
—Martin Luther King Jr.

SPEAKING TO THE GENERATIONS of a half-century ago, which look remarkably similar to the generations of today, Dr. Martin Luther King Jr. spoke of America's economic inequity as a crisis between the haves and have-nots, that required people to go beyond limited views of race and class to develop a worldview of connectedness. From the pulpit and with the pen, Dr. King preached against the evils of communism as well as oppressive capitalism. In his view a better social order had to be constructed. A system that honored both the community and individual. "Perhaps . . . he could take his country a step closer to the realization of an old dream: the forging of a Christian commonwealth that was neither capitalist nor Communist, but a synthesis of the best features of collective and individual enterprise, a commonwealth that cared for its weak and handicapped even as it encouraged its strong and gifted."[50]

---

50. Oates, *Let The Trumpet Sound*, 462.

An Edifice which Produces Beggars Needs Restructuring

The Poor People's Campaign (PPC) grew out of Dr. King's awareness of the need to address economic exploitation everywhere. With the passage of the Civil Rights Act in 1964, he felt the economic question was the next most crucial question that Black people, and poor people generally, were confronting.[51] For example, Dr. King observed, from the typical corporate perspective, mass unemployment in the White community was a crisis that required everyone's immediate attention to correct, while the same crisis in the Black community was merely a social problem brought on by that community and to be solved by that community.[52]

Dr. King understood market discrimination and economic inequality to be even more widespread and ingrained than racial inequality. The solution, Dr. King thought, should begin by cutting across racial lines and reaching the poor in every community across the nation: Native Americans in the Southwest; Chicanos in the West; Whites in Appalachia; Blacks and Hispanics in ghettos. Just as Jesse Jackson had earlier urged the Memphis community to support the striking sanitary workers so they would not have to bear the suffering and pain of the battle alone, the nation as a whole needed to become aware of and change the plight of the poor.

King also understood power. "The plantation and ghetto were created by those who had power, both to confine those who had no power and to perpetuate their powerlessness. The problem of transforming the ghetto, therefore, is a problem of power—confrontation of the forces of power demanding change and the forces of power dedicated to the preserving of the status quo."[53] Working upstream from the problem to its source, Dr. King saw the need to dramatize the importance of jobs and economic opportunities for the poor. With the needs of the poor starkly exposed and building on the successes of the civil rights movement, Dr. King envisioned launching a movement that would successfully speak truth to power by confronting the class and racial biases of economic discrimination.

Recognizing that equipping the poor to become regular consumers benefited both the poor and rich, Dr. King cast the vision of the Poor People's Campaign as a correction to market discrimination and set as its primary goal guaranteed jobs or income for all people. "We must develop a program that will drive the nation to a guaranteed annual income.... We've

---

51. Carson, ed., *The Autobiography of Martin Luther King Jr.*, 350.
52. Carson, ed., *The Autobiography of Martin Luther King Jr.*, 350.
53. Washington, ed., *Martin Luther King Jr.*, 172.

come a long way in our understanding of human motivation and of the blind operation of our economic system. Now we realize that dislocations in the market operations of our economy and the prevalence of discrimination thrust people into idleness and bind them in constant or frequent unemployment against their will."[54]

In his "Where Do We Go from Here?" speech of August 1967, Dr. King appeared to plumb and verbalize the core of economic inequality that shaped the response that became the PPC. This was his theme of restructuring. The civil rights movement "must address itself to the question of restructuring the whole of American society.... We are called upon to help the discouraged beggars in life's marketplace. But one day we must come to see that an edifice which produces beggars needs restructuring."[55] This means that questions regarding the whole of society must be raised, such as the root causes of racism, economic exploitation, and war. "These are the triple evils that are interrelated."[56]

Finding the Highest Good Through Love

We think it instructive, both theologically and operationally, to point out that in his speech the quotes below immediately preceded the quotes above. That is, before turning to "restructuring the whole of American society" Dr. King spoke of love. "And I say to you, I have also decided to stick with love. For I know that love is ultimately the only answer to mankind's problems.... I know it isn't popular to talk about it in some circles today.... I'm not talking about emotional bosh when I talk about love, I'm talking about a strong, demanding, love.... I have decided to love. If you are seeking the highest good, I think you can find it through love.[57]

The PPC's march to Washington, D.C. was originally scheduled to begin on April 1, 1968, but was postponed to accommodate Dr. King's visit at the same time to Memphis in support of the striking sanitation workers. After the shock of Dr. King's April 4 assassination and his funeral services, the PPC effort continued under the leadership of Dr. King's faithful: Abernathy, Young, Williams, and Jackson. On May 12, 1968, the first of the demonstrators descended on Washington, D.C. Thousands followed, arriving daily from across the nation and by every means possible. For a multitude of reasons, the PPC's message and demonstrators' protests failed to elicit any

54. Washington, ed., *Martin Luther King Jr.*, 173.
55. Washington, ed., *Martin Luther King Jr.*, 176.
56. Washington, ed., *Martin Luther King Jr.*, 177.
57. Washington, ed., *Martin Luther King Jr.*, 176.

immediate response from the President or Congress, and without Dr. King at the helm it was decided to shutter the effort just five weeks later.

Although the visionary was killed more than fifty years ago, the vision remains valid and implementable. Valid because looking back it still rings true through the echoes of the same need and hope. Implementable because looking forward it is more desirable to restructure an America that seeks the highest good through love than it is to continue the current course of hindered economic good and pervasive conflict. Just because a divinely inspired messenger was murdered does not mean the divine message or mission is dead.

In Dr. King's view there was only one true and sustainable solution: America needed a total, strong-and-demanding-love–based reconstruction of its economic system for the benefit of everyone. This was a bold step, envisioning to challenge the plantation inequities of American capitalism. It was an even bolder step to put voice, structure, and action to such a plan. In light of continuing plantation economics, might Dr. King appreciate an effort to dream afresh, to envision and implement Partnership Economics?

Homo Hermeneuticus—Interpreting Human

Let's briefly return to the helpful framing of behavioral economics and the factors of ignorance, uncertainty, and confusion that feature so prominently in our human economic experience. In Part 1 we dealt with ignorance by re-viewing our current form of economics (plantation) and making plain how problematic it is. If you weren't before, you should now be aware, rather than ignorant, of some destructive economic realities.

Part 2 now takes on the second step in better behavioral economics: addressing uncertainty. Uncertainty means that, when we do have some awareness of economic facts, we are uncertain about what those facts mean, uncertain of how to interpret and make sense of the facts. We must move from mere awareness and uncertainty about what the awareness means, to interpreting and understanding.

We're no longer ignorant, but a vacuum isn't helpful. The answer to bad economics isn't no economics but better economics. We need an intelligible solution, a constructive rethinking of economics. We need a sturdy interpretive framework (hermeneutic) and ethic that moves us beyond the problems of plantation economics toward a better capitalism. We deem this framework and ethic Partnership Economics and construct it in dialogue with the most influential economic voices of our civilization.

As you read and reflect on these voices and interpretations, we invite your collaboration, critiques, questions, comments, ideas, etc. at info@partnershipeconomics.com. We look forward to hearing from you and moving the conversation and action forward together.

Relentless Rules Reminder

1. Frictional costs are in every economic exchange.
2. Therefore merely transferring existing value is a losing proposition.
3. Therefore exchanges must create value greater than frictional costs to produce a true net gain.
4. We are they, and we, altogether, are average.
5. I gain/lose when we gain/lose, and we gain/lose when we all gain/lose.

CHAPTER 6

In God We Trust

"Religion without humanity is very poor human stuff."
—Sojourner Truth

Hebrew Bible

WE BEGIN TRACING THE thread of Partnership Economics in the ancient texts of the Hebrew Bible. For our readers who may want to get on with contemporary economics without much regard for biblical texts, it is important to recognize that Judeo-Christian influences have played a major part in shaping our world, so they can also be influences for reshaping it, including economically. Also, these texts and the traditions around them have stood the test of millennia, so at the very least it is worth considering how such durable wisdom could be helpful economically.

At the center of the Torah, Leviticus 17–26 is known as the "Holiness Code." This is an extended series of laws from God (YHWH) about holiness—how God's people are to live. Leviticus 19:1–2 makes the theme plain:

> And the LORD spoke to Moses, saying, "Speak to all the congregation of the people of Israel and say to them, You shall be holy, for I the LORD your God am holy."

This code of conduct, formalized into governing law for the Hebrew people, has theological grounding—the policies for the people flow from the nature of God. If such a divine basis for human policy-setting strikes you as foreign—a practice that could only belong to a long time ago in a land far, far away—remember that the Declaration of Independence also uses a divine basis for human policy-setting.

> WE hold these Truths to be self-evident, that all Men are created equal, that they are endowed by their Creator with certain unalienable Rights, that among these are Life, Liberty and the Pursuit of Happiness. —That to secure these Rights, Governments are instituted among Men, deriving their just Powers from the Consent of the Governed, that whenever any Form of Government becomes destructive of these Ends, it is the Right of the People to alter or to abolish it, and to institute new Government, laying its Foundation on such Principles, and organizing its Powers in such Form, as to them shall seem most likely to effect their Safety and Happiness.

This charter code, eventually formalized into governing law, has theological grounding—the desired nature of government among people flows from the nature of "their Creator." The "self-evident" truths of how "all men are created" and "endowed by their Creator" lead to the just nature of government among people, as well as to the right of the people to change the government when it becomes destructive. The Declaration goes on to provide a detailed list of examples of the failings of the government of Great Britain, giving very specific meaning to broad terms like *just* and *destructive*.

In fact, every code of conduct, every policy, has some grounding convictions (truths that are considered self-evident). Whether or not those convictions are explicitly theological, they involve one's sense of the nature of reality, what the world as a whole is like. No policy emerges from a vacuum; principles, ethics, and laws develop from the grounding convictions of worldviews. Better to acknowledge those grounding convictions and how they inform policies—as Leviticus and the Declaration of Independence do—than to operate in ignorance of underlying convictions.

Like *just* and *destructive*, *holy* is a broad term. What exactly does it mean to be "holy" in light of God's holiness? Just as the Declaration of Independence gives specific meaning to its key but broad terms through examples, Leviticus chapters 17–26 provide many concrete, specific examples of holiness. Chapter 19 in particular has clear examples of an economic nature that point to the principle we call Partnership Economics.

> Leviticus 19:9–10: When you reap the harvest of your land, you shall not reap your field right up to its edge, neither shall you gather the gleanings after your harvest. And you shall not strip your vineyard bare, neither shall you gather the fallen grapes

of your vineyard. You shall leave them for the poor and for the
sojourner: I am the LORD your God.

Don't take every last scrap for yourself without regard for others—don't "maximize" your own value at the expense of others. Instead of creating hardship for the poor and the stranger/foreigner by excessive self-seeking, those with resources are to cultivate them well and to consider others. Use excess resources to partner with others, particularly the poor and the stranger.

> Leviticus 19:11: You shall not steal; you shall not deal falsely;
> you shall not lie to one another.

Pretty straightforward. However, easy to understand does not mean easy to do. Not dealing falsely has the benefit of being far-reaching but the disadvantage of being unpopular. As one unfortunate example, consider the tortured history of the Department of Labor Fiduciary Rule, which in essence seeks to require retirement advisors to act in the best interest of their clients—to act in good faith toward the very people they advise. The rule was proposed in October 2010, faced numerous challenges, was vacated by an appeals court in June 2018, and remains unimplemented as of this writing. Contrary to the resistance to a fiduciary standard, partnership follows Leviticus and means *not* dealing falsely but instead dealing in good faith—faithfully seeking benefit for those entrusting you to do exactly that. (In this Part 2 we simply want to develop an understanding of Partnership Economics. We will return to ways to put it into specific practice, including more on fiduciary standards, in Part 3.)

> Leviticus 19:13: You shall not oppress your neighbor or rob him.
> The wages of a hired servant shall not remain with you all night
> until the morning.

Don't oppress neighbors or laborers, much less rob them. Partner by providing a non-oppressive wage, in full and on time.

> Leviticus 19:15: You shall do no injustice in court. You shall not
> be partial to the poor or defer to the great, but in righteousness
> shall you judge your neighbor.

Simple, straightforward, righteous decisions. Unlike "class warfare" that advocates the attacking of one class by another or the gaining of one class at another's expense, do not be unjust by being partial to either the poor or the great. One implication is that "the 1 percent" should not be mistreated simply because they are in the 1 percent. Henri Nouwen has rightly cautioned that a concern for the poor should not "carry with it a prejudice against the rich."[58] We should not idolize the rich and great, nor should we demonize them. We also should neither idolize nor demonize the poor. Partnership involves justly seeking the best interest of all partners, rich and poor alike.

> Leviticus 19:17: You shall not hate your brother in your heart, but you shall reason frankly with your neighbor, lest you incur sin because of him.

Another admonition against class warfare, as well as against interpersonal bitterness. Do not harbor resentment by allowing hate in your heart; be frank *with* your neighbor. Candid, in-person communication between aggrieved parties is called for. Shane Claiborne's line is unfortunately true: too often the problem isn't that rich and poor people don't care about each other but that rich and poor people don't know each other.[59] In our culture this disconnect is used for polarization, economic segregation, and technologically mediated communication; "reason frankly *with* your neighbor" is strong medicine. Partnership involves frankness *with* economic neighbors, not holding hateful attitudes *about* them or from a distance spouting unhelpful things *about* them.

> Leviticus 19:32: You shall stand up before the gray head and honor the face of an old man, and you shall fear your God: I am the Lord.

Respect your elders. People with more advanced age should not be discriminated against because of the innate characteristic of age but should be shown honor. Honoring our elders also provides the opportunity to hear and benefit from their wisdom, even the wisdom of what doesn't work gained from previous experience. Mutually beneficial partnership can involve people of any age.

> Leviticus 19:33–34: When a stranger sojourns with you in your land, you shall not do him wrong. You shall treat the stranger who sojourns with you as the native among you, and you shall love him as yourself, for you were strangers in the land of Egypt: I am the Lord your God.

Don't do wrong to strangers/foreigners—treat them as your own people, your partners. Love them as yourself—seek their benefit as well as your own. Partner, even with strangers, for mutual benefit.

---

58. Nouwen, *Spirituality of Fundraising*, 36.
59. Claiborne, *Irresistible Revolution*, 99–100.

Luke Bretherton's excellent article "'Neither a Borrower nor a Lender Be'?" insightfully shows that the apparent inconsistency of some Scriptures approving lending with interest and others forbidding that practice is resolved by considering the relational context. Within the covenant community there should be trust for repayment without charging interest; outside the covenant community, where trust is not yet well-established, the use of interest is allowed and encourages the formation of exchanges/relationships—dare we say partnerships—between people or groups who otherwise would not interact. Trust is necessary for mutual exchange; Bretherton demonstrates a scriptural basis for economic practices that help create that trust and mutuality among new partners.[60]

Strangers do not need to be excluded but can be lovingly engaged with sturdy finance practices that enable exchanges appropriate to the relationship and level of trust, leading toward increasing trust and partnership.

> Leviticus 19:35–36: You shall do no wrong in judgment, in measures, or length or weight or quantity. You shall have just balances, just weights, a just ephah [a measurement of volume], and a just hin [a smaller measurement of volume]. I am the LORD your God, who brought you out of the land of Egypt.

In assessing or measuring what you provide someone, do no wrong—how's that for a fiduciary standard? Do no wrong. Partnership means exchanges of goods and services have a just balance.

These examples all point to partnership, and they demonstrate what partnership looks like with various partners: the poor, strangers/foreigners, those entrusting you, neighbors, laborers, the poor *and* the great alike, brothers and sisters, the elderly, those receiving your assessments or measured goods and services. Leviticus 19:18 provides a brilliantly brief summary of these many laws: "love your neighbor as yourself: I am the LORD."

Already many types of economic "neighbors" have been addressed, so a broad understanding of "neighbor" makes this a far-reaching principle. "Love your (economic) neighbor as yourself" is the essence of Partnership Economics. It can be accurately restated as "benefit your (economic) neighbor as yourself" and "partner with your (economic) neighbor for mutual benefit."

If this concept were found only in Leviticus and afterward faded into obscurity, we should question its import. However, this core principle of partnership, including its economic aspects, is carried forward by a noteworthy teacher in the Hebrew tradition in the first century CE.

---

60. Bretherton, "Neither Borrower nor Lender."

Re-Thinking Jesus Preview

- Common but inaccurate understanding: Jesus advocates for the interests and concerns of others only ("other-interest"), without any regard for self-interest and no matter the cost or harm to self. To follow Jesus is to completely sacrifice self for the sake of others.
- Necessary correction: Don't passively absorb almost 2,000 years of second-hand portrayals about a significant person or his thought. Go to the source itself. What does Jesus actually say?
- More accurate understanding (see for yourself): Jesus does advocate for other-interest, and his view of other-interest is clearly paired with self-interest. Jesus's own summary of the whole of God's teaching, following the Hebrew scriptures and further exemplified in Jesus's most famous sermon, is to love God and to love your neighbor *as yourself*—within the love of God, pursue mutual self-interest and other-interest.

Sermon on the Mount

The New Testament also has much to say about economics. For focus among these wide-ranging texts, Jesus's instruction in the Sermon on the Mount serves as a keystone, a portion of material representative of and shedding light on the larger body of work.

Matthew 6:19–34 in the Sermon on the Mount presents a long block of explicitly economic teaching from Jesus, dealing with issues of money, food, and clothing. There are a variety of opinions about exactly how this block should be subdivided. These range from "disjointed units of tradition" to two units based on the preceding "Lord's Prayer" of vv. 9–13 to four units with 7:13–14 as the interpretive key.[61]

---

61. Robert Guelich notes that vv. 19–24 and vv. 25–34 can appear as "apparently disjointed units of tradition" with no interrelationship, but he follows Gunther Bornkamm in finding structure based on the preceding "Lord's Prayer" of vv. 9–13. In this approach, vv. 19–24 relate to the first three petitions of the prayer, and vv. 25–34 relate to the fourth petition. Ulrich Luz treats those same sections separately based on their internal coherences, vv. 19–24 as three related logia and the particularly unified vv. 25–34. Hans Dieter Betz includes this material in a larger Matthew 6:19–7:12 section and then takes 7:13–14 as the interpretive key. Each unit in the large section contains parenthetical material which can be understood as describing the "rough" path of 7:13–14 that leads to life. With this frame of reference, Betz then treats 6:19–21, 22–23, 24, and 25–34 as four distinct units. David Gushee and Glen Stassen make a slight adjustment, placing v. 24 with the second section. They view 6:19–23 and 6:24–34 as distinct but related sections, the eleventh and twelfth triads in their traditional righteousness/vicious cycle/transforming initiative model.

In our analysis we see and understand two major, economic parallel units—vv. 19–24 and vv. 25–33—with v. 34 encapsulating the full block of teaching. These two units provide complementary "from above" and "from below" economic parallels and perspectives that frame the gateway to Partnership Economics.

Verses 19 and 25 parallel each other by opening with negative commands—"Do not . . ." The Greek grammar is entirely parallel.[62] Verses 24 and 33 can also be read as parallel summary statements—"You cannot serve God and money" and "Seek first the kingdom of God." Each statement encapsulates its respective unit, and together they form a synthetic parallelism emphasizing the priority of the kingdom of God.[63]

These two sections could be treated separately and provide valuable insights, and there are many commentaries that do that well. We suggest, however, that they are better taken together. Many scholars note that both sections have economic themes, but we have not seen our particular approach, below, proposed elsewhere. It has sturdy grammatical and structural support as described above, and it also presents tremendous interpretive potential, particularly for economic ethics, inspired by Christ and beneficial to all.

We argue that Matthew 6:19–34 presents a single economic ethic viewed from two perspectives—"from above" and "from below." Matthew 6:19–24 is the view from above. Only people who have some economic prosperity need to be told to avoid treasuring for themselves on earth. Matthew 6:25–33 is the view from below. People of economic poverty are anxious about food and clothing. These two units address the distinct perspectives of prosperity and poverty, but they do not offer distinct ethics. Rather, Jesus points the prosperous and poor alike to the core economic conviction of his kingdom message: God provides.

The "from above" and "from below" perspectives do not pertain strictly to prosperity and poverty in a narrow monetary sense; this is not merely about how much or how little one has. These perspectives are best understood in terms of *one's relationship with their economic goods*. From above, one has the perspective of sufficiency if not abundance—having "enough," however much or little that may be. From below, one has the perspective of lack—not having "enough," however much or little that may

---

62. Both commands are formed with μή + a 2nd-person plural present imperative. This is the common form to express a prohibition.

63. We also think the second section should begin at v. 25, rather than v. 24 as some scholars suggest, because v. 25 opens with διὰ τοῦτο, which is widely translated as "therefore" but can be literally understood as "on account of this." Either way, this formulaic phrase with the singular neuter form of οὗτος is a clear reference to the previous material, bringing it to bear on a following unit.

be. The perspective from above is characterized by the sense of plenty—feeling prosperous and needing a way to securely employ that prosperity. The perspective from below is characterized by the sense of lack—feeling impoverished and needing a way to feel secure.

Structure of Matthew 6:19–34:
Integrating Parallel Perspectives Reveals a Single Economic Ethic

	From Above vv. 19–24	From Below vv. 25–33
Prohibition . . .	v. 19 Do not lay up for yourselves treasure on earth . . .	v. 25 Therefore I tell you, do not be anxious about your life, what you will eat or what you will drink, nor about your body, what you will put on. . . .
. . . with initial explanation	. . . where moth and rust destroy and where thieves break in and steal.	. . . Is not life more than food, and the body more than clothing?
Further instruction and explanation	v. 20 through all but last phrase of v. 24	vv. 26–32
Summary statements	end of v. 24 You cannot serve God and Mammon.	v. 33 But seek first the kingdom of God and his justice, and all these things will be added to you.
Encapsulation of full block of teaching	v.34 Therefore do not be anxious about tomorrow, for tomorrow will be anxious for itself. Sufficient for the day is its own trouble.	

It is of utmost importance to note that both "from above" and "from below" have needs related to security, whether securing one's prosperity or securing one's survival. Throughout this block of economic teaching, Jesus recognizes realities of human experience that underlie our economic actions—behavioral economics!—and he speaks to those deeper issues in deep ways. The final summary statement of the full block of teaching, "do not be anxious," which is grounded in serving God not money and in seeking the kingdom of God more than superficial economic comforts, goes to the core of the matter theologically and economically.

With this understanding, let's explore these two perspectives, united by the single conviction that God provides, flowing toward an ethic of partnership.

From Above

"There's no question in my mind that anyone's personal wealth is the product of a collective effort, and of social structures which present opportunities to some people, and obstacles to countless others."

—MacKenzie Scott[64]

From above, "God provides" means that treasuring for oneself is unwise, unproductive, and unfulfilling. Why risk the loss of stored treasures when God provides securely (vv. 19–21)? Ample receiving of God's provision must result in fruitful use of that provision (vv. 22–23). Why leave God's service to pursue what God already provides (v. 24)?

> Matthew 6:19–21: Do not lay up for yourselves treasures on earth, where moth and rust destroy and where thieves break in and steal, but lay up for yourselves treasures in heaven, where neither moth nor rust destroys and where thieves do not break in and steal. For where your treasure is, there your heart will be also.

This is investment advice—Jesus as investment advisor says invest for the long term, the really long term, invest in things of eternal value. Such advice fits well the "do not be anxious" theme—don't invest in things that make you lose sleep at night, don't invest in things that you have to keep worrying about—invest in things that are secure. In a financial world obsessed with so-called securities, Jesus teaches the kinds of investments that are truly secure—treasures in heaven.

What is meant by heaven? In the "Lord's Prayer" earlier in Matthew 6, Jesus teaches to pray, "Your kingdom come, your will be done, on earth as it is in heaven." *On earth as in heaven*. This serves as a strong caution against viewing heaven as exclusively otherworldly, completely detached from our current world. Investing in heaven, according to Jesus, is to be done in ways that are realized on earth! We are not to store up treasures on earth, but

---

64. The world's richest woman as of this writing, who has pledged to donate to others the majority of her fortune over her lifetime, and has donated almost $2 billion to date. See https://time.com/nextadvisor/banking/mackenzie-scott-charitable-giving/.

neither are we to ignore earthly things—we are to invest in heaven while seeking the realization of God's heavenly will on earth.[65]

These verses are also risk management advice. In financial investing alone, there are countless types of risk—interest-rate risk, default risk, fraud risk, volatility risk, political risk, inflation risk, competitive risk, innovation risk, liquidity risk, delisting risk, etc. Beyond strictly financial matters, risk management in the larger economic sense is a huge and complex field that admits by its very name just how limited it is—risk cannot be eliminated, only managed.

In our sea of constantly swirling risks, Jesus's words to counter the risks of moth and rust and thief may seem quaint—but if people had anxiety about those risks, we should not pretend that we are subject to any less anxiety given the risks we face. Jesus's idea of risk management is at once simpler and sturdier than most—invest in things that can't be destroyed (by moth, rust, virus—microbiological or digital, disease, storm, market downturn, economic bust, war, exchange rates, depreciation, and on and on). Invest in things that can't be stolen (by thieves, cyber thieves, thievery of fraud, the thief of inflation, and on and on). Invest in things that simply aren't subject to risk, at least not in an ultimate sense, because they are rooted in the ultimate reality of God.

> Matthew 6:22–23: The eye is the lamp of the body. So, if your eye is healthy, your whole body will be full of light, but if your eye is evil, your whole body will be full of darkness. If then the light in you is darkness, how great is the darkness!

The "evil eye" here is an expression for stinginess, and the good or healthy eye means generous. If your eye is good—you are good toward others—you have good relationships with others, then your whole body is full of light. There is less anxiety for you . . . and for them, meaning the collective "body" is better too. This corporate ethic lightens the whole "body"—both those dealing favorably and those favorably dealt with are lightened. Corporate bodies can be either stingy or generous and subject to the same teaching here about promoting light or darkness, creating anxiety or reducing it based on use of economic goods in relationship with others.

We often think of exploitation as happening by the rich toward the poor, and that is a problem to be resisted, yet the exploitation of others with economic ramifications happens both ways. Those with fewer resources are also subject to greed (the stingy eye) and motivations less than generous

---

65. In this vein we also note that Jesus said "the kingdom of heaven is among you" (Luke 17:21) and Matthew's use of "kingdom of heaven" as synonymous with "kingdom of God."

as they view those with more resources. This can result in trying to use resourced people for their resources (manipulative, self-seeking personal "relationships" and/or political agendas) rather than pursuing genuine relationships with them in the spirit of love your neighbor as yourself. Wealthy people often experience fear, worry, dare we say anxiety as they come to be suspicious of people's "evil eyes" toward them. Again, Nouwen rightly cautions that we not let our concern for the poor "carry with it a prejudice against the rich."[66]

> Matthew 6:24: No one can serve two masters, for either he will hate the one and love the other, or he will be devoted to the one and despise the other. You cannot serve God and Mammon.

A divided self creates great anxiety—no one can ultimately serve two masters, and trying to creates tremendous stress/anxiety. One of Jesus's opening lines in the Sermon on the Mount expresses the blessing of a fully unified self. "Blessed are the pure in heart, for they shall see God" (Matthew 5:8). Contrast this with the effects of living a double life. Imagine trying to work two full-time jobs for completely different companies/masters, much less keep up two different 24/7 agendas. There are numerous studies showing the negative impacts of stress from multi-tasking on even minor tasks; being pulled by two different ultimate agendas—God's and Mammon's—simply doesn't work.

"Mammon" is used very distinctively here, as a personification or even deification of monetary/material wealth. As a common noun, mammon is a neutral term for material goods, requiring modification as "unjust mammon" when under criticism (see Luke 16:9). Mammon in this usage is not neutral but a personified pursuit of wealth that demands religious devotion in place of God, resulting in loss of control and self-enslavement. Put plainly by Hans Dieter Betz, "One can either serve God in freedom or serve Mammon in slavery."[67] The full Luke 16:1–13 context of Jesus's teaching on mammon/Mammon is aptly summarized by Nick Spencer: "As a parable and a teaching, the story cuts the ground away from absolute property rights in favour of relationship. Earning stuff, owning stuff, lending stuff, owing stuff: that's all fine, just so long as it doesn't lead you to sacralise stuff."[68]

Day by day we all have to invest ourselves somewhere, put our trust for our resources and our very lives in something. Risk, and along with it anxiety, decrease as the trustworthiness of where we place our trust increases.

---

66. Nouwen, *Spirituality of Fundraising*, 36.
67. Betz, *Sermon on the Mount*, 458.
68. Spencer, "Use Worldly Wealth to Gain Friends."

From Below

"When I got religion, I found some work to do to benefit somebody."
—Sojourner Truth

From below, "God provides" means that economic anxiety has no place. Nature demonstrates that God provides for Creation, and people can expect the same—or more (vv. 25–30). God knows what we need (vv. 31–32). Seek the kingdom, and all will be provided (v. 33) . . . through partnership with those of the "from above" perspective!

> Matthew 6:25–30: Therefore I tell you, do not be anxious about your life, what you will eat or what you will drink, nor about your body, what you will put on. Is not life more than food, and the body more than clothing? Look at the birds of the air: they neither sow nor reap nor gather into barns, and yet your heavenly Father feeds them. Are you not of more value than they? And which of you by being anxious can add a single hour to his span of life? And why are you anxious about clothing? Consider the lilies of the field, how they grow: they neither toil nor spin, yet I tell you, even Solomon in all his glory was not arrayed like one of these. But if God so clothes the grass of the field, which today is alive and tomorrow is thrown into the oven, will he not much more clothe you, O you of little faith?

In the most concrete sense, Jesus here speaks to the basic material needs of human existence—food and clothing. And he does so "therefore"—because of the immediately preceding "from above" section. Because God provides for investing in heaven (6:19–21) such that God's will is done on earth as in heaven (6:10), because God provides and encourages "good eye" light instead of "evil eye" darkness (6:22–23), because God provides and we don't have to serve two masters (6:24)—therefore do not be anxious about your life. God provides, for the necessities of life just as for investment of plenty.

The basic needs of food and clothing are not just matters of physical existence, as Jesus is very clear—they can trigger anxiety. This anxiety about food and clothing is not limited to those who are in material poverty; one can have vast wealth yet also have a "from below" perspective if they feel they do not have enough, if they feel they are lacking. Indeed, insecurity can and does strike those who have much material wealth.

John D. Rockefeller, business titan of the Standard Oil Company, in the late nineteenth and early twentieth centuries amassed wealth of staggering proportions, by some accounts possessing a fortune of about 2 percent of America's GDP. (Based on America's 2019 GDP, that would be about $430 billion in 2019 dollars.) Journalist Ida Tarbell investigated his business dealings, exposing their shady aspects and becoming highly critical of the business and the man. Her words upon seeing Rockefeller in person in 1905 are striking:

> There was an awful age in his face—the oldest man I had ever seen, I thought, but what power! . . . My two hours study of Mr. Rockefeller aroused a feeling I had not expected, which time has intensified. I was sorry for him. I know no companion so terrible as fear. Mr. Rockefeller, for all the conscious power written in face and voice and figure, was afraid, I told myself, afraid of his own kind.[69]

Nouwen again has powerful words reminding us that even those who may appear to be very "from above," like Rockefeller, experience the "from below" perspective and need compassion and deeper security. "More and more, my experience is that rich people are also poor, but in other ways. Many rich people are very lonely. Many struggle with a sense of being used. Others suffer from feelings of rejection or depression. It may seem strange to say, but the rich need a lot of attention and care."[70]

> Matthew 6:31–32: Therefore do not be anxious, saying, "What shall we eat?" or "What shall we wear?" For the Gentiles seek after all these things, and your heavenly Father knows that you need them all.

Simply telling people to "not be anxious" would not be helpful, in fact could be invalidating and harmful, if the underlying cause of anxiety is not addressed. The "therefore" of these verses makes that connection. Because God feeds the multitude of birds, and people are more valuable than birds, therefore do not be anxious about what to eat—God knows what you need. Because God clothes the expanses of grass, and people are more valuable than grass, therefore do not be anxious about what to wear—God knows you need that too. However "from below" we may feel, Jesus reminds us that God provides for all aspects of the glorious Creation, so people (the divine image-bearers in the Creation) need not be anxious but at peace in receiving from the Creator who knows their true needs.

---

69. Chernow, *Titan*, 452.
70. Nouwen, *Spirituality of Fundraising*, 36.

The anxiety of what to eat and what to wear is not limited to those in material poverty; those who are materially wealthy may be poor in other ways, may also feel the "from below" insecurity of what to eat or wear. In our current culture we cannot miss the pressure among the "well-off"[71] in matters of food, drink, body, and clothing. Those who don't have anxiety as to whether or not they will have anything at all to eat, drink, or wear often replace that with anxiety about eating, drinking, or wearing "the right" things, however they may be defined by trends of the moment. The more material wealth one has, the worse this pressure can be. Even if you have no experience with red carpet celebrity attention, consider how simply speaking in front of a relatively small group of very supportive people increases your level of self-consciousness about your appearance. For those in the public spotlight, whose careers and psyches can be subjected to cruel scorn when any of their appearances is dubbed a "miss" rather than "hit," Jesus's words to not be anxious about what you eat, what your drink, your body, what you wear are sorely needed.

Social media now creates a showcase in which eating, drinking, body, and clothing are intensely scrutinized, and not just for public appearances by public figures. *You* can be minding your own business, unknowingly have your name and likeness posted by someone else, and experience anxiety from being on display in ways uncomfortable to you. Part of Jesus's remedy is the theological focus—don't worry about what critical people think moment by moment, trend by trend; don't worry what your interior insecurities say—focus on God who knows your true needs and cares for you in life-giving ways as part of the glorious Creation.

> Matthew 6:33: But seek first the kingdom of God and his justice,
> and all these things will be added to you.

Instead of anxiously seeking for yourself, whether by having material wealth but being in insecure servitude to it (6:19–25) or by experiencing insecurity in basic material needs or social expectations around those needs (6:25–32), seek first the kingdom of God. The cardinal teachings of the kingdom of God, echoed and expounded upon in the Sermon on the Mount teachings we are here examining, are to love God with all of all you've got and to love your neighbor as yourself (Deuteronomy 6:4–5; Leviticus 19:18; Matthew 22:34–40; Mark 12:28–34; Luke 10:25–37). This is what it means

---

71. Interesting phrase, isn't it—why do we assume having wealth equates to being well? This is just one data point, but it is worth noting that while Americans' overall use of antidepressants surges, there is no variation in antidepressant use based on income. See https://www.health.harvard.edu/blog/astounding-increase-in-antidepressant-use-by-americans-201110203624.

to seek first the kingdom of God, this is what it means for God's kingdom to come and God's will to be done on earth as in heaven.

For those who may be religiously devout in a way that has been detached from economics, we cannot overstate the significance of the fact that Jesus commands "seek first the kingdom of God" as part of a block of teaching that overtly and definitively deals with money and material resources. For those who may be economically inclined in a way that has been detached from religion, we cannot overstate the significance of the fact that Jesus offers a way for "all these things"—material resources and the behavioral aspects that drive people's approach to them—to be added to all who need them. Jesus says our dis-ease, material and relational, can be overcome by stopping the disease of serving Mammon and instead serving God, seeking first the kingdom of God, God's justice. That's quite an offer. Can it be taken seriously? How would it work?

We must highlight that Jesus says "all these things *will be added to you*"—the use of passive voice deliberately does not specify the agency by which all things are added. (Also note that "you," both in the imperative "[you] seek first the kingdom of God" and in "will be added to you" are plural. Throughout the full Matthew 6:19–34 block, in fact, the vast majority of "you" usage is plural, an important distinction to make for English readers who may read "you" only in an individual sense.) Jesus plainly does not say, "God will hand-deliver all these things to you individually."[72] After teaching about having resources and lacking them, and the perspectives of having enough and lacking, Jesus uses active voice to say that God knows all that you all need (6:32) and passive voice to say "all these things will be added to you all" (6:33).

Our scholarship unleashes the convicting and inescapable conclusion that the adding to us of all that we need (basic needs, wise investment, valuable relationship, peace rather than anxiety) *happens via partnership with our fellow human beings.* "All these things will be added to you all" when all of us from all across the "from above" and "from below" experiences come together with all our resources (material and relational) and all our needs (material and relational) to seek mutual benefit with each other. This is the enlightened mutuality of the kingdom of God. This is foundational to our Partnership Ethic.

---

72. Also, when Jesus used the example of birds in 6:26, he did not suggest that God's provision for the birds comes from glowing angels directly to their beaks; the birds go out and get their food. The early bird gets the worm. Just as Jesus recognizes God as the source of provision for birds through the medium of nature, so should we recognize God as the source of provision for us, whatever the economic medium may be (nature, money, trade, etc.).

Better Together

The core conviction that "God provides" fundamentally (re)shapes our relationship to economic goods and to our fellow human beings, whether from above or from below. From above, in the perspective of plenty, we receive God's provision and invest it securely and productively with one another rather than anxiously hoarding for our divided selves. From below, in the perspective of poverty, we receive God's provision gratefully as part of a glorious Creation rather than anxiously comparing ourselves with those who appear to have more. God provides for our needs—economic and relational, countering our underlying anxieties about both—through our partnership with each other. In partnership together, loving neighbor as self, God secures our material resources and our psychology that are otherwise prone to insecurity.

> Matthew 6:34: Therefore do not be anxious about tomorrow, for tomorrow will be anxious for itself. Sufficient for the day is its own trouble.

This verse summarizes all of 6:19–33, Jesus's profound, as-needed-in-the-twenty-first-century-as-the-first, life-giving teaching on loving your economic neighbor as yourself. "Do not be anxious about tomorrow" applies to those from above and those from below alike. Remember Nouwen's observation that materially rich people may be poor in other ways, and note the corollary that materially poor people may be rich in other ways. Don't be anxious about how to manage your plenty, materially or in other ways, nor about how to manage your poverty, materially or in other ways. Whether "from above" with the perspective of enough or "from below" with the perspective of lack, whether materially or in other ways, do not be anxious but trust that God provides what is needed and seek the realization of God's provision in the mutually beneficial partnering of those with plenty and those in need. The partnership of mutually beneficial interacting—love as a verb—among those who have various forms of plenty to meet each other's various forms of need makes for a sufficient and satisfying day.

This verse, and the teaching it summarizes, are not calls for short-sightedness or endorsements of poor planning; quite the opposite! Recall that the opening vv. 19–21 are about investments that truly last, and here in the closing v. 34 Jesus does not command an irresponsible ignoring of tomorrow but rather speaks against our anxious attempts to control tomorrow. "Begin with the end in mind" fits Jesus's teaching. Good strategy knows the long-term purpose to be achieved and how day-to-day activities move toward that purpose; Jesus points to the long-term purpose of the kingdom of God coming, the desired end of God's will being done on earth as in heaven—that is the "tomorrow" that we therefore do not need to be anxious about. With that end in mind, we can go through each day as a beginning that has sufficiency (and, yes, trouble—see Part 3 of this book) in moving toward that ultimate purpose. In Jesus's vision we don't irresponsibly live like there's no tomorrow, or aimlessly do things that lack alignment toward a meaningful tomorrow, or anxiously try to create tomorrow in our own image; we handle the trouble of the day knowing that it is a sufficient step toward the tomorrow that *God provides*.[73]

From God the Father to Another Father

The Leviticus command to love your neighbor as yourself, framed theologically, is echoed explicitly by Jesus in the Gospels of Matthew (22:34–40), Mark (12:28–34), and Luke (10:25–37), and with variation on the theme in the Gospel of John (13:34–35; 15:12–17). As just shown, even beyond direct quoting, this principle of mutually beneficial interaction is also at the heart of larger instruction from Jesus in the Sermon on the Mount, including in pointed ways for economic matters.

The command to love your neighbor as yourself is then further echoed in Jesus's followers in New Testament writings, both as concise instruction (Romans 13:8–10; Galatians 5:13–15; Philippians 2:4; Colossians 3:12–14; James 2:8; 1 Peter 4:8–10; 1 John 4:19–21) and in narrative form (such as the Acts 2:42–47 and 4:32–37 stories of *koinonia*[74] and accounts of the Apostle Paul's ministry).[75] This core biblical thread of "love your neighbor

---

73. Note the etymology of two key words. "Provide" stems from the Latin preposition *pro* plus the root *videre* and means to see before/ahead/forward. "Profit" stems from the same preposition *pro* plus the Latin root *facere* and means to move/do before/ahead/forward. God's provision then is God seeing ahead. Human profit is moving ahead into what God sees. Far from being a result of self-sufficiency or earning in a strict sense, "profit" is inextricably linked to "provision." Surely God's seeing ahead is not only for the rich. Surely profit, understood as ultimately being provided by God, should then be handled in a manner reflecting God's generous provision.

74. Justo Gonzalez notes that all the Greek verbs in these texts are in the imperfect rather than the aorist, indicating that the actions described were not one-off events but a continual, ongoing practice. He also demonstrates that the Greek term κοινωνια, *koinonia*, often translated as "fellowship," is not merely "the inner disposition of goodwill" but sharing and partnership, as in business ventures. Christian "fellowship" is not just warm fuzzies. Far more than merely enjoying being around one another, *koinonia* is a full-bodied concept and practice of material and relational, economic partnership. *Faith and Wealth*, 82.

75. Ronald J. Sider confirms the economic significance of *koinonia* lived in the Apostle Paul's ministry and reflected in much of his writing.

as yourself," which can be well understood as seek mutual benefit with your neighbor, or partner with your neighbor for mutual benefit—including your economic neighbor—continues beyond the biblical period into the eras of the early church, Roman Christendom, the Middle Ages, and Renaissance and Reformation.

Much more could be said about this core principle in each setting and if we had the luxury of more pages we'd do a deeper dive, but for now suffice it to say it is a principle that has proven its worth across an impressive variety of times and places from its grounding in ancient Hebrew devotion to YHWH and highlighting in Jesus. Even with such a track record, if this concept faded in more contemporary cultures, we could question its import for our own time and place. However, this core principle of partnership, including its economic aspects, is also carried forward by someone who holds no less a title than "father of capitalism."

Re-Thinking Jesus Recap

- Common but inaccurate understanding: Jesus advocates for the interests and concerns of others only ("other-interest"), without any regard for self-interest and no matter the cost or harm to self. To follow Jesus is to completely sacrifice self for the sake of others.

- Necessary correction: Don't passively absorb almost 2,000 years of second-hand portrayals about a significant person or his thought. Go to the source itself. What does Jesus actually say?

- More accurate understanding (see for yourself): Jesus does advocate for other-interest, but his view of other-interest is clearly paired with self-interest. Jesus's own summary of the whole of God's teaching, following the Hebrew Scriptures and further exemplified in Jesus's most famous sermon, is to love God and to love your neighbor *as yourself*—within the love of God, pursue mutual self-interest and other-interest.

CHAPTER 7

The Father of Capitalism—Adam Smith

ADAM SMITH (1723–1790) WAS the Scottish philosopher turned economist most famous for his 1776 magnum opus, *An Inquiry into the Nature and Causes of the Wealth of Nations* ("*Wealth of Nations*"). In American universities and publications Smith is frequently considered the father of capitalism, certainly America's version of capitalism, and *Wealth of Nations* is the capitalist's bible.

The enlightened mutuality of the kingdom of God is found in Smith's work too. In fact, among Smith's wide-ranging texts, mutuality serves as a keystone, a central concept representative of and shedding light on the larger body of work.

Re-Thinking Adam Smith Preview

- Common but inaccurate understanding: Smith advocates for self-interest and self-interest only, because the "invisible hand" and *laissez-faire* turn self-interest in unregulated markets into social good. To follow Smith is to completely focus on one's self-interest and ignore or even actively avoid seeking social good.

- Necessary correction: Don't passively absorb over two centuries of second-hand portrayals about a significant person or his thought. Go to the source itself. What does Smith actually say?

- More accurate understanding (see for yourself): Smith does advocate for self-interest, and his view of self-interest *inherently and inextricably includes* concern for others and the common good. His own words declare that both individuals and governments can *and should* seek mutual benefit. Smith's work centers upon and repeatedly emphasizes the mutuality of self-interest with other-interest and social good.

Moral Sentiments

Smith's previous bestselling book was first published in 1759. *The Theory of Moral Sentiments* ("*Moral Sentiments*"), this thought leader's masterpiece, written during the logic- and reason-centric Age of Enlightenment, is all but unknown to modern readers. In *Moral Sentiments* Smith introduced his social science breakthroughs that explained human behavior, including our behavior related to free market economics, as springing from our nature as social creatures. On the strong foundation of *Moral Sentiments* is where Smith placed and erected the economic breakthroughs he introduced in *Wealth of Nations*. John Rae, among Smith's earliest and best-known biographers, writes that Smith himself considered *Moral Sentiments* his superior work over *Wealth of Nations*.[76] Despite Smith's view of his own work, *Moral Sentiments* appears to be long absent from the education of American business students.

Given Smith's own assessment of his work, one needs an understanding of *Moral Sentiments* alongside *Wealth of Nations* to have an accurate interpretation of free market capitalism as envisioned by Smith.

We should not be surprised then, when our business leaders are unaware that Smith teaches the turbulent waters of free market economics include favorable currents. These currents are formed from the inherent values of humankind, which Smith derives and supports from our empathetic behavior as social creatures. These currents, like virtually all currents and trade winds at sea, are invisible to the eye. Neither should we be surprised when those same leaders run aground their organizations, even their entire national economy, because they fail to safely navigate in the currents of empathy, as Smith explains in *Moral Sentiments*.

Invisible Hand-Wringing

How might an understanding of *Moral Sentiments* lead to a clearer reading of *Wealth of Nations* and re-thinking of capitalism? There are many examples, from Smith's perspectives on the pursuit of wealth to the core purpose of government, but for our exploration and purpose it is enough

---

76. Rae, *Life of Adam Smith*, 436.

that we take up the example of his phrase "invisible hand." He uses that phrase *exactly one time* in the almost thousand-page entirety of *Wealth of Nations*. Used without definition and preceded by the clause "as in many other cases," the phrase is frequently misconstrued by later interpreters to imagine or advance a host of unfettered theories, mostly associated with supposed phenomena that influence supply, demand, and competition.

Here's the phrase "invisible hand" in context:

> By preferring the support of domestic to that of foreign industry, he intends only his own security; and by directing that industry in such a manner as its produce may be of the greatest value, he intends only his own gain, and he is in this, as in many other cases, led by an invisible hand to promote an end which was no part of his intention. Nor is it always the worse for the society that it was no part of it. By pursuing his own interest he frequently promotes that of the society more effectually than when he really intends to promote it.[77]

Since its meaning is neither clear from a plain reading nor from the context, and to avoid further speculation, let us take the scholarly turn to Smith for his explanation of the phrase. In *Moral Sentiments*, the lens through which Smith wrote and we properly interpret *Wealth of Nations*, we are introduced and guided to an understanding of Smith's use of the phrase "invisible hand."

Here's the phrase as found in *Moral Sentiments*, together with the two sentences before and after to provide context.

> The rich only select from the heap what is most precious and agreeable. They consume little more than the poor: and in spite of their natural selfishness and rapacity, though they mean only their own conveniency, though the sole end which they propose from the labours of all the thousands whom they employ be the gratification of their own vain and insatiable desires, they divide with the poor the produce of all their improvements. They are led by an *invisible hand* to make nearly the same distribution of the necessaries of life which would have been made had the earth been divided into equal portions among all its inhabitants; and thus, without intending it, without knowing it, advance the interest of the society, and afford means to the multiplication of the species. When providence divided the earth among a few lordly masters, it neither forgot nor abandoned those who

---

77. Smith, *Wealth of Nations*, book IV, chapter II, para. 9, 572.

seemed to have been left out in the partition. These last, too, enjoy their share of all that it produces. (Emphasis ours.)[78]

This passage is found in Part IV of *Moral Sentiments*. Here we see that an invisible hand leads the rich to distribute, and not withhold, the necessaries of life. A contextual reading of this section illustrates why this distribution is a desirable outcome. A broader contextual reading also firmly attaches the invisible hand to its invisible body—"the impartial spectator" introduced and discussed by Smith from the earliest pages.

The Hand of the Impartial Spectator

Moral Sentiments is a book of behavioral and social psychology. Smith introduces natural human emotions and feelings, for ourselves and for others, as the springboard for our actions and self-governance. For example, our natural inclination of self-interest, to put ourselves first, guides us to a sense of prudence. Similarly our natural inclination of empathy, our feelings for others, guides us to a sense of justice.[79] Smith recognizes that it is human nature for our emotions to be inaccurate given the situation, if not run extreme. Emotions can be unreasonably interpreted by us and toward our narrow benefit in the case of unfettered self-interest, or against another and to their detriment in the case of withholding justice. As a way to more accurately align our emotions with the situation that gives rise to those emotions, Smith introduces an invisible third party to each exchange, what he called "the impartial spectator."

The impartial spectator is a construct, a third-person emotionally detached from the situation at hand, imagined by someone as his or her guide and judge of the behavior in which that person is about to engage. Assume Person A has found Person B injured on the side of the road. Person B is going to have much stronger emotions about her situation than Person A. In fact, there is the possibility that while Person B is extremely distraught Person A may be so indifferent that she's considering moving on without helping Person B. The impartial spectator, an imaginary person observing both Person B's concern for herself and Person A's level of empathy for Person B, is a resource for both but particularly Person A. Persons A and B, each imagining how the impartial spectator will judge their respective actions, adjust their respective emotions to be more in line with the other. What

78. Smith, *Moral Sentiments*, part IV, chapter I, para. 9, 182.
79. Smith uses the word *sympathy* throughout *Moral Sentiments*. Today, and in accordance with his meaning, we use the word "empathy." See https://www.adamsmith.org/the-theory-of-moral-sentiments/.

Smith expects is that Person A will be guided by the imagined, impartial spectator and take action according to that guidance.

Here is Smith's earliest description of the influence of the impartial spectator, set in its own paragraph.

> In all such cases, that there may be some correspondence of sentiments between the spectator and the person principally concerned, the spectator must, first of all, endeavor, as much as he can to put himself in the situation of the other, and to bring home to himself every little circumstance of distress which can possibly occur to the sufferer. He must adopt the whole case of his companion, with all its minutest incidents; and strive to render as perfect as possible that imaginary change of situation upon which his sympathy is founded.[80]

The eighteenth-century English is sometimes difficult to parse, but it clears up after a few passes and as the ear becomes accustomed to the style. Notice the opening words "in all such cases." Smith often uses this phrase and close variations when considering the presence of the impartial spectator.

For example, in the second paragraph before the use of "invisible hand" in *Moral Sentiments*, Smith writes, "If he is to live in society, indeed, there can be no comparison, because in this, as *in all other cases*, we constantly pay more regard to the sentiments of the spectator, than to those of the person principally concerned, and consider rather how his situation will appear to other people than how it will appear to himself."[81] Notice the parallel use of the phrase in *Wealth of Nations*, "and he is in this, *as in many other cases*, led by an invisible hand" (emphasis ours).[82]

The impartial spectator—made in the image of you and me—is only imaginary, but Smith argues that it guides us over time and through our experiences to establish acceptable rules regarding behavior. In other words, our morality. Toward the end of *Moral Sentiments*, Smith offers a summary to that point.

> Concern for our own happiness recommends to us the virtue of prudence; concern for that of other people, the virtues of justice and beneficence—of which the one restrains us from hurting, the other prompts us to promote that happiness. . . . [A]nd no man, during either the whole of his life or that of any considerable part of it, ever trod steadily and uniformly in the paths of

---

80. Smith, *Moral Sentiments*, part I, section 1, chapter IV, para. 6, 16.
81. Smith, *Moral Sentiments*, part IV, chapter 1, para. 7, 180.
82. Smith, *Wealth of Nations*, book IV, chapter II, para. 9, 572.

prudence, of justice, or of proper beneficence, whose conduct was not principally directed by a regard to the sentiments of the supposed impartial spectator, of the great inmate of the breast, the great judge and arbiter of conduct.[83]

A reading of *Moral Sentiments* shows Smith's creation and use of the impartial spectator, an imaginary and invisible human standing "in all cases" as a witness, motivator, and judge of our actions. In *Moral Sentiments* the rich are led by *the impartial spectator's "invisible hand* to make nearly the same distribution of the necessaries of life which would have been made had the earth been divided into equal portions among all its inhabitants; and thus, without intending it, without knowing it, advance the interest of the society, and afford means to the multiplication of the species" (emphasis ours).[84]

Notice again the parallel language in *Wealth of Nations*.

[H]e intends only his own gain, and he is in this, as in many other cases, led by an invisible hand to promote an end which was no part of his intention. Nor is it always the worse for the society that it was no part of it. By pursuing his own interest he frequently promotes that of the society more effectually than when he really intends to promote it.[85]

Reading *Wealth of Nations* through the lens of *Moral Sentiments*, we can see that the "invisible hand" found in both are one and the same. Further, the invisible hand is not disembodied but belongs to an equally invisible spectator whose influence is tangible. This impartial spectator, *when heeded*, gives self-interest an intentional social dimension; it leads oneself to consider how a "situation will appear to other people."[86] This leading of the impartial spectator's invisible hand is how pursuing one's interest "more effectually" promotes that of the society—pursuing one's interest with a perspective of how others are affected is more effective at promoting social (others *and* self) interest than attempting to promote social interest somehow without self-interest. Contrary to flawed yet widespread misunderstanding, the invisible hand is not an inexplicable force that magically turns unfettered selfishness into social good. The invisible hand is the working of

---

83. Smith, *Moral Sentiments*, part VI, conclusion, para. 1, 263.
84. Smith, *Moral Sentiments*, part IV, chapter 1, para. 9, 182.
85. Smith, *Wealth of Nations*, book IV, chapter II, para. 9, 572.
86. Smith, *Moral Sentiments*, part IV, chapter 1, para. 7, 180.

the impartial spectator to intentionally align self-interest with the interests of others for mutual benefit.

American capitalism is well beyond the time and need for its thinkers and leaders to return to the mutual intention of Adam Smith. Your authors discovered and now show you the invisible hand as part of Smith's larger, insightful gift of mutual empathy, more fully "embodied" by the impartial spectator. Quite the opposite of a reason to ignore others, the concept of the impartial spectator's invisible hand is a gift intended to check against unfettered selfishness[87] lest we find ourselves where we are today, with the high levels of poverty and economic disparity that not only inhibit the well-being of individuals but gut without distinction the souls of both the recklessly rich and painfully poor. From our reading of Smith, he neither envisioned nor advocated for the brand of capitalism we practice today. Indeed, we assert he would reject being called its father.

Leave Laissez-Faire Alone

We remember our high school social studies teachers as the first to introduce us to the concept of *laissez-faire* government, especially regarding the marketplace. You know the concept: "an economic doctrine that opposes government regulation of or interference in commerce beyond the minimum necessary for a free-enterprise system to operate according to its own economic laws."[88] College and law school business professors follow suit, even doubling down as many explain this as Adam Smith's vision of capitalism and the meaning of his "invisible hand" phrase. But what does Smith actually say about the role of government? In relatively few words given his style,[89] Smith writes in *Moral Sentiments*:

> The perfection of police, the extension of trade and manufacturers, are noble and magnificent objects. The contemplation of them pleases us, and we are interested in whatever can tend to advance them. They make part of the great system of government, and the wheels of the political machine seem to move with more harmony and ease by means of them. We take pleasure in beholding the perfection of so beautiful and grand

---

87. As a contributor to the website Investopedia recently noted, in modern times the invisible hand is typically mangled as a shorthand reference to a supposed phenomenon that influences free markets, "rather than as something that results in the well-being of individuals." https://www.investopedia.com/updates/adam-smith-economics/.

88. https://www.thefreedictionary.com/laissez-faire.

89. His lengthier style expands the same concepts in *Wealth of Nations*.

a system, and we are uneasy till we remove any obstruction that can in the least disturb or encumber the regularity of its motions. *All constitutions of government, however, are valued only in proportion as they tend to promote the happiness of those who live under them. This is their sole use and end.* (Emphasis ours.)[90]

Smith did not advocate for *laissez-faire* government. (He uses that phrase even less in the almost thousand pages of *Wealth of Nations* than his one use of "invisible hand"!).[91] Just the opposite. In his own words, Smith sees the need and benefit of well-formed, functioning, and active governments. Notice that Smith refers to government functions as "noble" and "magnificent" and government as a "great system" that supports harmony and ease in politics. Politics refers to the administration of internal and external affairs on behalf of a body of people, not merely allegiance to a particular ideology or partisanship as it's typically understood today.

What of those readers, deeply ingrained in their training or ideology, who believe that a government should not interfere with the marketplace (except, of course, to protect their own property and wealth)? Or that a smaller government is always a better government? Or that an unregulated market knows better than a just and fair government? These are readers for whom Smith's vision of government is a truth trying to set them free.

Smith's vision of government is of one that runs without obstruction, not a government that supports markets to run without obstruction. Yes. Please read that again. Smith does not posit either hands-off government or bureaucratically bogged-down government as a virtue. No matter the exact form of government, Smith provides the yardstick by which to measure all governments' value: "in proportion as they tend to promote the happiness of those who live under them."

Should we further be surprised that the United States' Declaration of Independence, ratified a few years after Smith first published *Theory of Moral Sentiments*, opens with the pursuit of happiness as an unalienable right? To quote the Declaration, "That to secure these rights, Governments are instituted among Men, deriving their just powers from the consent of the governed, . . . to effect their safety and happiness."

No, we shouldn't be surprised that a primary role of government is to foster the pursuit of happiness by "the governed" (the masses, not the few), and when it fails that simple benchmark test it fails as a government. Lightning quick highlights of just some of those failures by our United States

---

90. Smith, *Moral Sentiments*, part IV, chapter 1, para. 11, 183.

91. That's right—zero times! Compared to the great number of pages discussing not just policies but *duties* of government.

government include the abuse of Native Americans, Africans as chattel, our Civil War, our Great Depression, inept protection of our environment, our Great Recession, and, as of this writing, infighting at both the federal and state levels that hinders the response to the COVID-19 public health crisis and related economic downturn.

How did our nation stray so far from the vision and words of the father of capitalism and America's Founding Fathers and Mothers? How did our society come to believe the lie that *laissez-faire* government is best for our nation and its people? We offer our two-part answer to that question: 1) Once influential voices recklessly repeat damaging ideologies often and long enough, a critical mass of people will learn to believe and embrace the damaging ideologies; and, 2) once the critical mass is aboard then it's easier for those who are influenced by special interests and have abandoned their gatekeeper roles to create policies and laws that support those damaging ideologies. The notion that a *laissez-faire* government is *de facto* best for our nation simply finds no support in Adam Smith, yet it has long been a damaging ideology that seeks to dismantle the mutually beneficial guardrails and circuit breakers meant to promote the happiness of "we the people."

The Mutuality of Nations

The theme of mutuality, strongly established by Smith in his *Moral Sentiments,* carries through his *Wealth of Nations*. His is a massive book; ours intends to be lighter, so we will only briefly highlight further examples of how the keystone of mutuality holds together the breadth of Smith's thought.

Mutuality among individuals:

- "But man has almost constant occasion for the help of his brethren, and it is in vain for him to expect it from their benevolence only. He will be more likely to prevail if he can interest their self-love in his favour, and shew them that it is for their own advantage to do for him what he requires of them."[92]
- "As it is by treaty, by barter, and by purchase, that we obtain from one another the greater part of those mutual good offices which we stand in need of, so it is this same trucking disposition which originally gives occasion to the division of labour."[93]

---

92. Smith, *Wealth of Nations*, book I, chapter II, para. 2, 23.
93. Smith, *Wealth of Nations*, book I, chapter II, para. 3, 24.

We note that division of labor does not by itself create gains—it is division of labor *and partnership exchanges among the specialized laborers* that creates mutual benefit and net gain.

Mutuality between "town and country"—urban and rural areas within a nation or commonwealth:

- "The gains of both are mutual and reciprocal, and the division of labour is in this, as in all other cases, advantageous to all the different persons employed in the various occupations into which it is subdivided."[94]
- "The inhabitants of the town and those of the country are mutually the servants of one another."[95]
- "Each tradesman or artificer derives his subsistence from the employment, not of one, but of a hundred or a thousand different customers. Though in some measure obliged to them all, therefore, he is not absolutely dependent upon any one of them."[96]

Mutuality between nations:

- "Commerce, which ought naturally to be, among nations, as among individuals, a bond of union and friendship, has become the most fertile source of discord and animosity . . . [due to] the impertinent jealousy of merchants and manufacturers."[97]
- "A nation that would enrich itself by foreign trade, is certainly most likely to do so when its neighbours are all rich, industrious, and commercial nations. A great nation surrounded on all sides by wandering savages and poor barbarians might, no doubt, acquire riches by the cultivation of its own lands, and by its own interior commerce, but not by foreign trade."[98]

Mutuality between producers and consumers:

- "Consumption is the sole end and purpose of all production; and the interest of the producer ought to be attended to, only so far as it may be necessary for promoting that of the consumer."[99]

Mutuality between governments and citizens:

94. Smith, *Wealth of Nations*, book III, chapter I, para. 1, 481.
95. Smith, *Wealth of Nations*, book III, chapter I, para. 5, 484.
96. Smith, *Wealth of Nations*, book III, chapter IV, para. 12, 527.
97. Smith, *Wealth of Nations*, book IV, chapter III, Part II, para. 9, 621.
98. Smith, *Wealth of Nations*, book IV, chapter III, Part II, para. 11, 623.
99. Smith, *Wealth of Nations*, book IV, chapter VIII, para. 45, 839.

- "The third and last duty of the sovereign or commonwealth is that of erecting and maintaining those public institutions and those public works, which, though they may be in the highest degree advantageous to a great society, are, however, of such a nature, that the profit could never repay the expence [expense] to any individual or small number of individuals, and which it therefore cannot be expected that any individual or small number of individuals should erect or maintain."[100]

- "When the institutions or public works which are beneficial to the whole society, either cannot be maintained altogether, or are not maintained altogether by the contribution of such particular members of the society as are most immediately benefited by them, the deficiency must in most cases be made up by the general contribution of the whole society."[101]

Smith even applies mutuality to interactions among religious groups and government:

- "The teachers of each little sect, finding themselves almost alone [supposing no state sponsorship], would be obliged to respect those of almost every other sect, and the concessions which they would mutually find it both convenient and agreeable to make to one another, might in time probably reduce the doctrine of the greater part of them to that pure and rational religion, free from every mixture of absurdity, imposture, or fanaticism, such as wise men in all ages of the world wished to see established."[102]

And pointedly, just a couple of pages before the invisible hand reference, Smith trumpets the natural and necessary mutuality of self-benefit and social benefit.

- "Every individual is continually exerting himself to find out the most advantageous employment for whatever capital he can command. It is his own advantage, indeed, and not that of the society, which he has in view. But the study of his own advantage naturally, or rather necessarily, leads him to prefer that employment which is most advantageous to the society."[103]

---

100. Smith, *Wealth of Nations*, book V, chapter I, part III, para. 1, 916.
101. Smith, *Wealth of Nations*, book V, chapter I, conclusion, para. 6, 1031.
102. Smith, *Wealth of Nations*, book V, chapter I, part III, article 3d, para. 7, 1001.
103. Smith, *Wealth of Nations*, book IV, chapter II, para. 4, 569–70.

So the core principle of mutuality, of partnering for self-interest *and* other/neighbor-interest, weaves not only through Scriptures but also throughout the wide-ranging considerations of the father of capitalism, from his impartial spectator's invisible hand to all combinations of exchange among individuals and nations. A yet more contemporary, and also influential voice, has more to say on this theme.

> "The core principle of mutuality, of partnership for self-interest *and* other/neighbor-interest, weaves not only through Scriptures but also throughout the wide-ranging considerations of the father of capitalism."

Re-Thinking Adam Smith Recap

- Common but inaccurate understanding: Smith advocates for self-interest and self-interest only, because the "invisible hand" and *laissez-faire* turn self-interest in unregulated markets into social good. To follow Smith is to completely focus on one's self-interest and ignore or even actively avoid seeking social good.

- Necessary correction: Don't passively absorb over two centuries of second-hand portrayals about a significant person or his thought. Go to the source itself. What does Smith actually say?

- More accurate understanding (see for yourself): Smith does advocate for self-interest, and his view of self-interest *inherently and inextricably includes* concern for others and the common good. His own words declare that both individuals and governments can *and should* seek mutual benefit. Smith's work centers upon and repeatedly emphasizes the mutuality of self-interest with other-interest and social good.

CHAPTER 8

The Mother of Capitalism—Ayn Rand

THE INFLUENCE OF AYN Rand's last novel, *Atlas Shrugged* (first published in 1957), simply can't be ignored. Rand called it, particularly the portion known as Galt's speech, a perfect fictional presentation of her philosophy.[104] A 1991 survey conducted for the U.S. Library of Congress and the Book-of-the-Month Club identified *Atlas Shrugged* as the second-most influential book in America, second only to the Bible.[105] In 2012 the U.S. Library of Congress included this novel in its eighty-eight-volume display of "Books That Shaped America."[106] With millions of copies sold, it has been a staple of bookstores and classroom curriculum since the early 1960s. Generations of college and graduate students have been drilled on this tome, instilling in them variations of moral codes and economic ethics they've since carried into the marketplace worlds of business and politics.

What should be read as a cautionary tale against the evils of collectivism and socialism she suffered as a child in her native Russia, *Atlas Shrugged* teaches Rand's philosophy of "Objectivism." Particularly through her description of the utopia she named Taggart Terminal (or the adopted name of Galt's Gulch) and the voice of John Galt's epic speech, Rand extols the benefits of her Objectivism. Some benefits received exponentially more attention than others by her adopted America and its postmodern audience, particularly radical self-interest, rugged individualism, and a limited

---

104. Encyclopedia.com, "Atlas Shrugged-Criticism."
105. Fein, "Book Notes."
106. Library of Congress, "Books That Shaped America."

government that does not interfere with individual liberty (unlike her native Russia).

The enlightened mutuality of the kingdom of God, prominent in Adam Smith, is likewise found in Rand's Objectivism. We recognize this claim may be surprising or even outlandish to some, but one's reaction doesn't make the claim any less accurate. We encourage and challenge you not to dismiss our claim without considering at least our threshold evidence with an open mind. Recall our earlier section on "A Clearer Vision"—usually all we need to achieve clearer vision is a receptive posture and to relax a little. We also recognize Rand can stir strong emotions, both for and against her views. We invite you to relax a little and find your receptive posture, so clearer vision into perspectives you were not looking for can surface.

Based on Rand's own assessment of the significance of *Atlas Shrugged*, as noted above, we focus on Galt's Gulch and Galt's speech as keystones among her voluminous and wide-ranging texts. These keystones, representative of and shedding light on her larger body of work, speak powerfully of mutuality, even if to the surprise of many readers. In this way, Rand, too, carries forward the thread of partnership.

Re-Thinking Ayn Rand Preview

- Common but inaccurate understanding: Rand advocates for self-interest and self-interest only, without any regard for others' interest and no matter the cost or harm to others. To follow Rand is to completely sacrifice others for the sake of self.

- Necessary correction: Don't passively absorb more than six decades of second-hand portrayals about a significant person or her thought. Go to the source itself. What does Rand actually say?

- More accurate understanding (see for yourself): Rand does advocate for self-interest, and her view of self-interest involves relationships with *other* selves *also* ably pursuing their interest. Her self-interest position is not gain for self to the detriment of others, but various selves mutually seeking aligned benefit. In the portion of her work that she herself identified as the perfect presentation of her philosophy via a novel, she explicitly rejects gaining for self at the expense of others and explicitly advocates for exchanging in mutually beneficial ways with others.

The Utopia?

As a society America has been largely persuaded by the utopia Rand presents, which includes the sign of the dollar as the primary focus if not the gauge of every thought and action. Indeed, a careless reading of Rand might have us believe every interaction has an economic basis and should not occur without an accompanying payment. Given how interpretations and misinterpretations of *Atlas Shrugged* have profoundly shaped the American corporate ethic, we dub Rand "the mother of capitalism," at least the version currently perceived and practiced by very many.

Utopias can be laudable, if not beneficially visionary and inspirational. Given the influence of *Atlas Struggled* on America and the shaping of its modern culture, Galt's Gulch may be among the most influential of utopian visions. Space does not permit a complete description of Galt's Gulch. But one passage, through the eyes of the protagonist Dagny Taggart as she enters and explores Galt's Gulch, fairly summarizes a core ideology of this utopia:

> And then she [Dagny Taggart] gasped, because the trail had turned and from the height of an open ledge she saw the town on the floor of the valley. . . . Far in the distance, some structures seemed taller, and the faint coils of smoke above them suggested an industrial district. But close before her, rising on a slender granite column from a ledge below to the level of her eyes, blinding her by its glare, dimming the rest, stood a dollar sign three feet tall, made of solid gold. It hung in space above the town, as its coat-of-arms, its trademark, its beacon—and it caught the sunrays, like some transmitter of energy that sent them in shining blessing to stretch horizontally through the air above the roofs.[107]

Given the impact and influence of *Atlas Shrugged*, it's surprising that half a century passed before a critical eye questioned the viability of Galt's Gulch. Alan Clardy, writing in the journal *Utopian Studies*, rightly argues that when a utopia is offered as a vision for a future that requires social or political action today, that utopia must be able to withstand a strong scrutiny.[108] Galt's Gulch, offered as Rand's vision for the future, is a utopia in need of strong scrutiny. Clardy sets out a two-part test by which to critically evaluate a utopia. We provide a brief description below of Clardy's two test elements applied to Galt's Gulch.

---

107. Rand, *Atlas Shrugged*, 647.
108. Clardy, "Galt's Gulch," 258.

First, Clardy tests and analyzes the description of Galt's Gulch in terms of logical consistency, completeness, and continuity. Among the fault lines he points to are values and rules by which Galt's Gulch operates that are contradicted by the characters' actions, and assertions that prove incorrect.[109] Summarizing his analysis of the first part of the test, he writes, "there is no appreciation of internal contradictions or externally imposed challenges that will stress—and in all likelihood, destroy—the fundamental principles on which her utopia is created. We are shown an idyllic still life, not a plausible scenario."[110]

The second part of Clardy's test considers the utopia's psychology and sociology. He asserts that Galt's Gulch is fatally flawed because of its gross misclassification of all humans into the limited categories of hero industrialist, looters, or sheep. Similarly, he asserts Galt's Gulch fails under its own weight of Rand's label as a voluntary association (run by and for the benefit of like-minded hero industrialists) and not a society, yet describing it with the basic elements of a society. More pointedly, he concludes, her utopia is "simply not plausible in reality. Her idealized version of society is flawed in terms of sociological and economic and political laws and rests on a distorted view of human psychology."[111]

In light of critical scholarship should we continue to accept, or even aspire to, Rand's utopia based on Objectivism? To do so seems unwise. The question is increasingly relevant as America continues its march into ever deeper moral and economic divides, and its persona as a society where every relationship is increasingly judged only by its economic value.

The Speech

Even if Rand's case for Objectivism in the "utopian" form of Galt's Gulch proves unsustainable, we uncovered and now point you to insights within Objectivism that steer us away from plantation economics and toward Partnership Economics. Those insights are found in John Galt's nationwide radio speech, the fifty-six-page summary of Rand's Objectivism philosophy set toward the end of *Atlas Shrugged*.[112]

Galt's speech opens with a fiery introduction that lays his fictional world's social and economic collapse at the feet of its failed moral code. He asserts that moral code failed and caused the present calamity because it was

109. Clardy, "Galt's Gulch," 258.
110. Clardy, "Galt's Gulch," 259.
111. Clardy, "Galt's Gulch," 258.
112. Rand, *Atlas Shrugged*, 923–79.

founded on a misguided faith, buttressed by force, that specifically rejects humankind's abilities to think and reason. Galt then begins his argument to replace that failed moral code for his own (Rand's Objectivism), a code that anchors in and springs from the human ability to think and reason.

We can be quick to agree with Galt's reasons and reasoning for humans to live according to a substantially consistent moral code (see especially our chapters 3 and 6.) Those include the human mind and ability to think as the basic tool of survival, that thinking is a purposeful choice, and that people are creatures of "volitional consciousness."[113] As creatures of volitional consciousness with no automatic course of behavior, Galt argues, humans need a code of values to guide our actions.[114] After making the case that humankind has no automatic code of survival, but can determine such a code through the rational process of decision-making between choices, Galt asserts, "[a] code of values accepted by choice is a code of morality."[115] Galt emphasizes the issue of choice by underscoring the nature of a moral code as being chosen, not forced; and as being understood, not merely obeyed.[116] Indeed, as if to ensure his audience does not confuse his criticism of their failed moral code with the absolute need of a sustainable moral code, he states, "It is for the purpose of self-preservation that [humankind] needs a code of morality."[117] Again, we agree (see especially our chapters 3 and 6).

With the old moral code dismissed and the need for a moral code clearly established, Galt quickly transitions to presenting his remedy. Explaining the structure of his code of morality, Galt begins with the three supreme and ruling values of life: reason, purpose, and self-esteem.[118] These values imply and require seven virtues, he asserts, virtues that he introduces and briefly explains. A *value*, Galt explains, is that which one acts to gain and keep, while a *virtue* is the action by which one gains and keeps the value.[119]

Reasonable minds may differ over the values and virtues by which to frame a code of morality, and we certainly find places to differ with Galt. Rather than underscore the differences, however, we point to important common ground. For example, honesty. Galt describes honesty, one of the seven virtues that frames his code of morality, with a paragraph-long single

---

113. Rand, *Atlas Shrugged*, 926.
114. Rand, *Atlas Shrugged*, 926.
115. Rand, *Atlas Shrugged*, 927.
116. Rand, *Atlas Shrugged*, 931–32.
117. Rand, *Atlas Shrugged*, 928–29.
118. Rand, *Atlas Shrugged*, 932.
119. Rand, *Atlas Shrugged*, 926.

sentence that argues "neither love nor fame nor cash is a value if obtained by fraud . . . [and] . . . that honesty is not a social duty, not a sacrifice for the sake of others, but the most profoundly selfish virtue man can practice . . ."[120] To be honest with oneself and to be honest with the other is supported by the weight of scholarship and of tradition, including Hebrew Scriptures, Jesus, and Adam Smith. Honesty, which is the gateway to transparency, is a threshold virtue that moves us from plantation systems to Partnership Economics.

Neither in her illustration of Objectivism in action through the construct of Galt's Gulch, nor in her teaching and defense of Objectivism through the voice of John Galt does Rand set out many absolute rules. Like values and virtues, reasonable minds may differ over the rules by which to frame a code of morality. Again, we find places to differ with Galt but prefer to point to important common ground around mutuality. For example, Galt's rule against the use of physical force against others. Galt emphatically argues that no matter what else might be open to disagreement, the use or even threat of force to make a person act against his or her will is an act of *evil* that cannot be tolerated.[121] In fact, Galt argues, to force a person to act against his or her will—the judgment to do what is in his or her best interest—is to negate and paralyze his or her means of survival. To do so destroys that person's capacity to live.

Galt illustrates this evil with the visual of a pointed gun forcing a person to act against his or her will. To strip a person of free will through force is to coerce them to surrender their life. This "your mind or your life" coercion is antithetical to his code of morality—and it is antithetical to mutually beneficial partnership. Galt gives the additional example of the "politician who confronts a country with the ultimatum: 'Your children's education or your life'" as an example of a "your mind or your life" coercion. Indeed, Galt affirms, "Force and mind are opposites; morality ends where a gun begins."[122]

As the human experience has long and painfully taught, coercive force as effective as a gun can take any form. Let's illustrate with two familiar examples consistent with Galt's "your mind or your life" coercion.

The southern American slavery system reduced humans from Africa to chattel and forced them to physical labor. While these humans were coerced to work with physical force, the underlying reason was economic: it was cheaper to make slaves of people and force them to work than to hire

120. Rand, *Atlas Shrugged*, 932–33.
121. Rand, *Atlas Shrugged*, 936–37.
122. Rand, *Atlas Shrugged*, 936.

and pay them a living wage. An important recognition here is that the force was economic and the means was physical.

In modern capitalism we find a glaring parallel. Take for example a laborer at a nationwide retailer whose executives have chosen to limit wages of its laborer class of employees to under $10 an hour. It is beyond reasonable debate that $10 an hour is not a full-time living and sustainable wage in the United States for the average working adult. With no alternatives, because the executives at many nationwide retailers have collectively made similar decisions, the adult laborer is forced to accept and work against his or her will for a wage that not only negates and paralyzes his or her means of survival, but destroys that person's capacity to live. An important recognition here is that both the force and means is economic.

As Galt should logically agree, whatever shape the gun takes—physical in the form of a gun-bearing taskmaster, or economic in the form of a collectively suppressive lack of options—to force a person to choose against his or her will in exchange for his or her life is an evil that cannot be tolerated. The opposite of this evil of coercion, the corrective remedy and cure to this and similar evils is the mutually beneficial alignment—partnership—that Galt points to.

The Power of a Conjunction

What Rand also rails against, stridently via her alter-ego character of Galt, is the "morality of sacrifice," sacrificing one's entire self-interest. We agree that failing to love oneself is detrimental. We likewise see that loving only oneself, and therefore failing to also love others, is detrimental. Between these two equal and opposite failings is the path of partnership, mutuality, loving your neighbor as yourself.

Early in Galt's speech, Rand lambasts the morality she opposes:

> You have been taught that morality is a code of behavior imposed on you by whim, the whim of a supernatural power or the whim of society, to serve God's purpose or your neighbor's welfare, to please an authority beyond the grave or else next door—but not to serve *your* life or pleasure.[123]

We aren't here to argue what Rand herself was taught, or what she supposes her audience had been taught, but she is clear that the morality she rails against frowns upon serving "your life or pleasure." It is that

---

123. Rand, *Atlas Shrugged*, 925.

conjunction—her use of the word "but"—that drew our attention to seek clearer vision into Rand's hunger for mutuality.

Rand brings fire and brimstone against serving "God's purpose or your neighbor's welfare" *but* denying "your life or pleasure." We agree against such a morality, whatever morality that is, that requires service to God and others *but* not service to oneself. Understanding Rand's demand for a morality that doesn't require sacrificing one's self for the benefit of others or God, we see her demand consistent with the moralities taught by Jesus and Adam Smith: to love God, love your neighbor, *and* love yourself—to love your neighbor as yourself.[124]

What does Rand's mutuality look like? Despite her strong language in places that would seem to demonize so much as a second thought about another person, Rand does in fact, like Jesus and Smith, advocate explicitly for the mutuality of self-interest and other-interest. This fuller context of Rand's words must be kept in view. Contrary to popular (mis)conceptions of Rand as espousing a dog-eat-dog, brutally selfish style of self-interest, Rand's own words—in the keystone speech of her perfect fictional representation of her philosophy—say otherwise. From Galt's speech:

> Just as I support my life, neither by robbery nor alms, but by my own effort, so I do not seek to derive my happiness from the injury or the favor of others, but earn it by my own achievement. Just as I do not consider the pleasure of others as the goal of my life, so I do not consider my pleasure as the goal of the lives of others. Just as there are no contradictions in my values and no conflicts among my desires—so there are no victims and no conflicts of interest among rational men, men who do not desire the unearned and do not view one another with a cannibal's lust, men who neither make sacrifices nor accept them.[125]

In strong contrast to the "dog-eat-dog" philosophy that has come to be how Rand is characterized, both spitefully by her opponents and adoringly by her advocates, here Rand plainly disavows such "cannibals's lust." Our challenge to both those who oppose the who-cares-about-anyone-else view of Rand, and to those who praise it, is to see that it is in an incomplete, and therefore inaccurate, view.

Rather than taking sides on a debate unhelpfully centered on false "Randian" premises, we strongly encourage you to begin thinking afresh about Rand and how she, too, speaks for aligning self-interest and

---

124. Matthew 22:34–40, Mark 12:28–34, and Luke 10:25–37, and numerous echoes as described in chapter 6, the "From God the Father to Another Father" section.

125. Rand, *Atlas Shrugged*, 935.

others-interest. Rand's prominence and influence would be far more valuable, not to mention accurate, redirected toward mutuality rather than misinterpretations around self-interest. In the above passage she speaks plainly against standard elements of plantation economics—robbery, injury of others, others' lives serving one's pleasure, victims, desiring the unearned, viewing one another with a cannibal's lust—in favor of seeking self-interest in mutuality with others.

Continuing with the next paragraph in Galt's speech:

> The symbol of all relationships among such men, the moral symbol of respect for human beings, is the trader. We, who live by values, not by loot, are traders, both in matter and in spirit. A trader is a man who earns what he gets and does not give or take the undeserved.[126]

First we note the use of the word *relationships*, itself a counter to any notion of self-interest without regard for others. Rand then explicitly espouses respect for human beings and names her moral ideal "traders," those who live by values and do not loot others. Those who do not give or take the undeserved but earn in fair exchanges by trading value for value. What Rand calls traders, we call partners—people we are confident will find solutions and power in Partnership Economics.

From the next paragraph in Galt's speech:

> I deal with men as my nature and theirs demands: by means of reason. I seek or desire nothing from them except such relations as they care to enter of their own voluntary choice. It is only with their mind that I can deal and only for my own self-interest, when they see that my interest coincides with theirs. When they don't, I enter into no relationship . . . I have nothing to gain from fools or cowards; I have no benefits to seek from human vices: from stupidity, dishonesty or fear.[127]

Opposite of taking advantage of others in the name of self-interest, Rand again plainly disavows gaining at the expense of others: "I seek or desire nothing from them except such relations as they care to enter of their own voluntary choice." She advocates for dealing with others and engaging in relationships voluntarily when self-interest coincides with the other's interest. This is, as we've also seen in Leviticus, Jesus, and Adam Smith, enlightened mutuality. These lines of Rand are also particularly resonant with Martin Luther King Jr.'s description of true alliances, which are "based upon

126. Rand, *Atlas Shrugged*, 935.
127. Rand, *Atlas Shrugged*, 936.

some self-interest of each component group and a common interest into which they merge. For an alliance to have permanence and loyal commitment from its various elements, each of them must have a goal from which it benefits and none must have an outlook in basic conflict with the others."[128]

We expect that, even in this limited space, we've reasonably carried the burden of proof for our claim that enlightened mutuality is firmly present in Rand's Objectivism. For any readers not yet convinced or concerned that we cherry picked texts, recall that 1) Rand herself identified Galt's speech as the perfect presentation of her philosophy, and 2) we quoted and examined from that speech not selectively severed phrases but groupings of full sentences, including some from three consecutive paragraphs. With clearer vision, Rand's prominent voice can be understood as part of the chorus pointing away from what we call plantation systems and toward what we call Partnership Economics.

If our position still seems a bridge too far, we strongly encourage you to read Galt's speech for yourself. We're not asking you to accept our interpretation until you're convinced, but we're insisting that you don't dismiss it until you've fully investigated it. See for yourself, then email us. We are glad for ongoing conversation and debate at info@partnershipeconomics.com.

Re-Thinking Ayn Rand Recap

- Common but inaccurate understanding: Rand advocates for self-interest and self-interest only, without any regard for others' interest and no matter the cost or harm to others. To follow Rand is to completely sacrifice others for the sake of self.

- Necessary correction: Don't passively absorb more than six decades of second-hand portrayals about a significant person or her thought. Go to the source itself. What does Rand actually say?

- More accurate understanding (see for yourself): Rand does advocate for self-interest, and her view of self-interest involves relationships with *other* selves *also* ably pursuing their interest. Her self-interest position is not gain for self to the detriment of others, but various selves mutually seeking aligned benefit. In the portion of her work that she herself identified as the perfect presentation of her philosophy via a novel, she explicitly rejects gaining for self at the expense of others and explicitly advocates for exchanging in mutually beneficial ways with others.

128. Washington, ed., *Martin Luther King Jr*, 162.

Where Do We Go from Here?

So the core principle of mutuality, of partnering for self-interest *and* other/neighbor-interest, weaves not only through Scriptures and the father of capitalism but also through this mother of capitalism. Even with such a track record, if this concept couldn't translate into our own time and place, what good would it be?

We are ready to articulate this principle for our time and bring it into full expression for contemporary consideration (and action—that's the purpose of Part 3). Re-thinking economics can gain much from the wisdom of such major voices from the past (a form of partnership in itself). To realize the promise of partnership, though, we cannot merely look back. We must re-think economics for here and now.

Chapter 9

The Partnership Economic Ethic

"Any time you try to introduce a new idea, first it's it'll never work. Then, it'll work but only for a short time. Then, the guy's really lucky. And finally, you know, he's right."

—John Bogle

AT THE ROOT OF plantation system thinking and markets are widespread and entrenched misconceptions about the true nature of Adam Smith's vision and version of capitalism. Indeed, to even associate Adam Smith with what modern society has collectively implemented and calls capitalism is akin to trademark infringement—like sewing a deceptive label to a plastic knockoff purse and trying to pass it off as a genuine Prada purse. Before long the hapless owner needs to apply needle and thread, glue, and finally duct tape to keep the imitation purse pieced together enough to even call it a bag.

In our mission to recognize and replace with genuine options the damaging limitations of capitalism as it's currently practiced, early in this book we identified and explained the relentless rules of economics. The relentless rules are clear, established, and beyond reasonable debate. (Nevertheless, we understand that some people—especially invested people—will push back, argue, and debate against anything. Some just for the sport of it.) Comparable to Bogle's "relentless rules of humble [investment] arithmetic," the relentless rules of economics presented here simply are what they are. Better to think and work with them than continue to be run over by them.

How do we best work with the relentless rules of economics? Given the nature of those relentless rules, we've sought to identify and explain an economic ethic that works. That ethic, which we have developed from dialogue with the preceding voices, we've termed the Partnership Economic Ethic. Now we present it plainly on its own terms. As we did with the relentless rules, we'll list the elements of the ethic and then flesh out each part.

- God provides and we partner.
- To partner is to seek mutual benefit.
- Mutual benefit is created by engaging in exchanges that are profitable for the self *and* the other—pursuing our economic neighbor's interest *and* our self-interest.
- Corporately our purpose is to sustain profitability for all stakeholders.

In sum, the Partnership Economic Ethic is to love your economic neighbor as yourself.

God Provides and We Partner

The story is told of an extraordinarily talented woman who could think her way through any problem and make anything. So talented was she, that after figuring out how to make animals and finally a human from dirt she confidentially and continuously began to petition God for a contest. She wanted to prove that she was as capable a creator as her Creator.

One summer day while hiking in a remote wilderness, God entertained her many petitions by meeting her on the trail and agreeing to consider her talents as a creator. She had honed her skills during the years of petitioning and was beyond excited to prove her abilities. Dropping her pack and then to her knees, she began scooping up dirt.

"Whoa, whoa, whoa," said God, "what are you doing?"

"I'm. You know. Scooping up dirt to make a person," she replied, a bit startled.

"No, no, not so fast," God patiently smiled. "I fully admire your gifts and accomplishments. I truly do. I'm also sympathetic to your perspective. It's why I'm here to encourage you but also explain, if you want to be a Creator at my level you need to first create your own dirt. What you're holding is mine."

She took more time than usual to process those words—that truth trying to set her free. After becoming angry she recognized she had to set aside her ego, and then she could see her role from the Divine perspective. It is God who provides the context and resources—"the earth and all that is in it"[129]—for her to exercise her talents and abilities. She (or anyone else) can't literally create anew; the best she (and everyone else) can do is apply her God-given imagination to the God-given resources made available.

The work that is ours to do, indeed our highest and best work, is to be the very best partners possible with God and with what God has provided.

To Partner is to Seek Mutual Benefit

The definition of the noun *partner* is simple and familiar. A common dictionary definition is "one that is united or associated with another or others in an activity or a sphere of common interest." The verb form typically just places the partner in his or her role (e.g., partnered, partnering, partners). The popular dictionary consulted for this definition offers six examples of partners: a member of a business partnership, a spouse, a domestic partner, a lover, either of two persons dancing together, and one of a pair or a team in a sport such as tennis.

Of course, all of these definition examples involve relationships. Family, a familiar form of relationship, is a good context to illustrate partnering to seek mutual benefit.

In healthy family systems and dynamics, each of the family members, to the best of his or her abilities, tries to help and protect the other(s). In helping and protecting our family members, we mutually help and protect ourselves. The benefits run both ways to all involved, and this is true whether the partners operate within a family relationship or an economic relationship.

Contrast the mutual benefit model with the parent who does not care for his child and soon finds himself facing criminal charges of child negligence. Or the unlicensed minor who decides to sneak out of the house at midnight with the family's car only to wreck it. The parent and the unlicensed minor are partners who do not seek mutual benefit and as a result cause harm. The harm runs both ways to all involved, and this is true whether the partners operate within a family relationship or an economic relationship.

Economies are larger than families, but both center on people in relationship. To partner is to recognize the reality of relationships, understand

---

129. Deuteronomy 10.14; Psalm 24:1; 1 Corinthians 10:26.

that what affects one person in a relationship necessarily affects the other(s) too, and act in ways that mutually benefit all involved in the relationship.

Mutual Benefit is Created by Engaging in Exchanges That are Profitable for Our Self *and* the Other— Pursuing Our Economic Neighbor's Interest *and* Our Self-Interest

The Rev. Dr. James King is the pastor of a church Paul and Aaron attended together. A sermon of his titled "It's Crazy, Right?" is about the parable of the rich landowner.[130] A story from that sermon so perfectly illustrates this element of mutual benefit that we share it here.

> There is an old story, told in many cultures, about two brothers who were farmers. They shared and worked and together farmed the land that their father had left them. One of the brothers was unmarried and lived alone in a small house on one side of their fields. The other brother was married, he and his wife had a large family of six children, and they lived in a larger house on the other side of their fields.
>
> Every day the brothers worked side by side in the fields, and every harvest they divided the grain they harvested evenly between them, half and half. It had always been so.
>
> One night, the brother who lived alone found himself thinking that it was unfair that they should divide the grain evenly because he had only himself to feed and his brother had his large family to feed. *"He should receive more of the grain than I,"* this brother decided. So that night he took a sack of grain from his own barn, crept across the star-lit fields, and secretly put it into his brother's barn.
>
> That same night the brother who was married sat looking into the faces of his beloved family and found himself thinking that it was unfair that he and his brother should divide the grain evenly, because every day he himself was surrounded by his large loving family, and had so many children who could help care for him when he grew too old to work—while his brother lived all alone, and had no children to care for him in his old age.
>
> *"He should take more than half of the harvest so that he could store some for the future or sell it and have the money for his old age,"* this brother decided. So later that night after his family

---

130. Luke 12:13–21. King, "It's Crazy, Right?"

was asleep, he took a sack of grain from his own barn and crept across the star-lit fields and put it into his brother's barn.

Both brothers slept well and satisfied that night, but each was shocked and puzzled the next morning, when counting the sacks of grain (as they did every morning), to discover that one sack was *not* missing, as it should have been, but there was the same number of sacks of grain as the day before.

This went on for several nights until one night they each started taking that night's grain over to his brother's barn at the same time—and met in the middle of the field. And each saw immediately what the answer to the puzzling mystery was. They set down their sacks and embraced each other.

And God looked down from heaven and proclaimed, "This will be forever a holy place, for here I have witnessed great love."

This story illustrates "pursuing our economic neighbor's interest *and* our self-interest." The care shown to the economic neighbor, literally the brother in this story but applicable to any economic neighbor, is obvious. Perhaps less obvious but every bit as significant is the self-interest. By caring for the other, each brother also benefits himself—he ensures that his business partner is well-supplied and therefore healthy, happy, willing, and able to continue as a productive partner. The benefit is mutual; both sides gain from each exchange. Caring for the other creates productivity that benefits the self and is the basis for continued caring/investing in the mutually beneficial partnership.

To partner does not mean to prop others up with destructive selflessness (loving neighbor and not self), nor does it mean to push others down with destructive selfishness (loving self and not neighbor). Partnering is about mutual benefit, created by exchanging in ways that are profitable for self *and* other(s). To partner is to pursue self-interest and neighbor's interest, care for neighbor and self.

What Martin Luther King Jr. wrote about "true political alliances" is also true of economic partnerships. They are "based upon some self-interest of each component group and a common interest into which they merge. For an alliance to have permanence and loyal commitment from its various elements, each of them must have a goal from which it benefits and none must have an outlook in basic conflict with the others."[131]

Some personalities and philosophies are so self-centered that they lose sight of the economic neighbor; other personalities and philosophies are so other-focused that they lose sight of the self. Partnership is about keeping both the self and the other in view, and acting profitably for both together.

---

131. Washington, ed., *Martin Luther King Jr.*, 162.

Corporately Our Purpose is to Sustain Profitability for All Stakeholders

Corporately—whether corporal the economic body or corporate the legal entity—each of us operates within a context that we did not create but that we stepped into as stakeholders. We cannot deny this reality, whether regarding our family of origin, our local community, our country, or our global environment. In this way we are each a stakeholder in a continuum of stakeholders engaged with issues across the economic spectrum. As such, each stakeholder has a responsibility to other stakeholders.

But in our present-day version of capitalism, not all stakeholders are created equal. Some stakeholders are also shareholders, like George Orwell's novel *Animal Farm* where some animals are "more equal" than others. Milton Friedman's article "The Social Responsibility of Business Is to Increase Its Profits," (earlier discussed in Part 1, chapter 3) ignited the mind-set that calcified the fiction (right up to present day) that the only social responsibility of the corporation is to maximize profits for the shareholders. From this mind-set and fiction, shareholder value was elevated to the highest if not only priority, and shareholders were elevated to virtually the only relevant stakeholders.

Encouraging signs are appearing that some corporations are throttling back on the myopic focus of maximizing shareholder value. Over the past several years articles such as "The Origin of 'The World's Dumbest Idea': Milton Friedman" have appeared in respected business publications like *Forbes*,[132] and individual corporations have been taking steps to voluntarily consider their other stakeholders. Further and surprisingly, the Business Roundtable, a lobbying organization that represents many of America's largest companies, recently issued its newly revised "Statement on the Purposes of a Corporation."[133]

Signed by 181 member CEOs of corporations from A. O. Smith to Zebra Technologies that comprise nearly 30 percent of the United States stock market, the Roundtable's Statement breaks with nearly fifty years of the corporate orthodoxy launched by Friedman, as well as with its own previous official position. In what appears is an explicit rebuke of the notion that the role of the corporation is to maximize shareholder value at all costs, the Roundtable's Statement argues that corporations should no longer advance only the interest of shareholders, but invest in their employees, deliver value to their customers, deal fairly and ethically with their suppliers, and

---

132. Denning, "World's Dumbest Idea."
133. Business Roundtable, "Purpose of a Corporation."

protect the environment. We are encouraged; it sounds like the Business Roundtable is poised to consider a Partnership Economic Ethic.

Skeptics are right to wonder whether the Roundtable Statement is lofty but hollow lip service. On the other hand, perhaps one day, after its members integrate a Partnership Economic Ethic, historians will be able to point back and say, "August 19, 2019, when the Roundtable issued that Statement, that was the day capitalism again began to reinvent itself and this time to be a blessing for everyone." What will likely prevent the Roundtable Statement from getting traction? Quoting a *New York Times* article that ran virtually immediately after the Statement issued,

> "The ideology of shareholder primacy has contributed to the economic inequality we see today in America," Darren Walker, the president of the Ford Foundation and a Pepsi board member, said in an interview. "The Chicago school of economics is so embedded in the psyche of investors and legal theory and the C.E.O. mind-set. Overcoming that won't be easy.[134]

Indeed, the long specter of Milton Friedman's shareholder exclusivity, coupled with the raging image of Gordon Gekko screaming "Greed is Good" in the movie *Wall Street* will not be easy to overcome, if we collectively continue to ignore the avalanching evidence that these perspectives are in fact astoundingly damaging ethics. Otherwise, overcoming can be made easier and then possible by framing the Roundtable Statement goals according to the blueprint of Partnership Economic Ethics. Making the Partnership Ethic change, away from shareholder exclusivity and toward sustainable stakeholder profitability, is clearly the responsibility of and is just as clearly within the ability of every partner and every stakeholder, which is all of us!

Recap

"Act only on that maxim which can at the same time become a universal law. . . . So act as to treat humanity, whether in your own person or in another, always as an end and never as only a means."

—Immanuel Kant

---

134 Gelles and Yaffe-Bellany, "Shareholder Value."

The Declaration of Independence, in light of the nature of the Creator and the rights endowed by that Creator to all people, declares that a certain form of government is justified. In light of the nature of the divine Provider and the provision made by the Provider for all people, a certain form of economics is justified: Partnership Economics. This form of economics is "good" in an important double sense: it is morally upright, and it works—better than the non-partnership forms currently on offer. It is morally effective and beneficial; it is economically effective and beneficial. Partnership Economics hits a sweet spot where moral wisdom and economic value, or we could just as well say moral value and economic wisdom, overlap. Remember that the relentless rules of economics are what they are; Partnership Economics offers a way of thinking and acting that is holistically beneficial in light of those relentless rules.

In sum, Partnership Economics boils down to love your economic neighbor as yourself.

Chapter 10

Our Corporate Work, Working!

"How do you stop corporate fraud? The only way is ethics."
—*The Economist*

WE ARE TEMPTED TO conclude here our writing about the concept of a Partnership Economic Ethic because we think the point has been made. However, because of the pervasiveness of corporate influence and the entrenched predominance of the maximize shareholder value ethic, we see the need to further address the idea of the Partnership Ethic specifically within the corporate structure before turning to the action items of Part 3.

Canadian law professor Joel Bakan, in his book *Childhood Under Siege: How Big Business Targets Children*, makes the compelling illustration of a hockey game that spills out of the arena into the rest of society. We echo the power of his concept using the imagery of American football. In the specific, well-defined context of American football, people can slam into, push, and tackle each other, and these actions are part of society that takes place in the football arena. It would not be beneficial, though, if you were slammed into on the highway, or pushed down on a walk in your neighborhood, or tackled at school or work or the gas station!

Similarly, there is a context where special rules, conferred by democratically elected governments, allow corporations to act in ways that mere individuals could not and do things for society that otherwise would not be possible. The problem is that these "special interests" have forgotten they have a "*spec*ial"—that is, *spec*ific, pertaining to their *spec*ies—context within society. They try to make all of society play by their rules instead of playing by the rules society has given for the corporate arena.

We do not need to destroy corporations nor would anyone benefit from that, but for our own—individual and collective—protection we must not delay in reestablishing the "arena" within which they operate.

Practically Ideal

There is no shortage of opinions about economic ethics. This should not be surprising, considering the deep and broad influence of economics—everyone has something at stake, so everyone has something to say. One risk of such proliferation of perspectives is that it becomes impossible to weigh the merits of all options in the midst of daily practical considerations that must be processed quickly. Any economic ethic that will gain meaningful traction in corporate transactions must be practical. It must be clear; it must be actionable; and it must work—that is, it must be feasible in the corporate environment.

"Corporations should maximize profits for shareholders" is the prevailing corporate ethic of our day because it is clear, actionable, and works—at least in a narrow and short-term sense. It is utterly practical, so it is practiced. As described earlier, however, this ethic falls short on recognizing all true stakeholders, sustaining long-term effectiveness, and considering moral matters. We need a new corporate ethic that addresses these shortcomings and is at least as practically functional.

In our Partnership Economics approach, the corporate ethic is to sustain profitability for all stakeholders, and intelligently partner to use the corporation's excess for mutual benefit (the millions or billions, beyond any reasonable emergency or reserve fund, held unproductively in cash), rather than stagnate uselessly on a balance sheet. This is a better corporate economic ethic. It is faithful to Christian Scriptures and history. It has support among prominent economic thought leaders. It corrects the failings of cyclical economic experience. It draws us away from the plantation system mentality. It works with, rather than against, the relentless rules of economics. This ethic is beneficial for corporations, individuals, and the common good and is viable in practice, as we explore in Part 3.

Sustained profitability for all stakeholders is the ideal overlapping of moral uprightness, entrepreneurial character, and economic effectiveness. It is consistent with core theological convictions, enlivens human aspirations, and generates greater value from our resources. This is ideal, but not pie-in-the-sky wishful thinking—it is an ideal that can and must be put into practice.

How did we arrive at this ideal of sustained profitability for all stakeholders? Recall the unified ethical decision-making model first described and illustrated in Part 1 chapter 3. The ideal set in the Venn diagram is the result of actions that are morally sound, in character, and advance the cause.

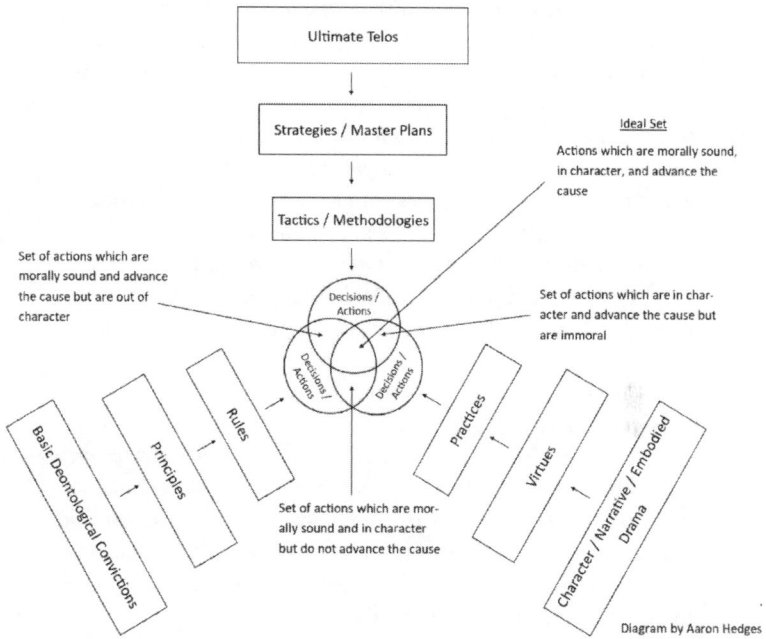

Unified Ethical Decision-Making Diagram, or Unified Ethical Modes

In this case the ideal is a better partnership capitalism including corporations designed to benefit as many as possible, that replaces the inequitable plantation capitalism designed to benefit as few as possible. This ideal is the starting point for corporate strategic planning and engagement and is the platform on which to develop concrete transforming initiatives that build that better capitalism.

Let us return to and continue the unified ethical decision-making explanation of Gushee and Stassen in *Kingdom Ethics* for further insight on how to develop both the ideal and its concrete transforming initiatives:

> The difference between deontologists [rules-based], teleologists [goal-based], and characterologists [character-based] is not whether they emphasize particular judgments, rules, principles,

or basic convictions or even what moral norms they value; the difference pertains to what they base their moral norms on, or, as we are saying here, the *mode* in which they reason: obligation to do right [rules-based], pursuit of a good end [goal-based], or embodying God's character [character-based] . . .

The fact that a Jesus- and kingdom-centered ethic includes concerns about consequences may trouble those who are determined to oppose teleological [goal-based] ethics. Yet "Seek ye first the Kingdom of God" (Mt 6:33 KJV) clearly posits a good end. Jesus presents a goal—verily, *the* goal—for which all Christians are to strive, and he sets us to work pursuing that goal. Actions that advance the kingdom of God are obligatory; actions that hinder it are forbidden. Rightly understood, this kind of goal-oriented concern meshes with a healthy Christian deontology [rules-based] and characterology [character-based]. . . .

The best overall term for the substantive content of Christian ethics is the broadest available—*Christian ethics is about the entire "way of life" of the people of faith* (Eph. 2:10; cf. Dt 30:19–20). . . .

The familiar language of "moral norms" thus comes to feel too passive, static, and theoretical. The church's moral task is not merely to develop right beliefs about issues and then make sure that every member holds them. Nor is it to uphold the right set of virtues and hope that every member will be virtuous. Instead, our central task is to be useful servants of the reign of God, and thus with all our heart we seek to discern and put into practice a total way of life in tune with God's kingdom.

Jesus's moral teaching in the Sermon on the Mount is focused precisely in this way. He does not instruct his listeners merely in *right beliefs* about moral issues but trains them in those behaviors, those *practices*, that characterize the reign of God and offers concrete *transforming initiatives* that advance it.[135]

What might it look like to examine the life and role of the corporation through the lens of Gushee and Stassen's unified ethical decision-making? Rewriting just the two paragraphs immediately above in view of the corporate entity yields an attractively practical corporate perspective:

> The familiar language of "employee handbooks" thus comes to feel too passive, static, and theoretical. The corporation's moral task is not merely to develop right policies about issues and then make sure that every employee holds them. Nor is it to have

---

135. Gushee and Stassen, *Kingdom Ethics*, 79–81.

lawyers draft the right set of procedures and hope that every employee follows them. Instead, our central task is to be useful servants of stakeholder resources, and thus with all our ability we seek to discern and put into practice a total way of doing business in tune with partnership.

Jesus's moral teaching in the Sermon on the Mount is focused precisely in this way. He does not instruct corporate leaders merely in *right beliefs* about moral issues but also shows how they can train in those behaviors, those *practices*, that characterize partnership and offers concrete *transforming initiatives* that advance it.

As an economic ethic our partnership approach is practical, clear, actionable, and it works—it is feasible in the corporate environment. As we noted earlier, the inventor and futurist Buckminster Fuller famously said, "You never change things by fighting the existing reality. To change something, build a new model [reality] that makes the existing model [reality] obsolete." Partnership Economics is that new model that makes the old model of plantation economics obsolete.

In the corporate context, sustained profitability for all stakeholders also directly addresses and improves upon the three failings of the current (plantation) corporate ethic. Having examined those three problems in chapter 3, we turn now to the correlated three improvements Partnership Economics offers corporations.

Improvement 1: All for One, and One for All

Recognition that God provides lends itself to sustaining profitability for *all stakeholders*. If provision is in the nature of the eternal God, then it will continue. God's provision does not boom and bust, as we've come to accept with plantation economics, but reflects steady care as Jesus observed in Matthew 6. The fact that Creation still provides the sort of life-sustaining resources Jesus noted two millennia ago is a powerful testament to the enduring nature of God's provision. Our Partnership Ethic does not demonize profit but recognizes that profit and particularly the ability to profit—profitability—are a result of God's provision.

Profitability in and of itself is not evil. It is provided by God. Those receiving profit experience this economic ethic "from above" and are to partner with those "from below." Sustained profitability is provided by God and is to be partnered with—with all stakeholders, not just shareholders. These are several truths working together to set us free. Once they are initiated and practiced, the anxiety experienced by both those "from above" and "from below" will be put away.

Have you wondered why it is written, "You shall generously give to him, and your heart shall not be grieved when you give to him, because for this thing the LORD your God will bless you in all your work and in all your undertakings. For the poor will never cease to be in the land; therefore I command you, saying, 'You *shall* freely open your hand to your brother, to your needy and poor in your land'" (Deuteronomy 15:10–11, NASB, emphasis ours)? Or why Jesus said, "Let her alone; why do you bother her? She has done a good deed to me. For you always have the poor with you, and *whenever you wish* you can do good to them; but you do not always have Me" (Mark 14:7, NASB, emphasis ours)? We have wondered.

We have wondered and now embarrassingly confess that, like countless previous generations, we dismissed these passages with popular excuses such as "they're a mystery" or "they're too difficult to understand and act on." We no longer find these clear instructions difficult to understand or act on, let alone mysteries, because a plain reading of the text makes clear that God's plan for economic sustainability depends on everyone living from the privilege of "from above" being willing to partner and share. God provides those people with profits to partner and share with the poor—everyone living "from below." Together there is enough to provide for at least everyone's needs, if not more, when we share. It really is that simple and doable.

The Deuteronomic text directs us, "You *shall* freely open your hand" and the Markan text invites us, "*whenever you wish* you can do good." Might we always have the poor so that those living "from above" can learn to partner with those living "from below"? We suspect this is another truth seeking to set us free, particularly from systemic economic inequality.

You remember sharing. Sharing is one of those foundational lessons we were all supposed to have learned by kindergarten. Remember when our five-year-old selves wouldn't share and some parent or teacher would take away the toy and give it to the other, or put it out of reach altogether? Remember the tears and tantrum that followed? We are older now and, hopefully, more emotionally intelligent. The toys cost much more and the stakes are much higher. In fact, many times the stakes are lives. The theme is substantially similar and simple, whether at age five or forty-five. If we are penalized at age five for not sharing, by what rational logic can we think we're going to escape being penalized at age forty-five? If anything, rational logic would suggest the penalties will be more severe. Those of us "from above" must now begin to fully share, partner, with those of us "from below" or, as experience teaches, the pain will increase until the student learns.

Interestingly, given the interconnectedness of economics (RR4), we are collectively a single student increasingly feeling the pain (RR5).

Corporation shareholders are not inherently bad, and the current corporate ethic is not wrong for seeking shareholder benefit. The problem is in seeking benefit for shareholders *only*. We, too, want shareholders to benefit—along with *all stakeholders*. Sustained profitability for all stakeholders is partnership that promotes both shareholders and the common good. In fact, it promotes them better than the current corporate ethic.

Improvement 2: More than Maximized

Frequently it's helpful to restate or rephrase a challenging concept in different words. Especially if the restatement comes from a different angle, then the concept might resonate differently with the reader or listener. With that intent, we offer the following restatement: Partnership Economics is not an anti-business ethic that seeks to stick it to shareholders while others mooch off their wealth.

Note that we are advocating *for* profitability—for business that creates value. The proposition here is not to reject profitability, but to pursue a profitability that is sustainable and benefits as many stakeholders as possible so that maximum value is added over time, rather than so-called "maximizing" profit in the short term (thereby undercutting its longer-term value). Ours is a pro-profit ethic—moreso, in fact, than the currently predominant corporate ethic.

Ironically, the ethic of so-called "maximizing shareholder value" falls short of its own claim—value that is not sustained is also not maximized. To truly maximize value corporations must pursue a sustainable profitability. By emphasizing sustaining profitability, the Partnership Ethic leads to more value than myopic attempts at "maximizing." More than maximized value for shareholders and all stakeholders—who wouldn't want that?!

As desirable as this end is, our Partnership Economic Ethic also improves upon the current corporate ethic in terms of how the end is achieved.

Improvement 3: Justified Ends *and* Means

Unlike the prevailing corporate ethic of profit maximization for shareholders, the Partnership Economic Ethic is not amoral. Rather, it achieves a desirable end within moral frameworks and admirable character. It supports reasonable rules and standards rather than ignoring or trampling them. It involves character that is caring rather than predatory.

We illustrate the difference in these two ethics by continuing with and then re-envisioning the example of Pacific Gas & Electric Company (PG&E), first discussed in Part 1 chapter 3. (Recall that we selected the example of PG&E simply because it was the corporate crisis publicly unfolding as we were writing chapter 3.) As of this writing, almost two years after the Camp Fire and a few months after filing for Chapter 11 bankruptcy, PG&E has pled guilty to eighty-four counts of involuntary manslaughter and one count of unlawfully starting the Camp Fire blaze.

According to related court documents and local media reporting, PG&E has agreed to negotiated penalty and settlement terms for those eighty-five counts, comprising: 1) bankruptcy terms that include an overhaul of PG&E's board selection process, financial structure, and oversight; 2) establishing a trust in the amount of $13.5 billion to compensate fire victims; 3) paying fines capped at just under $3.5 million; 4) reimbursing the Butte County District Attorney's Office $500,000 for its costs of investigation into the Camp Fire; 5) paying hundreds of millions to the town of Paradise, California, and Butte County, California; 6) cooperating with prosecutors' continuing investigations; and, 7) waiving its right to appeal. Hidden but boldly underscoring these financial penalties and acquiescence of its self-determination are the collateral damages and costs for breaching shareholder, stakeholder, and the broader public trust. Neither PG&E, nor anyone else, can buy back trust.

Appearing before Butte County Superior Court Judge Michael Deems on behalf of the corporation to accept the counts and affirm the settlements, PG&E's then-CEO and President Bill Johnson reportedly told the court that the corporation would never again put profits ahead of safety. Johnson also said that the corporation took responsibility for the devastation "with eyes wide open to what happened and to what must never happen again." (Johnson has since left PG&E after serving about thirteen months, so PG&E stakeholders can only hope Johnson's repentant representations of reform successfully transfer to and resonate with his successors in office.) PG&E's destruction, subsequent liabilities, and breach of trust are all object lessons for the kinds of increasingly untenable results produced by the prevailing corporate ethic of shareholder profit maximization.

Consider the ethic and course the previous PG&E leadership crafted that ultimately led to its CEO standing before Judge Deems. In 2005 PG&E's senior leaders introduced a newly defined vision and values, illustrated as:[136]

---

136. PG&E Corporation, "2007 Corporate Responsibility."

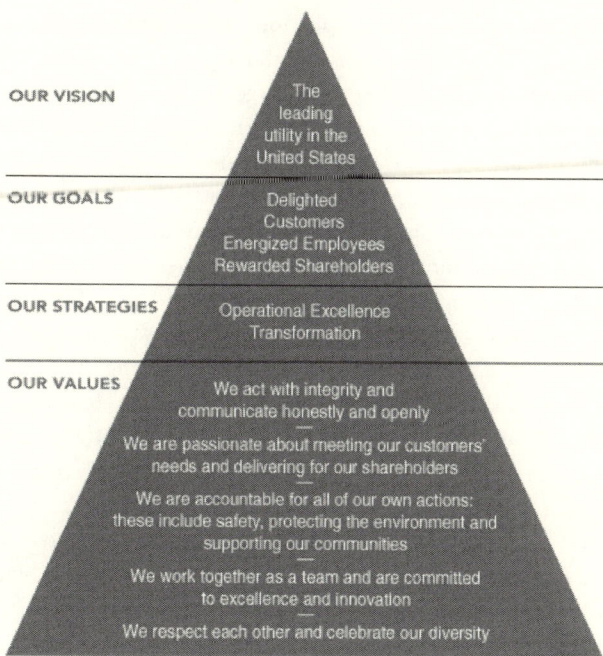

As proudly explained in its 2007 Corporate Responsibility Report, PG&E continued to pursue its vision to become the nation's leading utility, with its vision and goals "driven by [the following] series of strategic imperatives that inform both our day-to-day operations and strategic planning for the future:

- Creating a satisfying customer experience at all times at every touch point
- Investing in our employees and rewarding them for results
- Securing a sufficient and affordable energy supply
- Aggressively managing our cost structure
- Shaping the markets in which we operate
- Reducing our carbon footprint
- Creating regulatory and legislative alignment
- Supporting our communities
- Growing the enterprise"

We understand the use of aspirational but undefined vision statements such as "leading utility in the United States," we understand PG&E's goals and values as shown in the vision pyramid above, and we understand the strategic imperatives designed to drive those goals and values. Given the recent courtroom results of these visions, goals, and strategic imperatives, it would be easy but unproductive here to criticize PG&E's ethic and course using hindsight analysis, so we decline. We do, however, think it fair and reasonable to make two observations that do not depend on hindsight before turning to a re-envisioned PG&E ethic and results.

Our first observation is the emotionally connected language in its values and strategic imperatives that are a red-flag indicator of future trouble. The use of emotionally connected language in business is not by itself problematic, but PG&E's use is problematic and is revealing. Note the PG&E value that rises to the level of "passion" is attached to "delivering for our shareholders." Note also the only PG&E strategic imperative that rises (or lowers) to the level of "aggressively" is attached to "managing our cost structure." Passion typically speaks to object and intensity (e.g., he became her passion), and aggression typically speaks to hostile or destructive behavior or attitudes (e.g., she turned aggressive toward him). The combination of passion and aggression is familiar to abusive relationships.[137]

Drawing from the psychologist Marshall Rosenberg and his work that connects language to feelings then to needs and then to strategies, it is foreseeable, without hindsight analysis, that PG&E senior leadership would tie an underlying need (fear of not delivering to shareholders) to a misguided strategy (aggressively cutting the costs of maintaining PG&E's mammoth infrastructure) in an effort to meet the shareholder delivery need. Senior leadership's strategy to passionately deliver to shareholders worked for more than ten years as PCG (the stock ticker symbol for PG&E) increased over 500 percent. Until it finally imploded under the weight of its own misguided ethic and lit northern California on fire.

Our second and broader observation is that the ethic and course set by PG&E's senior leadership is not an example of unified ethical decision-making. Recall that a unified ethical decision-making model comprises the goal-based (teleological), rules-based (deontological), and character-based (characterological) modes.

Let's rethink, using the unified ethical decision-making model, what success would look like for PG&E leadership, who are presumed to be familiar with at least the basic facts regarding the corporation's physical assets circa 2020: it serves approximately 16 million customers in an area that

---

137. We acknowledge the use of the emotion-connected word *delighted* to refer to the goal of "delighted customers" but distinguish it because it's a desired result that depends on the customers as opposed to a stated value or driver within the purview of the corporation.

covers over 70,000 square miles of northern and central California; its electrical transmission infrastructure comprises over 106,000 circuit miles of distribution lines and over 18,000 circuit miles of interconnected transmission lines; its natural gas distribution infrastructure comprises over 42,000 miles of distribution pipelines and over 6,000 miles of transmission pipelines; its facilities include gas, electric, hydroelectric, and nuclear plants; and all this infrastructure sits atop seven significant geologic faults (including the massive San Andreas Fault) within one of the most active seismic zones on the planet.[138]

A reasonable goal-based mode for PG&E is "dependably and safely deliver energy to every customer." We acknowledge this is not a glamorous goal or end, but PG&E's leadership and shareholders have to be at peace with the reality that for PG&E to wow its customers with a flash is not the same as its Bay Area neighbor Pixar wowing its customers with a flash. With every flip of a light switch and turn of a gas dial human beings are grateful far more often for PG&E's mundane dependability in safely delivering energy to their homes and businesses than they are for occasionally watching or rewatching the latest Pixar spectacle. This is a goal-based mode PG&E can readily embrace that supports its stated goal of delighted customers.

Rational rules-based convictions for PG&E would spring from "best in class engineering practices." The kinds of engineers and maintenance crews employed by PG&E are trained to prevent risks like power plants exploding, dams failing, and power or gas lines catching fire. These kinds of engineers and maintenance crews are the spine to PG&E's skeleton and should never be hampered by the motives of financial officers or hedge fund managers. Unlike their Pixar engineering brethren, whose function and purpose are worlds away, PG&E engineers don't likely want their names lit up on a screen or news feed because that usually means something has gone terribly wrong. A rules-based mode of best-in-class engineering practices for PG&E is consistent with a goal-based mode of dependably and safely delivering energy to delighted customers.

A rational, if not core, character-based virtue of every PG&E employee and contractor must be a devout commitment to their roles as caretakers and their duty to maintain the well-being of the corporation's massive physical assets. This character-based mode, especially for PG&E leaders, is inextricably anchored to a relentless sense of asset care (at a minimum for the corporation's infrastructure and customers) and creation care (at a minimum for the environment in which the corporation infrastructure and customers are situated). A virtue of care and a character-based mode

---

138. PG&E Corporation, "Corporate Profile."

comprising asset and creation care is congruent with a duty to faithfully execute the goal-based and rules-based modes envisioned here for PG&E.

The unified ethical modes envisioned for PG&E form the structure for its transforming initiative. This goal of safe dependability, rules of best-in-class engineering, and character of care are an ideal set of decisions and actions that are morally sound, in character, and advance PG&E's vision of being "the leading utility in the United States." We think it reasonable to envision this ideal set would have avoided the many northern California wildfires attributed to failing PG&E electrical equipment in the Fall of 2017 and again in the Fall of 2018, particularly the Camp Fire.

Recall that investigations into the causes of these 2017 and 2018 fires revealed grossly negligent maintenance on the part of PG&E. In the case of the Camp Fire, no records of required maintenance for the piece of failed equipment linked to igniting that blaze could be located for the prior seventeen years. Igniting fires was apparently considered an acceptable risk for PG&E, whose CEO Johnson acknowledged before Judge Deems the corporation's ethic of putting profits ahead of safety. Envisioning a different ethic for PG&E is reasonable based on Johnson's promise to never again put profits ahead of safety, and therefore reduce if not eliminate deadly fires.

Also recall PG&E's goals of delighted customers, energized employees, and rewarded shareholders. We assert this unified ethic and transforming initiative for PG&E would have led to satisfying those goals. We now support that assertion by focusing on the goal of "rewarded shareholders" because share price is the metric we can most objectively access and address.

What might shareholders' return on PG&E stock (which trades with the ticker symbol PCG) have been if the company had followed the unified ethical modes approach? While we think it reasonable to expect that the well-rounded, mutually beneficial Partnership Economics approach would generate performance above the current (plantation) corporate norm, there is not yet an index of Partnership Economics firms. So we will compare to the S&P 500 as a widely accepted benchmark for corporate stock performance. We consider this a conservative basis for our comparison given that the S&P 500 firms are burdened by the suboptimal plantation corporate ethic, but it provides objective data and is eye-opening even with the conservatism.

For the twenty years ending June 30, 2019 (about eight months after the Camp Fire), the S&P 500's annualized return[139] was 3.99 percent. For the

---

139. This does not include dividends. Dividend yields for the S&P 500 and for PCG were similar in these time periods, so simply comparing their returns based on share price is accurate and compelling.

ten years ending June 30, 2019, the S&P 500's annualized return was 12.05 percent.[140]

Around November 8, 2018, immediately after the start of the Camp Fire, PCG fell to $39.92/share. Around January 18, 2019, as fines, penalties, and bankruptcy loomed, PCG fell to just $7.23/share. Beginning with a PCG price of $10.68/per share around November 8, 2002,[141] and assuming an annualized rate of return of 3.99 percent for the sixteen years and two months, a rethought PCG in January 2019 would have traded at $20.10—a 178 percent improvement over the actual $7.23. Assuming an annualized rate of return of 12.05 percent for the same period, a rethought PCG in January 2019 would have traded at $67.18—an 829 percent improvement over the actual $7.23.

We consider one more way of comparing the performance data between the actual PG&E ethic and the rethought PG&E unified ethic. Under the actual PG&E ethic for the time span we can most closely correlate to the fires in 2017 and 2018 and bankruptcy, PCG share price *decreased* from $10.68/share in November 2002 to $7.23/share around January 18, 2019, for a 32 percent *loss*. Under the rethought PG&E unified ethic for the same time span and assuming share prices that simply follow the S&P 500 average (which, again, we expect represents a lower performance than firms using Partnership Economics would achieve, so is a conservative benchmark), PCG share value would have *increased* to a range of $20.10–$67.18, for *gains* ranging from 88 percent—529 percent. That level of return is sufficient to satisfy the goal of "rewarded shareholder" *and*—here comes the bonus!—without igniting northern California or declaring bankruptcy.

As demonstrated by the straight-from-the-headlines example of PG&E, Partnership Economics and its unified ethic is the transforming initiative that empowers us, individually and collectively, to step away from the myopically focused and destructive ethic of "maximizing" shareholder value. Partnership Economics provides the structure and framework for the "what's next" we're all looking for in order to develop and sustain solutions that are more enriching and more equitable for more people.

---

140. https://dqydj.com/sp-500-historical-return-calculator/.

141. Our preference to select the price per share on November 8, 2001, exactly seventeen years prior to the Camp Fire in order to correspond to the seventeen years of missing maintenance records, deferred to our recognition of the proximity to the attacks of September 11, 2001 and the impact those attacks had on market indexes. We selected instead the following year, sixteen years prior to the Camp Fire, as a reasonable date and data point (near the time PG&E unveiled its ethic, after the 9/11 market reaction, and near the time period of the missing maintenance records).

Of the People, by the People, for the People

When you understand, you love. And when you love, you naturally act in a way that can relieve the suffering of people.

—Thich Nhat Hanh

We the People are developing humans. So why, after all these millennia, do we still spend comparatively so little engaged in human-enriching efforts and so much in dehumanizing efforts? How have we reached a point that human beings can consider other human beings "fungible billings units"? More importantly, how can we live into greater partnership with our fellow human beings?

In this Part 2 we have explored the (mis)interpretations of prominent influences on capitalism and economics and how inaccurate understandings have contributed to destructive distortions. A bit more historical context will further show how we got here and set the stage for how we can move forward better.

At least as far back as Augustine in the fifth century CE, Western thought has featured a two-tiered approach to the world. Augustine portrayed two "cities": one heavenly and one earthly, co-existing through history. Middle Ages Christendom conceived of two "estates": the spiritual and the secular, both under church authority but with a preference for the spiritual and the spiritual ideal being monastic detachment. In the sixteenth century, Martin Luther developed the doctrine of two "kingdoms": the spiritual and the worldly, both established by God but with private spiritualized piety distinct from public and material activities. The 1648 Peace of Westphalia and Thomas Hobbes's 1651 publication of *Leviathan* laid the groundwork for two separate authorities: the public authority of the modern nation-state, grounded in a human-centric social contract, and the private authority of religion. The two-tiered framework of public state and private religion was influential in the nation-building of the seventeenth and eighteenth centuries, including the rise of America, and remains to our current day.

Through all the variations, one result of this deep-seated and long-standing two-tiered approach is divisiveness. It is impossible to develop unity—oneness—when reality is fundamentally believed to have two tiers. It is impossible to integrate and cooperate—partner—when it is believed there are sides to take with ultimate stakes. Whether you remember Abraham

Lincoln's speech or the Gospels, or both, "a house divided against itself cannot stand" should be a lesson we take to heart.

In contrast to the two-tiered approach that is the ocean we all swim in, Partnership Economics is the beachhead to a unifying firmer ground. Grounded in relentless rules of economics that simply "are," and "are" *for everyone* just as gravity "is" for everyone, and building on provision and mutual benefit *for everyone*, here is the opportunity to bridge the "great divides" and, to borrow Bogle's call to action, "begin the world anew." Partnership Economics is a way to embrace our shared humanity, in light of God's provision. It is how we can make FBUs a thing of the past and move forward as partners with mutual benefit.

Thus we emphasize here the importance of the cohesiveness of the Partnership Economic Ethic. It is not two ethics; it is a single ethic which functions with the two integrated vantage points of "from above" and "from below." Joined and in balance with each other, like the drawbridge from our Introduction, there is mutually beneficial connectedness. This matters in some specific ways.

First, it removes stigmatizing and dehumanizing based on money. Economic modesty ("from below") is not necessarily a higher or nobler way than economic prosperity ("from above"), nor is economic prosperity a higher or nobler way than economic modesty. Rather than demeaning "the poor" or "FBUs," rather than demeaning "the rich" or "the 1 percent," we must always see people as people and recognize that both simplicity and prosperity can be responses to God's provision. We must see that partnership is the human-enriching practice in which these two responses from different positions integrate with mutual benefit.

Second, refuting the two-tier approach matters pastorally and practically. Practically, not everyone is poor, nor is universal poverty desirable. Pastorally, giving poverty a higher "moral" status results in a second-class status for masses of people who find themselves in prosperity. The only options available in the two-tiered approach are 1) becoming poor, 2) bearing a continuous burden of guilt before God for being prosperous, or 3) enjoying prosperity without any regard for God.

Effectively, the two-tier approach results in prosperous people either suffering a guilty conscience before God, or detaching themselves from God to avoid the awareness of guilt. Our integrated Partnership Ethic restores human-enriching relationship between the prosperous and the poverty-stricken. Prosperity and poverty are not competing approaches to holiness—they are complementary and should be integrated. The prosperous need not become poor, bear guilt, or detach from God. Rather, the more they recognize God's provision, the more they partner with that provision and create mutual benefit with the poor, joining the two in the holy communion of partnership.

The consequences of the two-tiered approach writ large, particularly the negative stigma it gives to prosperity, are significant for publicly held corporations. Corporations, by and large, are prosperous, in many cases massively so. Now consider the only three options available in the two-tier model for a corporation that actually aspires to a higher way. Becoming poor ends the corporation's existence. Bearing guilt is unlikely in collective entities, as Reinhold Niebuhr illustrates in *Moral Man and Immoral Society*.

The first two options are not available to corporations, leaving them no alternative but the third option: detach from God and pursue their prosperity. The pejorative "soulless corporation," then, is not just a figure of speech, but the logical result of a faulty yet pervasive two-tiered worldview. Simply put, a two-tiered ethic that honors poverty at the expense of prosperity is unlikely to create either prosperous Christ-followers or Christ-following corporations.

On the bright side, the integrated approach of partnership bridges this gap. Just as prosperous individuals can recognize God's provision and enter mutually beneficial partnership with the poor, so too can prosperous corporations. This breaks through tired, unhelpful, polarized debates of prosperity versus poverty, which sometimes is even framed as capitalism versus Christianity. No longer must we take sides in an artificial dualism in which both sides lose. Demonizing prosperous corporations encourages them to operate apart from God which leads to further demonization. This is a vicious cycle, but there is another way.

Prosperous corporations, the crowning achievement of capitalism, can and should recognize their profitability as resulting from God's provision. As such, they can and should seek to sustain that profitability. They sustain that profitability by seeking mutual benefit with all their stakeholders—employees, customers, suppliers, distributors, communities, Creation, future generations, and shareholders. Well-provided-for stakeholders become the foundation of an enduring, prosperous corporation in the form of productive employees, fertile markets, bountiful resources—and happy shareholders. This is the virtuous cycle of partnership.

Relentless Rules and Partnership Economic Ethic Reminder

1. Frictional costs are in every economic exchange.
2. Therefore merely transferring existing value is a losing proposition.

3. Therefore exchanges must create value greater than frictional costs to produce a true net gain.
4. We are they, and we, altogether, are average.
5. I gain/lose when we gain/lose, and we gain/lose when we all gain/lose.

- God provides and we partner.
- To partner is to seek mutual benefit.
- Mutual benefit is created by engaging in exchanges that are profitable for our self *and* the other—pursuing our economic neighbor's interest *and* our self-interest.
- Corporately our purpose is to sustain profitability for all stakeholders.

Because of the relentless rules of economics, the Partnership Economic Ethic is to love your economic neighbor as yourself.

Part 3

Putting Partnership into Practice—*Re-Living* Economics

"Big thinkers don't just ask the big questions. They answer them."
—Paul and Aaron

"First they ignore you, then they laugh at you, then they fight you, then you win."
—Nicholas Klein[142]

CAN SUCH A VISION become reality? Can a Christian economic ethic, far from a contradiction in terms, in fact be a great hope for both Christianity and capitalism? Can Christ and corporations flourish together? With the Partnership Economic Ethic now thoughtfully in view, how do we bring it to life?

Part 3 is where the rubber meets the road. This is a *re-living* of economics. For awareness and understanding to be valuable, they must result in action. The truth fully makes us free only if the truth is known, understood, *and* enacted. This admittedly was the most difficult section to write—the

---

142. Attributed to American attorney and labor union advocate Nicholas Klein from a 1914 speech (and most often misattributed to Mahatma Gandhi). See https://www.snopes.com/fact-check/first-they-ignore-you/.

devil really is in the details, the details of how an ethic is put into practice. This also is the most important section, precisely because it dares to give specific, actionable guidance, and because here we invite you to participate by contributing specific, actionable guidance that you create in your context.

The Partnership Economics guidance begun here is centered on corporations but extends from individuals (who, paradoxically, must take personal responsibility to partner with others in corporate forms) to governments, professions, and culture (which influence and are influenced by corporations). A stanza Johnny Cash sings in his classic "Man in Black" reads:

> Well, there's things that never will be right, I know,
> And things need changin' everywhere we go,
> But 'til we start to make a move to make a few things right,
> You'll never see me wear a suit of white.

From that kind of perspective your authors' "move to make a few things right" begins with our first cut at addressing topical aspects of plantation economics that cry out for change—nay *transformation*—in the partnership mode. Beginning with chapter 12, "The Rubber Meets the Road" for key economic entities, we then provide actionable ways forward with the Partnership Ethic, designed to actualize positive and sustainable transformation. These action items are bullet-pointed at the end of each topic under the label "Partnership in Practice."

We are limited in the topics we can address in this intentionally length-conscious book, so we start with a few things now and look forward to continuing the conversation and action beyond this book. Let us know your critiques and suggestions for action items at info@partnershipeconomics.com.

CHAPTER 11

What the Powers of the Country Will Kill You For

PUTTING NOT-YET-WIDELY-PRACTICED ECONOMICS INTO practice is not only difficult to write; more importantly it is difficult, sometimes costly and even dangerous to do. Returning to the shining example of Dr. King: he admitted the challenge of adapting local lessons gleaned from the civil rights movement to widespread economic matters was going to be a mammoth job.[143] It was one challenge to stage a sit-in at a lunch counter or mobilize a city against a bus system. Could those lessons be scaled up to stage a sit-in of the nation's capital or mobilize a full nation against its own economic system?

"Though much thinking and planning remained, 'there was an awareness,' recalled Dr. King's advisers, 'that we were going to confront the economic foundations of the system and demand reforms'—in short, said Bernard Lee, 'what the powers of the country will kill you for.'"[144]

Homo Agens—Acting Human

Let's return one more time to the helpful framing of behavioral economics and the factors of ignorance, uncertainty, and confusion that feature so prominently in our human economic experience. In Part 1 we dealt with ignorance by re-viewing our current form of economics (plantation) and making plain how problematic it is. In Part 2 we dealt with uncertainty by

---

143. Oates, *Let The Trumpet Sound*, 461.
144. Oates, *Let The Trumpet Sound*, 462.

re-thinking economics through the sturdy and promising lens of partnership. You should now be aware of destructive economic realities, rather than ignorant, and have an understanding of how to constructively interpret and understand economics, rather than uncertainty.

Part 3 now takes on the final step in better behavioral economics: addressing confusion. Confusion means that when we, individually or collectively, have some awareness of economic facts and also some understanding of their meaning, we are confused about how to put that understanding into practice—we aren't sure what to *do*. We must move from mere awareness and understanding, to confronting confusion about how to act on that understanding, then to confident action. We must exercise our agency, acting as intentional agents rather than hapless bystanders. We must decide and do.

We, individually or collectively, are no longer ignorant or uncertain, but confused action—or more likely, confused inaction—isn't helpful. The answer to bad economics isn't continuing passive decline into worse economics, but active engagement toward better economics. We all need an actionable solution, a constructive re-living of economics. We all need to bring to life our life-giving ethic by exercising active agency in the economic arena. We all need to live as intentional agents of a Partnership Economics so profitable, sustainable, and mutually beneficial that it spreads through the interconnected web of economic partners (RR4) and renders plantation economics obsolete.

To adapt John Bogle's inspiring language, it is time to "begin the world anew" and build a partnership society in which mutual benefit is our talisman. We begin with a warning.

Caveat Lector—Let the Reader Beware

"I tell you I can't read a book, but I can read de people."

—Sojourner Truth

Below we explore four major areas in which Partnership Economics can be pursued—companies themselves, government that both influences and is influenced by companies, professions, and culture that likewise has a two-way relationship of influence with the other areas. Notable by a presumed absence among the actionable areas of Partnership Economics is the individual. However, this is not because the individual is insignificant in this pursuit—quite to the contrary, the individual is the most critical factor for the implementation of Partnership Economics. Individual decisions and actions are so foundational that they cannot be isolated as a separate category but underlie each of the areas explored below. The individual is ubiquitous. Corporations, governments, professions, and culture are collective entities, but they all consist of individuals, and it is individuals ultimately who make decisions and take action. No collective entity changes except by the intentional efforts of We the People.

Let the reader beware: the role of the individual is likely to step on some toes as specific actions are proposed. We may feel righteous indignation about what "those corporations" should do—but we, individually, are the employees, customers, and investors (owners) who comprise "those" corporations. Even if you don't work for a big company, small organizations matter too, and you use products or services of big corporations every day. Who made the clothes you're wearing right now? The vehicle you drive or ride in? The materials from which the building you are in was made? The glowing "smart" rectangle you have in your hand so often? Who connects you to endless streams of data for communication and entertainment? Who among us doesn't have some financial stake in companies, through stocks/mutual funds held personally or by our employer or by institutions (universities, charities, religious organizations, service organizations) we care about?

It is easy to complain about government, and polls in recent years show remarkably low approval ratings for elected officials—but those officials weren't born into those roles and foisted upon us. We elected them! Instead of saying that Congress has a low approval rating, it would be more accurate, and more helpful (but less selfishly comforting), to say that we have done a poor job of voting. There are also polls indicating that we have a low level of trust in corporations, especially following the 2008–2009 crash. Again, because corporations consist of people—us—joined corporately, this effectively is us saying we don't trust ourselves.

And culture is a favorite punching bag of anyone who has any recognition that the world isn't exactly as they think it ought to be. "Culture wars" is an unfortunately common phrase—but we collectively are responsible for our culture and for our wars. There are cultural factors that affect economics, and need to be changed toward Partnership Economics, and those cultural changes will happen by individuals making changes.

All that to say we are "they." Although this is not a flattering realization, it is necessary so that instead of casting aspersions and waiting for others to do something about the problems, we can hold the mirror up and see our own participation in the problems. With this perspective, we can translate some of the energy vainly spent complaining about "them" into the hard but fruitful work of changing our own decisions and actions for mutual benefit.

Caveat Emptor—Let the Buyer Beware
—New Normals

Although it is easy and common to pose individual responsibility and collective good as opposing dynamics, they are interrelated. As described above, collective entities consist of individuals. This means that individuals cannot hide from the demands of individual responsibility in the name of collective matters, and it also means that collective standards cannot be ignored in the name of narrowly conceived (and completely unrealistic) individualism. While we place high demands on the individual, we also recognize that no individual is expert in everything, so it simply is not feasible for each individual to thrive in all areas individually.

The essence of Partnership Economics is that individuals use their expertise not only for their own benefit but also to lend their expertise for the benefit of others. When those who have expertise in an area help create standards and norms in that area to benefit those who lack that expertise, many benefit from the good standard (RR3). When this occurs in many areas as many individuals use their unique expertise, all benefit—we are all better off when we can pursue our strengths with trust that our non-strengths are being maintained well by others (RR5). In this way partnership is a virtuous cycle—the more individuals pursue their strengths, the more they have to benefit others, and the more others benefit individuals in ways individuals can't do for themselves, the more individuals can pursue their strengths. Partnership Economics thus offers mutual and increasing benefit to individuals *and* the common good.

Some specific examples help illustrate the interrelatedness of individual responsibility and collective good. Only a small percentage of individuals have the expertise to evaluate the safety of medications, but we all purchase and use medicines—generally without having to spend time or energy to determine if the medicine will have any ill effects other than those described on the label. The few individuals who lend their pharmaceutical expertise benefit the rest of society not only by keeping us safe but also by saving tremendous amounts of time and energy. Their work, done well, creates standards and norms that enable many others to avoid harm and apply themselves to other productive efforts.

Some of the non-pharmaceutical others are those individuals who have the expertise to design and construct buildings. We all spend major portions of our lives indoors, but we don't all have to spend time and energy creating our buildings or even inspecting their safety, nor would we be effective in those efforts. (Imagine if you had to verify that every floor you encountered would support your weight before walking on it.) Instead, we can trust that the structure is sound and apply our time and effort within buildings to work (and personal lives) in which we are effective and create value for others according to our individual strengths. Again, we see the social benefit from standards and norms established by the responsible work of relatively few individuals.

And how might the individuals with pharmaceutical expertise or those with architectural expertise communicate with each other, much less with those who disperse their expertise across society? Most likely they communicate with phones and computers, devices they were not individually responsible for designing or manufacturing, using cellular and internet networks that they also did not individually create. They, like all of us, benefit from the relatively few individuals who lend their expertise to the creation of such communication tools.

Perhaps there are some especially gifted individuals out there who have the capability, and just as remarkably, the time and energy to exercise expert responsibility in matters pharmaceutical, architectural, and telecommunicational. That would be exceptional, and of course these are only three areas where expertise is needed. There are innumerable matters that affect our lives—the 2017 North American Industry Classification System lists 1,057 different industry categories. No individual on the planet, no matter how responsible he or she is, could possibly exercise full responsibility for all the decisions and behaviors needed to thrive in all of those areas in a lifetime, much less in the demands of daily life. (Even Superman doesn't build the buildings he leaps over in a single bound.) By mutually using our individual responsibility for others to develop beneficial standards and norms, we all benefit. The better our standards and norms, the more we thrive individually, and the more we thrive individually, the more we are empowered to improve standards and norms. This is the promise of partnership—self-interest and common good reinforcing one another in a virtuous cycle of increasing value creation.

This promise is recognized to some extent, as evidenced by government officials, elected by We the People, creating and enforcing regulations in transportation, communication, food and drugs, healthcare, housing, various consumer products, environment, etc. There are two major limitations to the realization of this promise, though. One is the claim that self-interest should be unhindered by considerations of common good (and the opposite but equally problematic claim that the common good should or could advance apart from self-interest). The second is that financial matters mostly have not been brought into the virtuous cycle of better standards and norms, leading to thriving individuals, leading to better standards and norms.

Approaches that favor either self-interest or the common good at the expense of the other fail to see the beneficial interrelatedness described above. This is not just a conceptual failure but, literally, a fatal flaw. The experiences of Boeing beginning in 2018 with its 737 Max jet plane make an unfortunate case in point. There are regulations in aviation for the common good, but at least some decision-makers at Boeing pursued self-interest (in the form of reduced testing time and cost) at the expense of the common good (of rigorously verified safety of all equipment and scenarios). This has resulted in, at the time of this writing, two crashes, hundreds of dead stakeholders (crew and passengers), a grounding of all 737 Max planes, cancelling of new plane orders, and no new sales of this previously bestselling jet plane—setbacks for the common good *and* the supposedly self-interested company.

Regulations and standards may be perceived as irritations or hindrances to a company's self-interest, but who would argue that Boeing's self-interest was advanced by its shirking of such standards? By pursuing "self-interest" apart from the common good, Boeing harmed its own brand and business relationships—and killed people. When self-interest and the common good are separated, *both* are diminished, and the results are destructive, even deadly. Had Boeing pursued true self-interest in partnership with the common good, it would have continued to incur the cost of testing yet been in an infinitely stronger business position.

We mentioned stepping on toes earlier, and we can't let any of us (or ourselves) off the hook. It's easy to point the finger when there are disasters as dramatic as Boeing's, but . . . Boeing is a publicly traded company, meaning it is owned by the public—us. Hundreds of thousands of us are the owners of Boeing, whether through direct shares, mutual funds that hold shares, and/or our involvement with institutions whose endowments hold shares or mutual funds. How many of us resisted Boeing's regulation-avoidance before these recent crashes? How many of us, after the 2018 and 2019 aircraft crashes, have worked to make change at the company we collectively own? And lest we say that is the Federal Aviation Administration's job, the FAA is part of the government we elect. It is our job to elect public servants who serve well. The major players in this episode may nominally be Boeing and the FAA, but we must recognize our collective role at the root of both, no matter how much toe-stepping that involves.

Plane crashes are dramatic events that generate a lot of attention and are easy to recognize as destructive. Similarly, when someone consumes toxic food or medicine, or is exposed to a toxic chemical, the consequences are quick, visceral, and obviously harmful. Toxic financial products—loans unlikely or unable to be repaid, whether held individually or sliced and diced beyond recognition into derivatives—have consequences every bit as dangerous. Maybe because toxic financial products may take years to come to light and play out, or perhaps because their effects don't have the graphically visual, gut-wrenching impact of mangled planes or poisoned bodies, financial products are currently less regulated than other products. There is no reason that should remain the status quo, especially since the Great Recession spectacularly proved toxic financial products can be so destructive.

In the wake of the 2008–2009 recession and market meltdown that involved mass amounts of toxic financial products, there was some public energy for better standards and norms in finance. Such initiatives would be good to make the financial sector benefit from the partnership dynamics of aligned self-interest and common good. Much ink has spilled about financial regulation following those years, and voluminous new regulation has been proposed, debated, modified, and eventually passed, with implementation, enforcement, legal challenges, and legislative revisions still being developed and debated. This is not the place to go into detail about it all, nor would many readers be eager to cozy up to detailed analysis of, for instance, the 2,300-page Dodd-Frank Act of 2010. Indeed such massive size is part of the challenge.

We dispute the notion that financial institutions are "too big to fail" (plainly they did fail and we question why they should be saved only to continue with a plantation ethic that assures they will fail again), but financial legislation has become too big to read, much less implement and enforce effectively. This creates confusion rather than clarity, incentivizing well-resourced financial experts to take advantage of complexity for themselves rather than establish standards and norms that would be helpful to society. The remainder of this book explores brief, clear, and actionable standards and norms for mutual benefit. For now, please recognize and trust that much opportunity remains for greater realization of partnership dynamics between self-interest and the common good in finance.

In the realm of finance, claims of caveat emptor—"let the buyer beware," effectively having people fend for themselves rather than aligning self-interest and common good—remain more common than in other areas. For loans, insurance, investments, and the like, more than a few voices resist any kind of regulation on the basis that people should be free to make their own choices, apart from any interference from a regulator. That has a surface appeal, but it only works well if everyone is an expert in finance. Just because some people can make expert financial decisions no matter how many or how confusing the choice may be does not mean all people can do that or should have to. Who would argue that people should be "free" to make their own choices for medications, apart from any "interference" from a regulator who ensures at least a baseline of safety in all available choices? Or that we should be "free" to make our own choices for buildings, apart from any "interference" from a regulator who ensures at least a baseline of structural integrity and functional electricity and plumbing in all options? Or that we should be "free" to make our own choices for aircraft, apart from any "interference" from a regulator who ensures that we won't have a deadly crash?

Yet crashes occur regularly in finance, and their consequences are at least as deadly as plane crashes. People lose their homes, their healthcare, their retirement savings, all leading to diminishment and loss of life. And, as in the Boeing example, this does no favors for the companies either. When people experience destruction from finance, they lose trust in it and are less willing to engage it. As with Boeing, financial companies cannot neglect the common good without also damaging their self-interest. For the sake of mutual benefit between companies and society, to further both self-interest and the common good, we need to bring finance into the partnership model. Those who have financial expertise must recognize that they benefit from the standards and norms established by others in 1,000+ lines of work, allowing them to pursue their financial abilities. In turn, they should not exploit their financial expertise for "self-interest" at the expense of the common good, which is ultimately self-defeating, but establish standards and norms that benefit everyone. Imagine the benefit to society and financial companies if walking into a regulation-approved financial product were as trustworthy as walking into a regulation-approved building.

Winston Churchill had a line about making sure that no good crisis is wasted. Although financial markets have recovered from the 2008–2009 crash, we should not be content with Band-Aid fixes while leaving deeper issues unchanged. As with Boeing, the underlying equipment must be addressed before we take flight again, as must the reasons the bad equipment came into being in the first place. Partnership Economics addresses the deep issue of destructively detached self-interest and common good. We have the opportunity to restructure this fundamental relationship, and there is no need to wait for the next crisis, whether individual or societal!

Read on for specific, actionable ways partnership can be more fully realized in companies, government, professions, and culture. As you read and consider how you will partner to shape the next new normal, we encourage you to keep top of mind our simple mantra: "There's nothing to it but to do it."

Chapter 12

The Rubber Meets the Road— Companies

"Everyone, in every business, and in every position within a company, can be constantly learning and strengthening the values that drive good profit."

—Charles Koch

Building to Last

JIM COLLINS HAS GIFTED the corporate world with two bestselling books, *Good to Great* and *Built to Last*. The concept of "core ideology" is one of the four key ideas that emerged from the built-to-last research that is supported by the good-to-great research, and is the extra dimension that helps elevate a company to the elite state of enduring great company.[145] Core ideology points to the principles and grand vision—never perfectly followed but always answering the question of why the company exists and inspiring its people over the generations. A company's core ideology comprises and instills its core values and core purpose. As defined by the research, core

---

145. Collins, *Good to Great*, 194.

values are the essential and enduring tenets and core purpose is the fundamental reason for being, beyond just making money.[146]

Important things are worth repeating and restating in different ways, so they stand a better chance of being understood by all ears. The *core purpose* of an enduring great company—beginning with its conceptual days as a start-up—is its fundamental reason for being *beyond just making money*. One more time, a different way, with a direct quote. "Enduring great companies don't exist merely to deliver returns to shareholders. Indeed, in a truly great company, profits and cash flow become like blood and water to a healthy body: They are absolutely essential for life, but they are not the very *point* of life" (emphasis in original).[147]

Collins reports that one of the most paradoxical findings from *Built to Last* is that while core values are essential for enduring greatness, greatness and profitability don't seem to depend on what those core values are.[148] One does not have to fear lack of profitability when designing and creating a company that benefits as many stakeholders as possible. Stated another way, core ideology does not have to include maximizing shareholder value in order to realize profit or increase shareholder value.

In our view these important research findings and examples—that profitability doesn't depend on what the core values are, and choosing to benefit as many stakeholders as possible can provide for exceptional profitability—begs a critical question. "Shouldn't founders and leaders choose a core ideology that creates an enduring great company—a profitable company that sustains benefit for as many stakeholders as possible—over a core ideology that merely seeks to maximize shareholder profit on a quarterly basis?" The short answer is, "Yes." The slightly longer answer is, "Yes, and the unified ethical decision-making model is a powerful tool by which to develop a sustainable core ideology."

That is the first and among the most crucial action items we offer: that one can confidently design and run an enduring great company for the benefit of as many stakeholders as possible and also be exceptionally profitable. One simply chooses to make the decision to step back from following the historic status quo of maximizing shareholder value and move in a more enlightened direction.

In the last few pages of *Good to Great*, Collins shares the story of a question posed during a professional seminar by one of his former Stanford University students. This was an accomplished student, both academically

---

146. Collins, *Good to Great*, 198.
147. Collins, *Good to Great*, 194.
148. Collins, *Good to Great*, 195.

and later as an entrepreneur, and someone Collins says he has come to respect. So, Collins took this business owner seriously when he asked, "Why should I try to build a great company? What if I just want to be successful?"[149] Hypothetically, you might ask a similar question, "Why should I choose to build or run a company that benefits as many stakeholders as possible, rather than just maximize shareholder profit?" Collins' twofold response to that entrepreneur's question is instructive for your hypothetical.

First, Collins is of the opinion that it is no harder to build a great company than it is to build a good company. In fact, as suggested by some of the comparison companies in his study, building a great company "involves less suffering and perhaps even less work."[150] Second, Collins is also of the opinion that the quest for greatness equates to the search for meaningful work. If you are engaged in something you care about with a purpose that you believe deeply in, "then it is impossible to imagine *not* trying to make it great. It's just a given"[151] (emphasis in original). Collins's response, knowingly or unknowingly, speaks to spirituality and the spiritual journey.

Paul is an attorney and frequent speaker at law practice-related seminars where he introduces spirituality and the spiritual journey as a dimension of the legal practice. The definition of spirituality he provides these lawyer audiences is "the nature of every person to possess an inner trust and strength, which in turn gives meaning to work and life." The definition of spiritual journey that he provides these audiences is "the process of developing inner trust and strength, which manifests in being increasingly empowered and fulfilled." These definitions, as well as the proposition of spirituality as a dimension of the legal practice, are overwhelmingly accepted by these typically most critical of audiences. Based on this experience, as well as feedback from peers in the legal profession, a person's intentional spirituality and spiritual journey pushes him or her to excel, if not setting them on an active quest to be great.

Collins's response to the rewards of pursuing greatness, supported by both his sets of research, is compelling and bolsters what we wrote above about the rewards of pursuing sustained profitability for all stakeholders and the significant risks of other approaches.

Partnership in Practice:

- Choose a core ideology that comprises core values and purpose beyond just making money.

149. Collins, *Good to Great*, 205.
150. Collins, *Good to Great*, 205.
151. Collins, *Good to Great*, 208.

- Write and explain your core ideology, which includes sustaining profitability for all stakeholders.
- Embed your core ideology in your business or strategic plans. Draft and implement strategies, plans, and policies that support your core ideology. This becomes the DNA of your culture.
- Become grounded in and never waiver from your core ideology, which cultivates a company culture that circles back to inform and support your core ideology. Culture dominates and beats strategies, plans, and policies every time. (More on culture in Part 3, chapter 15.)
- Integrating your lived culture and official policies based on core ideology provides you the successful both/and rather than the more mediocre either/or.

Of course, if you don't like these action items or have better ideas, we invite you to email us at info@partnershipeconomics.com with your thoughts.

What is Enough?

"Enough is equal to a feast."

—Henry Fielding

"There are sufficient resources in the world for the needs of everybody, but not enough for the greed of even a significant minority."

—Millard Fuller

Millard Fuller is the attorney-entrepreneur turned founder and president of Habitat for Humanity during its several decades of stunning worldwide growth. In his book *Theology of the Hammer,* Fuller relates the story of a very wealthy man who built for himself and his immediate family an extravagant house in Atlanta. Admirers compared it to a royal palace. Explaining himself and his decision to build so opulently, the man said, "Because I'm a born-again Christian and I wanted to glorify God."

Really? Fuller prods. "Is God really glorified? Or, is God glorified more when a wealthy family exercises restraint, builds more modestly for its needs, and uses the excess funds to build additional modest houses for less fortunate families?"[152] Fuller's illustration regards housing and connects to Habitat's vision of a world where everyone has a decent place to live, but the theology at the center of his question is a Partnership Ethic that is universally applicable.

Explaining the development of his perspective and grounds for questioning the rich man's defense, Fuller reflects on a childhood that included a Christian home, active church life, and an early ambition to be a Christian rich man. According to his youthful reading of Scriptures to be a Christian rich man would be difficult, but in his youthful exuberance he was willing to take on the challenge. He certainly drove himself into that challenge, eventually building with his business partner both a law firm and a direct-mail marketing company through which he amassed significant wealth and possessions. The "being rich" part of Fuller's plan was working, but he didn't realize he had fallen flat on the "being Christian" part until his wife told him that he'd been absent from their marriage for so long that she'd fallen out of love and didn't think they had a future together.

To rescue their marriage the Fullers eventually agreed to a "burn the ships" strategy. He sold his interests in his business and they gave all their money away, in order to force themselves to focus on each other and their faith. They also soon found themselves at Koinonia Farm near Americus, Georgia, under the spiritual leadership of Clarence Jordan. During his time with Jordan, and before he was equipped to found Habitat, Fuller had to undergo spiritual and theological reconditioning. Those attentive to the spiritual journey will recognize this order-disorder-reorder pattern of growth.

Fuller reports two scriptural references, later read and understood through the lenses of newfound wisdom, were especially influential to reconditioning his theology around wealth. The one is the Apostle Paul's guidance to Timothy, "Command those who are rich in this present world . . . to do good, to be rich in good deeds, and to be generous and willing to share" (1 Timothy 6:17–19). The other is the Apostle Paul's guidance to the Corinthians, "Our desire is not that others might be relieved while you are hard pressed, but that there might be equality. At the present time your plenty will supply what they need, so that in turn their plenty will supply what you need. Then there will be equality . . ." (2 Corinthians 8:9–15). Doesn't that millennia-old vision for economic parity sound like a solution for most of the crises in this morning's news feed?

These references, together with more like them, are part of Fuller's "theology of the hammer." This is Fuller's understanding, and we think his confidence behind the Habitat partnership model, that "God has put all that

---

152. Fuller, *Hammer*, 31.

is needed on the earth—in human, natural, and financial resources—to solve completely the problems of poverty housing and homelessness." Indeed, in the forty-plus years of its existence (1976–2019) Habitat has helped more than 22 million people build or improve the place they call home,[153] and Habitat is now frequently listed as America's largest private homebuilder.[154]

So why is poverty housing and homelessness a problem still not yet solved? Because theology of the hammer, like countless other workable solutions to our systemic social ills, has a flip side. That flip side is the theology at the center of the question in the story opening this section, and which is universally applicable. Fuller names it, "theology of enough." "One of the big impediments to solving the problem [pick your problem] is that too few talented and wealthy people have a developed 'theology of enough.' They keep striving, struggling, and scrambling for more and more things for themselves and are too short-sighted and immature spiritually to see the futility of that type of grasping lifestyle."[155] While writing this section we couldn't help but recall the self-regulating wisdom of Proverbs 23:4–5—"Do not toil to acquire wealth; be discerning enough to desist. When your eyes light on it, it is gone, for suddenly it sprouts wings, flying like an eagle toward heaven."

It was an enlightened Fuller, almost twenty years as the president of Habitat—an exemplary case study in Partnership Economics—considering the primary obstacle to this otherwise juggernaut ministry, who wrote: "Simply put, the message is that we must have a well-developed 'theology of enough.' God's order of things holds no place for hoarding and greed. There are sufficient resources in the world for the needs of everybody, *but not enough for the greed of even a significant minority*" (emphasis added).[156] For us to develop a theology of enough, Fuller acknowledges "many hearts and minds must go through a radical transformation. With God, all things truly are possible!"[157]

As Fuller was toiling at Koinonia Farm and preparing to launch Habitat, in the figurative and financial a world away of Philadelphia, Pennsylvania, John Bogle founded and launched his juggernaut mutual fund company, The Vanguard Group. Like twins of different mothers but sons of the same Spirit, both men came to understand and write about a theology of enough. Fuller penned his book chapter titled "Theology of Enough" in 1994, while

---

153. Habitat, "Annual Reports."
154. Croce, "Builder 100."
155. Fuller, *Hammer*, 36.
156. Fuller, *Hammer*, 38.
157. Fuller, *Hammer*, 39.

Bogle wrote his book *Enough* in 2009. A couple of paragraphs from Bogle's Introduction show the resonance between him and Fuller.

> At a party given by a billionaire on Shelter Island, Kurt Vonnegut informs his pal, Joseph Heller, that their host, a hedge fund manager, had made more money in a single day than Heller had earned from his wildly popular novel *Catch-22* over its whole history. Heller responds, "Yes, but I have something he will never have . . . enough." . . .
>
> But the rampant greed that threatens to overwhelm our financial system and corporate world runs deeper than money. Not knowing what *enough* is subverts our professional values. . . . Worse, this confusion about *enough* leads us astray in our larger lives. We chase the false rabbits of success; we too often bow down at the altar of the transitory and finally meaningless and fail to cherish what is beyond calculation, indeed eternal.[158]

To make the concept of enough more actionable, we will be proposing clear and specific "enough-ratios" for various contexts in following sections and chapters.

Partnership in Practice:

- Don't seek *more* endlessly and meaninglessly. Shift your focus to *enough*.
- Determine, specifically and measurably, what is enough for you personally—see Part 3 chapter 15.
- Determine, specifically and measurably, what is enough for your corporate entity—see the next section.

Of course, if you don't like these action items or have better ideas, we invite you to email us at info@partnershipeconomics.com with your thoughts.

---

158. Bogle, *Enough*, 1–2.

Just a little bit more.

The Devil is in the Details

What about corporate financial capital—what is enough? We do not suggest that companies risk financial instability in the name of partnership with all stakeholders (not that this is a problem at present). Much of the source of the 2008 economic crisis was unwise debt accumulation; there is value in maintaining some cash reserves as a buffer against unexpected expenses and downturns. Wise capital allocation is in fact a necessary component of sustainable profitability.

Earlier, using 2008 as a snapshot, we drew attention to the fact that American corporations controlled $76.8 trillion of assets. To put it mildly, there would seem to be room for partnering within that magnitude of wealth without risking financial instability. Perhaps the most egregious example currently is the Alphabet corporation, parent of Google, YouTube, Chrome, Gmail, Android, and numerous other products and services. (Full disclosure: Aaron is an Alphabet shareholder at the time of writing.) As of June 2020, Alphabet boasted $121 billion in cash and short-term investments against only $16 billion in debt, for net cash of $105 billion. That sounds like a lot—because it is, truly is.

Alphabet has experienced massive success in creating services that people love to use; nine of its products each have over a billion users. But what value is a twelve-figure cash hoard? Alphabet's total profit in 2019 was $34 billion, so if it stopped all operations overnight its cash reserve could match its 2019 profit for three years. Such an amount of cash fails to benefit Alphabet shareholders as it earns only a negligible amount of interest and does not expand operations. It is not benefiting employees or customers or Alphabet's communities. Noah himself could not imagine a rainy day that would require such reserve resources. There are no benefits, to any stakeholders, to having this much cash on hand.

So how much reserve is too much? There is abundant literature in the field of corporate finance about capital allocation, and opinions fill a wide spectrum. In general the principle we suggest is that when a corporation has more capital than it knows how to allocate, resulting in cash storage as a default for the excess, then sharing (dividends, employee bonuses, customer and/or community appreciations) is more beneficial to shareholders and all other stakeholders. The devil is in the details, though—an apt idiom for ethical considerations.

We propose a specific metric, an enough-ratio for corporations. Cash reserves are fully sufficient when they can replace six months of revenue. That is, a corporation could fail to earn a single dollar of revenue for six months yet have sufficient cash on hand to maintain its full operations. If a corporation experiences a 50 percent decline in revenue—which would represent a catastrophe—it could still continue operating for a full year because of its cash. This is not a stingy measure. Most corporations in most circumstances would be fine with lower cash reserves because their ongoing operations provide cash flow, but we propose this as a maximum threshold. If a company has cash below this threshold, mutually beneficial sharing should still be considered. If a company has cash above this threshold, then sharing is indisputably best for all stakeholders, including shareholders. This metric is not sophisticated—intentionally so. It is simple, clear, actionable, and it works, even from a financially conservative perspective.

To connect this metric with a story from Jesus, consider Luke 12:13–21, typically called the parable of the Rich Fool. A rich man gained abundance from his land, so much so that he did not even have the capacity to store it all. Rather than share, he tore down his barns to build larger ones, resulting in strong condemnation from God. In our time, storage capacity is no longer a concern due to electronic currency management. The danger of excessive hoarding (greed), on the other hand, has aged well. We find it interesting and instructive that the text gives no explicit judgment against the rich man's storage of the crop in the original barns. Storage is not bad in and of itself—the problem is in increasing storage beyond what had ever been necessary. There is a threshold of storage that is wise, and beyond that threshold lies greed. The man's barns were good enough to help him manage his resources to become rich. When blessed with an exceptional abundance (according to the story, the *land* produced the plenty—God's provision), but the rich man failed to partner with those in need. Alphabet and others are in danger of being rich, foolish corporations.

Beyond the threshold of usability, the enough-ratio, resources lose their value. Cash sitting in an account never to be deployed has no more value than food sitting in a barn never to be eaten. Food that does not feed is no longer really food, and money that does not remunerate is no longer really capital. This may sound strange, but understand that money held in reserve beyond our proposed threshold is not worth its stated value. Money never used is as worthless as food that is never eaten. If, in the case of Alphabet, you hold $121 billion but will never, even through an extended catastrophe, use more than $81 billion (50 percent of Alphabet's 2019 revenue), you have effectively reduced $40 billion to $0. You have destroyed the value of an asset. This is an offense (dare we say "sin"?) against shareholders, all other stakeholders, and the God who provided the asset.

This approach can be applied to American corporations as a whole using available data from the Census Bureau. Total corporate revenue in 2008 was $28.6 trillion. Total cash and cash equivalents was $31.6 trillion.[159] There is enough cash reserve on hand to cover more than a full year of revenue replacement—more than twice the amount we recommend. The 50 percent sufficiency threshold for this composite corporate entity is $14.3 trillion, meaning that $17.3 trillion in financial capital is held that will never be used. Corporate America as a whole, by this standard of sufficiency-based value, has reduced $17.3 trillion to nothing. This is a massive destruction, both in direct financial terms and in the opportunity cost of neglected exchanges for mutual benefit. This should not be. This is easily remedied. There is no shortage of people for whom every dollar fully counts and who would be glad to partner in mutually beneficial ways with corporations in danger of having many dollars count for nothing.

Partnership in Practice:

- Maintain cash reserves as a buffer against unexpected expenses and downturns.
- Cap those reserves at six months of revenue = 50 percent of the previous year's revenue.
- When your cash exceeds that threshold, congratulations on your success, and deploy the excess in mutually beneficial ways with your stakeholders, including shareholders.

159. Census, "Table 753."

Of course, if you don't like these action items or have better ideas, we invite you to email us at info@partnershipeconomics.com with your thoughts.

Partnership Has a Price

"If this book were strictly for academic or business audiences we'd have followed the traditional route and stuffed it full of case studies. But we find stories of courage more persuasive, and Dan Price's story most persuasive."

—Paul and Aaron

I'm a performance piece titled "Living on a Market-Rate Wage."

Dan Price had a truth set him free, but first it certainly ticked him off. The co-founder and CEO of Gravity Payments, Dan launched a media frenzy and exploded onto the national stage in 2015, when he announced a $70,000 minimum annual wage for all the employees of his Seattle-based company. Moreover, in order to fund the wage increase without layoffs of employees or price increases to customers, Dan slashed his own annual salary of $1.1M to $70,000.

As of this writing, almost five years after implementing that announcement, Gravity just opened a second location and is successful by every typical business metric (i.e., year-over-year revenue growth and profits, customer satisfaction and retention, employee satisfaction and retention). You can refresh your memory and learn more on the company's website.[160] Gravity is also successful as measured by non-traditional but significantly meaningful employee-centric metrics (i.e., happiness, engagement, increased home ownership, decreased commute time, increased 401(k) contributions, increased family formation and stability, and the fact that the employees bought Dan a new Tesla car as a thank you gift).[161]

What was the truth that set Dan free? Paul Keegan tells of it in his *Inc.* magazine story, published a few months after the announcement.[162] Dan spotted Jason Haley on a break, an entry-level employee making about $35,000/year, and saw that Jason was in a foul mood. When Dan approached and asked Jason what's up, the truth spewed out. "You're ripping me off," Jason responded. When Dan pushed back with his defense of Jason being paid market rates, Jason bared his soul if not a national psyche. "You brag about how financially disciplined you are, but that just translates into me not making enough money to lead a decent life."

What was Dan's response? Keegan relates:

> Price walked away shocked and hurt. For three days, he groused about the encounter to family and friends. "I felt horrible, he says. "Like a victim." . . . Yet the more people tried to cheer him up about this wage policy, the worse Price felt.
>
> Finally, he realized why: Haley was right—not only about being underpaid, but also about Price's intentions [keeping a lid on wages even after the economy recovered from the recession, reasoning low wages would help the company survive in the event of another downturn.] "I was so scarred by the recession that I was proactively, and proudly, hurting my staff," he says. Thus began Price's transformation . . .

This backstory nicely illustrates one journey and a basic model from plantation system to Partnership Economics. First, Dan is confronted with

---

160. Gravity, "Dan Price."
161. Gravity, "$70K Minimum Wage Results."
162. Keegan, "What Really Happened."

a truth that ticks him off. Notice that the CEO says he "felt horrible" and "like a victim." But because he's willing to face and wrestle with his emotions over the encounter, Dan's transformed to a place of understanding about the underlying truth. In this case he realizes and acknowledges he's in fact fostering a plantation system, even if he's without that specific intention. Courageously revisiting and exploring his childhood Christian training and ethics (described elsewhere in Keegan's article and in a more recent article in *Forbes*)[163] Dan concludes a form of Partnership Economics is a better path and begins to make the tangible changes toward that new model, even at an initial personal cost. The new model benefits Gravity's stakeholders, not just its shareholder(s), and is proving to be sustainable. In this way Dan fulfills the wisdom of Buckminster Fuller, who urged "build a new model that makes the existing obsolete."

The critics immediately attacked Dan and are expected to continue to attack, as you would expect of everyone invested in the plantation system and fearful of letting it go. As of this writing, however, Dan leads a successful organization of engaged employees, his annual salary is over seven figures when he wants, and his example of Partnership Ethics continues to attract business owners and leaders seeking a guiding light out of the plantation system model. Indeed, the most difficult part of Dan's journey appears to have been his merely having to steel himself with the courage to make the change he knew was necessary. And Jason? As of this writing he's still at Gravity. Whether Jason remains at Gravity his whole career or not, he's pleased that he steeled himself with the courage to be honest with Dan.

Partnership in Practice:

- Learn from being confronted by someone or something about the way you set policy or lead others; confrontations often point to or reveal aspects of plantation system flaws.
- Instead of turning away or turning in defense to the confrontation, or continuing to hide the flaw, turn toward your emotional response and wrestle with it until you figure out a Partnership Ethic response.
- Steel yourself with the courage to take the first step toward the change you know is necessary.
- Confidently and courageously move forward implementing your response—that resonates first with your heart and then with your mind.

---

163. Ludema and Johnson, "Dan Price."

- Send Dan Price a LinkedIn invite to connect—he'll accept, and gain insight from every comment posted in the best real-time case study available.

Of course, if you don't like these action items or have better ideas, we invite you to email us at info@partnershipeconomics.com with your thoughts.

Above Board

In theory a board of directors (board) is charged with making decisions as a fiduciary on behalf of the owners (shareholders) of a corporation. In practice this is far from the case. Currently, a typical American corporate board appears to make decisions on behalf of its own self-interest and in favor of the CEO it supports. Such myopic behavior fails the fiduciary duty laugh test. This especially becomes self-evident after a corporate crisis publicly erupts.

Instead, to act as a fiduciary—to represent the corporation's owners well—all aspects of the corporation, all stakeholders must be considered. Yet stakeholders are frequently neglected. Why? A page of history is worth a tome of explanation.

Several photos taken during a GM shareholder meeting held in May 1970 accompanied the *New York Times* Friedman article of September 13, 1970 (described in Part 1, chapter 3). The caption that ran next to the photo of then-GM Chairman James Roche described efforts to "name three new directors to represent 'the public interest' and set up a committee to study the company's performance in such areas of public concern as safety and pollution." The shareholders overwhelmingly defeated those efforts, but in response to a sense of social responsibility, GM's management soon afterward did name five directors to a "public-policy committee."

The caption also described Friedman attacking such efforts toward corporate social responsibility as "pure and unadulterated socialism," adding, "Businessmen who talk this way are unwitting puppets of the intellectual forces that have been undermining the basis of a free society." Little wonder that boards quickly retreated from corporate concerns over social responsibility and became more subject to the pull of narrow self-serving. Friedman's fearmongering and bullying was ultimately successful. But that was fifty years ago. We've since collectively lived through and painfully awakened to the reality that the Friedman profit-only doctrine is unsustainable and can no longer be permitted to run its damaging course.

What's a path forward for boards willing to seriously live into their fiduciary duty? What's a path forward for those who will truly serve the interests of the shareholders they represent by attending to sustained profitability for all *stake*holders? Calling attention to the reality that too many corporate board members benefit from the status quo at the expense of those they are supposed to serve, we offer two specific and simple proposals to transform the status quo, two beneficial disruptions.

First, the practice of reciprocal board seats—executives sitting on each other's boards[164]—has birthed an inept cronyism that strips directors of the courage and independence to be bold leaders. Why would Company A director offer a painful but correct suggestion to the CEO of Company A when that CEO could retaliate as part of the board of Company B, where Company A director is an executive? Why not instead play nice (albeit self-serving) and suggest the CEO of Company A should have an increased compensation package, knowing that she will have influence on Company B's board decisions about executive compensation? To increase independence and accountability among boards and executives, and to encourage executive compensation that is actually tied to whatever benefits the executives actually deliver to a company, executives simply should not sit on the boards of each other's companies.

Second, and related to the first, is the untenable practice of directors sitting on the boards of multiple companies in the same industry.[165] Yes, this is a long-standing practice under the guise of "expertise" and is exceedingly profitable for the directors. Through the lens of ethical clarity, however, it is clear that such directors truncate if not sacrifice their fiduciary duty to each corporation they claim to serve. You simply can't serve the best interest of each of multiple competitors in the same competition.

In addition, this aggregating of multiple platforms places those directors in the powerful positions of influencing if not manipulating an entire industry, if not segment of a national economy. Yes, in theory manipulation

---

164. Direct reciprocity—Company A executive is on the board of Company B and Company B executive is on the board of Company A—affects 12 percent of firms: https://digitalcommons.ilr.cornell.edu/cgi/viewcontent.cgi?referer=https://www.google.com/&httpsredir=1&article=1236&context=articles. Indirect reciprocity—Company A executive is on the board of Company B, Company B executive is on the board of Company C, and Company C executive is on the board of Company A—has similar detriments and is more common: https://www.sciencedaily.com/releases/2015/04/150409120449.htm. Expand the criteria to include retired executives, and the percentages keep going up.

165. One in eight instances of a director sitting on multiple boards involves corporations that are supposedly competitors: https://insights.diligent.com/board-succession-planning/what-are-interlocking-directorates.

could be benevolent and for the benefit of a greater number of others, but more likely and historically the opportunity to manipulate at this level is to the detriment of most stakeholders, industries, and economies. And it clearly is not the way to encourage "open and free competition," as even Friedman thought was best for business.

Beyond the immediate benefits of increasing fiduciary duty, the two above proposals would open otherwise calcified board seats to qualified candidates with fresh perspectives and new voices. If we really want innovation, including diversity of thought, and dynamic profitability on American corporate boards, these are clear opportunities to open up seats.

A third proposal, requiring not much more courage and planning than the first two, and that could more fully swing open the doors of transformation toward Partnership Economics, is *co-determination*. Co-determination (sometimes called co-partnership, making explicit its partnership nature) is a form of corporate governance that, as primarily practiced today, includes employee representatives on a supervisory board. This form of governance is integral to Germany's economic success story of at least the last forty years, and enjoys widespread practice in prosperous and stable economies such as Sweden, Denmark, and the Netherlands.

Dr. Felix Hörisch is a professor at Heidelberg University whose research and work includes co-determination. In one article, where Dr. Hörisch considers whether co-determination could be viable in American capitalism, he writes,

> On the other hand, the implementation of co-determination could substantially contribute to stronger and more sustainable long-term corporate policies compared to the current short-term focus on pure shareholder value. Over time, this shift of focus could prove to be beneficial to both employees and the economy, as the implementation of co-determination could strengthen the social aspects of market economies and soften the blows of future financial crises.[166]

In related work, Dr. Hörisch's research indicates co-determination rights lead to higher income equality.[167] This makes perfect sense, given the dynamics of executive compensation, described above, that too often occur when board seats are reciprocal and not accountable to stakeholder interests.

Given its successes, why limit co-determination to employees as stakeholders? What about other stakeholders, such as customers, suppliers,

---

166. Hörisch, "Co-Determining the Future."
167. Hörisch, "Macro-economic Effect."

vendors, residents of areas the corporation affects? In addition to the direct benefit such interested stakeholders could bring to corporate boards, they could also benefit corporations that seek to avoid government regulation. Government regulation might reasonably be parried if a corporation could demonstrate that it is robustly co-determined. What need would there be for additional government oversight when all groups with something at stake are already meaningfully involved?

As this chapter is being written, Facebook is in the throes of another round of trying to regain public trust and avoid government regulation, this time by creatively offering a form of co-determination. Recently Facebook announced the formation of its global oversight board for content moderation, on behalf of stakeholders concerned about content. As this chapter was being written, Facebook released its bylaws for its oversight board.

In a real-time *Harvard Business Review* e-article, Mark Latonero notes that while Facebook wants its oversight board to take responsibility for decisions regarding the removal of content, he insightfully observed fiduciary duty conflicts within the bylaws. Nevertheless, striking a potentially optimistic tone, he quotes a legal scholar as noting, "Ideally, the board can be an important but small step forward."[168]

Similarly, an e-article of the same day and on the same issue in *The Economist*, but with a broader view of stakeholders worldwide and the industry as a whole, opined, "At a time when the internet is torn between its non-commercial roots and its hyper-commercial present, Facebook's [oversight board] experiment is worth pursuing."[169]

Mark Latonero closes his article with the observation, "If the board fails to self-govern, it would leave one clear and extremely challenging message for lawmakers: Facebook must be regulated." Because the weight of evidence indicates co-determination done well serves well, many observers—us included—hope Facebook succeeds in this effort and becomes an exemplar of faithful self-governance on behalf of and for the benefit of stakeholders, including but not limited to shareholders, worldwide.

Partnership in Practice:

- Stop seeking rock star directors from outside. Start developing your bench of effective directors from within the organization through internal training and ascension planning.
- Start building a rock star board by installing directors prepared to create and support a board culture consistent with the organization's core

168. Latonero, "Can Facebook's Oversight Board Win People's Trust?"
169. *The Economist*, "Facebook Unveils Details."

ideology, and that includes strong transparency, accurate communication, committed oversight, and rigorous compliance.

- Install directors with the critical skill set of familiarity with the organization's unique classes of top stakeholders (e.g., employees, customers, retailers, supply chain vendors, community representatives from largest markets, regulators, etc.).
- Invite your loudest critic(s) to present directly to the board at least once every year. The board is not promising to implement every idea, but it is promising to listen and take every opportunity to improve the corporation.

Of course, if you don't like these action items or have better ideas, we invite you to email us at info@partnershipeconomics.com with your thoughts.

Pensions—We Should Reap What We Sow

Frequently, governmental bodies (e.g., states, municipalities, school systems, police departments, etc.) and corporations offer pension plans as a benefit to attract and retain employees. Especially for governmental bodies, a well-known type of pension plan is termed a "defined-benefit" (DB) plan. DB plans were once common in major corporations and labor unions, but there the trend is now toward "defined-contribution" (DC) plans.

At its core, a DB plan is an employer-sponsored retirement plan where the benefits are defined by predetermined formulas regarding amount and timing, well in advance of the actual payout. In this regard DBs are guaranteed by and become a liability for the employer. DB plans, with their pre-determined and guaranteed payouts, differ from other types of retirement accounts, such as 401(k) plans (a type of DC plan), where the payouts depend entirely on investment returns. Another important distinction of DB plans is that the employer, rather than the employee, is responsible for all the investment planning and risk. In DC plans the investment risk is shifted to the employee.

Just as faulty assumptions and calculations or poor investment returns can result in individuals falling short of our funding goals in our personal portfolios, so can they result in a DB plan funding shortfall (known as underfunded). Over-simplifying for the present purposes, an underfunded DB plan is typically the result of the underperformance of the investments selected by the pension manager; or the pension manager having overestimated plan performance projections; or, and perhaps most frequently, a combination of both underperforming investments and overestimating projections. Controlling and monitoring costs in retirement plans is another key factor in achieving ultimate returns.

As Julia Kagan explains, "A pension shortfall is a significant event that requires the company offering a defined benefit plan to take steps to rectify the situation.... If the money is not there when people are ready to retire, it can imperil both the company and employees alike."[170] Corrective measures are possible, such as the company allocating profits to fill the DB plan hole. In cases where that isn't possible, the company can try to get relief through an ERISA (Employee Retirement Income Security Act of 1974) program known as the Pension Benefit Guaranty Corporation (PBCG). But what happens when relief or a bail out from PBCG doesn't come?

In a November 2019 article, *The Economist* noted, "Pension shortfalls are common across America, with the average public scheme monitored by the Centre for Retirement Research just 72.4% funded. That adds up to a collective shortfall of more than $1.6trn."[171] Before reaching its closing paragraph, which notes widespread public-sector pension deficit "is a crisis no one wants to solve" and "[t]he bill for taxpayers seems certain to rise substantially," the article points to the problem of overly optimistic forecasting. For example, "many assume nominal returns on their portfolio of 7% or more after fees. This optimism has a big impact."

At least fifteen years before that *Economist* article, in a presentation before The Investment Analysts Society of Chicago and The EnnisKnupp Client Conference, John Bogle spoke to and offered a corrective to the dangers of the optimism and big impact *The Economist* points to. After repeating the warning from Lord Keynes regarding the speculation of extrapolating future returns based on historical returns, and the relentless rule of frictional costs (RR1), Bogle gave a real-life example of how overly optimistic forecasting was threatening pension funds. He writes,

> Consider these typical words, verbatim from the 2001 annual report of one of America's largest manufacturing corporations, and forecasting a 10% future return on its pension plan: "Our asset return assumption is derived from a detailed study conducted by our actuaries and our asset management group, and *is based on long-term historical returns.*" This methodology could hardly be plainer Or more wrong.
>
> Rather than accepting this firm's assumed future return on its pension plan, let's see what returns might be generated using

---

170. Kagan, "Pension Shortfall."
171. *The Economist*, "Pension Schemes Trillions Short."

> the realistic expectation—and realistic costs—described earlier [in Bogle's presentation]. Assume that 60% of the portfolio is in stocks earning 7½% (contributing 4.5 percentage points to returns), and 40% in bonds earning 4½% (another 1.8 percentage points), for a total return of 6.3% before costs. Subtract 1.5 percentage points of costs and the result is an annual net return of 4.8%, less than *one-half(!)* of the firm's 10% prediction![172] (Emphasis in original.)

Bogle's primary point regarding pension plans to this audience of professionals was not about the actual returns of plan investments, but about the long-standing danger to the owners (employer and employees) because of the lack of realism and accuracy regarding plan projections. Faulty and overly optimistic assumptions are widely used in the formulas that calculate benefits. As those who teach how to code often say, "garbage in—garbage out." Then—and what we like about Bogle and similar thinkers—after identifying the problem he offers an elegantly simple solution.

> But my point is not that no one can be sure [of the rate of return]. Rather it is that each corporation's annual financial statement should present to shareholders a simple table such as this one [shown below] so that its owners can make a fair determination of the reasonableness of the pension plan's earning assumptions. After all, to do otherwise is, using Keynes' well-chosen word, "dangerous." I'd put such a report high on my list of financial statement priorities. *It is an idea whose time has come.* (Emphasis in original.)

---

172. Bogle, "Era of Subdued Returns."

Getting to a 9% Return:
A Template for Corporate Annual Reports

	1.	2.	3.	4.	5. (2+3-4)	6. (1 x 5)
Class	Allocation	Projected Return	Value Added	Expenses	Net Return	Return Impact
Equities	30%	7.5%	3.5%	2.0%	9.0%	2.7%
Bonds	30	4.5	0.25	1.0	3.75	1.1
Venture Cap.	20	12.0	6.0	3.0	15.0	3.0
Hedge Funds	20	10.0	7.0	6.0	11.0	2.2
					Total Return:	9.0%

Here are the assumptions such a chart makes visible. Allocation is the portion of the pension's funds allocated to each asset class. This involves no assumption; it is a simple matter of fact based on how the pension managers choose to allocate assets. Projected Return is what the pension managers assume each asset class will return as average performance—a big assumption. Value Added is how much the pension managers assume they can get above average performance in that asset class by picking above average asset managers—a really big assumption. As Bogle often reminded, asset managers as a whole are by definition average; it is mathematically impossible for every pension to hire "above average" asset managers (RR4). Yet such assumptions are distorting millions of peoples' pensions. Expenses are the cost to manage each asset class—putting these in view as the table does would help pension holders see how much they pay to let other people manage their money and provide accountability for pension managers to bring down expenses. Net Return is the calculation of Projected Return + Value Added Expenses, so for Equities the math is 7.5 percent + 3.5 percent - 2.0 percent = 9.0 percent. Return Impact is the impact the asset class has on the overall portfolio and is the calculation of Net Return x Allocation. So for Equities a 9.0 percent Net Return x 30 percent Allocation of the overall portfolio = 2.7 percent of return for the overall holdings.

Pension shortfalls are a crisis that is beginning to get some attention but not nearly enough. Those already dependent on a pension or heavily invested are likely living the crisis. The rest of us need to become aware, especially those early in their careers who are considering pension plan participation. For pensions both private and public, the assumptions used to calculate the projected returns are frequently both unrealistic and opaque.

For the benefit of pension holders (many people), the viability of the companies offering pensions (even more people), and the solvency of the governments offering pensions (virtually everyone), the basis of projected returns should, at the very least, be made public and clear through simple reporting such as Bogle demonstrates. Such clarity and transparency would at the very least allow people to determine if they want to entrust their savings to management making such projections, and would likely influence management to make more realistic projections.

Transparency matters. Understanding the math on which your retirement future rests is critical.

Partnership in Practice:

- Serious analysts need to take the issue of pension funding directly to corporation management and governmental bodies and challenge the assumptions being made.
- Corporate boards and governmental bodies that have not addressed and resolved this issue for their plans need to do so.
- Plan participants and shareholders need to insist on reasonable and transparent assumptions for the returns and liabilities of both DB and DC plans.

Of course, if you don't like these action items or have better ideas, we invite you to email us at info@partnershipeconomics.com with your thoughts.

Educational Companies

The large and growing problem of student debt presents a major need, and opportunity, for economic improvement based on partnership principles. One very intriguing idea, which we first came across in Luigi Zingales's *A Capitalism for the People,* is to finance education through equity rather than loans. Funding to a student would be given in exchange for a portion of their future income for some number of years, or better for a portion of the increase in their future income due to the education funded.

This approach creates significantly better alignment in incentives and informed decision-making across all participants—partners—in the educational enterprise. In the current debt-based approach, poorly informed and inexperienced young students bear the full weight of the decision to get a loan, and well-informed lenders always give the loan—regardless of the type or quality of education it may fund—because the government (taxpayers) guarantees them. Those lenders either get a fixed repayment or, if the student defaults, taxpayers are left holding the bag. In an equity financing model, the lenders are incentivized to actually advise students on educational investments that will generate good future value (helping the students) and provide funding where it offers increased value and not where it doesn't (helping the funders and students and society generally). These aligned funders and students will exert pressure on educators to deliver increasing value (helping the funders and students and educators and society generally) rather than continue in entrenched methods that have guaranteed subsidies regardless of results.

The equity approach also transfers risk from government (taxpayer-backed) loans decided on by young students and handed out by intermediaries with little skin in the game, to equity funders exercising informed investment decision-making with their own money. If a student's investment doesn't pay off, the cost will be borne by the equity funder rather than taxpayer subsidy (bailout). Similarly, reward is transferred from being based simply on making the most loans (regardless of quality or ability to repay) to making the best funding decisions with both cost and benefit considered. Current incentives favor behaviors that involve poor decisions and increase taxpayer risk and burden; the equity method would give greater rewards to superior performance and put risk for poor performance on the poor performers rather than taxpayers.

The parallels between the current approach to financing student education and government-subsidized housing loans are striking, and we should not too quickly forget the painful lessons learned when those poorly informed, mis-incentivized loans went bad on a large scale beginning in 2007. Equity financing presents an opportunity to mitigate the growing bubble and perhaps avoid collapse across student debtors (parallel to mortgage takers), colleges (mortgage-issuing banks), and government guaranteed subsidizers (Sallie Mae and Fannie Mae).

Equity financing for higher education is now being implemented in some places, so the idea is being put to the test and refined in practice. One notable example is Purdue University, which has an income sharing agreement (ISA) that started in 2016. More broadly, there is an ISA marketplace called edly[173] that connects schools and their students with investors in this new "asset class." The idea is gaining traction and prominence among schools and news outlets. As is to be expected with anything that threatens the status quo where such large amounts of money are involved, not all of the attention is favorable.

173. Edly, "Invest in Student Success."

Criticisms of ISAs tend to revolve around their not being equally available to all students, regardless of major, school, or other factors. This critique is voiced by Jessica Thompson, director of policy and planning at the Institute for College Access & Success. "The basic premise of the model is that they will derive a profit. And they will differentially price the terms of the agreement based on factors like the type of school you attend, its outcomes, the major you choose and who knows what else."[174] Thompson said she is also concerned that ISAs could deter students from taking out federal loans, which can also have income-driven repayment options and offer the same terms and conditions regardless of students' backgrounds. She says she doesn't "doubt that folks in this space are well intentioned," but fears that ISAs could favor low-risk students who have better potential for high earnings, and that could pull these students out of the federal student loan portfolio.

This critique is easily overcome. In fact, it contains the merits of what it attempts to criticize—by acknowledging that ISAs could favor low-risk educational ventures, the obvious implication is that some students' educational enterprises are high-risk. Financing high-risk ventures with the same terms and conditions as low-risk ones, as federal loans do, could be Exhibit A of economic foolishness. Financing should be, and almost always is, risk-adjusted—lower-risk candidates receive financing at lower costs; higher-risk candidates can receive financing but must pay more to justify the risk they bring. Risk-sensitive pricing benefits both the financier and the financee. Financiers are compensated according to the risk they incur. Financees are rewarded for lowering risk or are made aware of the true cost of their high risk. Financing that is not priced with risk-sensitivity imposes too high a cost on those who involve lower risk than the fixed price threshold and allows too low a cost for those who involve higher risk. This is a great attraction for higher-risk endeavors to inadequately priced funding. As of the third quarter of 2019, the record $1.56 trillion in student debt taken on by Americans,[175] many with insufficient ability to repay in a timely manner, is profound testament to the perverse incentive of fixed-price funding.

Imagine if car insurance cost the same for all drivers, regardless of driving history, type of vehicle, or ability to pay. Mature, safe drivers with high-safety vehicles and immature motorcyclists with numerous wrecks all get the same coverage at the same cost. The safe drivers would be unfairly paying more than they benefit from, and would thus be deterred from using such insurance at all. The unskilled and dangerous motorcyclist, on the

---

174. Johnson, "Wall Street Wants in on Income-share Agreements."
175. Friedman, "Student Loan Debt Statistics In 2020."

other hand, would get far more benefit than what they paid, and would thus be incentivized to use such insurance. The result is damaging to all—safe drivers are overcharged, unsafe riders are not made to reckon with the true cost of their recklessness and thus continue in unsafe behavior without the restraints true costs would impose, and the insurance company is on the hook for a disproportionately high number of risky clients with a disproportionately low payment from them.

Unfortunately this scenario is not hypothetical in the arena of student loans, particularly federal student loans. They cost the same for all students, regardless of educational history, type of education, or ability to pay based on the expected education. Mature students making good grades on educational tracks that generate proven value and immature students making bad grades in worthless programs all get the same loans at the same cost. Because the cost is fixed, the deal is sweetest for those with the least promising educational prospects. Students are not made to reckon with the true costs and value of their education and make more informed choices based on responsive (differential) costs, but for the same cost can pursue nuclear physics or basket weaving. The lending company, most often backed by the federal government and therefore American taxpayers, is on the hook for a disproportionately high number of risky student ventures with a disproportionately low payment from them. Either those students fail to pay the loans they didn't earn, harming taxpayers, or they scrape by and pay them at great opportunity cost—using significant amounts of money and time to repay something that generated little value instead of putting those resources toward endeavors more valuable for themselves and for overall economic impact. This is the antithesis of Partnership Economics—all parties involved come out worse.

All that to say: differential pricing, which some criticize about equity financing for education, is truly part of the approach—and that's a good thing. Pricing that reflects true values and costs is not a flaw but a feature.

Returning to the critique that ISAs may favor lower-risk students with higher earning potential: if a student is in an educational situation that does not create increased earning potential (because of school and/or program and/or major and/or the student's performance), that is not due to the form of financing. The financial value of that education is what it is, and the cost is also a fixed quantity. The financial cost-benefit difference therefore is what it is for each student and their chosen educational path, quite apart from how it is financed. Those without enough promise to attract an ISA do not magically become more promising by receiving a loan. With loans, the (lack of) value of the educational enterprise is simply borne entirely by the student. Instead of sharing educational costs and benefits with an investor   literally someone with a vested interest—loans make students bear the full costs, plus interest. If the benefits are not sufficient to attract a partner's investment, neither are they sufficient to justify the student's indebtedness.

Giving financing to all students, regardless of value created, as ISA critics/loan advocates suggest, does not benefit unpromising educational enterprises—it just saddles them with debt, with no regard for the ability to repay that debt, much less generate a reasonable return on it. "Giving" debt to fund an enterprise that doesn't generate value is like "giving" gasoline to put out a fire—not only are you burning money on a non-value-generating activity, you get to pay interest and inflame the value loss.

We are not advocating that ISAs should be required or be the exclusive form of educational financing. There is no compelling reason, though, why they should not be available to all students as an option for financing. If an investor sees potential value in financing a student's education, and the student agrees, this is a partnership model. If no investor sees potential value in financing a particular student's education, we should question why a lender would see value in financing it. (Answer: with government support, the lender, and the school accepting the student's loan-based payments, are compensated *for merely making the loan*, not for the value the loan actually generates.)

Again, we see that a major critique of ISAs—that their financiers would not finance endeavors lacking in value—is in fact a virtue. Something lacking in value should not be supported. Discriminating use of funds is a good thing—indiscriminate financing of non-valuable endeavors is the real danger. Schools that fear lower enrollment if rubber-stamped loans become less commonplace are guilty of not properly valuing the best interest of students. Lenders who give rubber-stamped loans without serious consideration of the students' ability to repay also are self-serving rather than operating in partnership.

Increasing the prominence of ISAs also means that how to finance education would become more of a true choice for students. Currently, for students not funded by scholarships or grants (or personal finances), loans are entrenched as the "normal" option, so much so that few students consider whether or not a loan is a good choice for them—they simply take the loans because that is the commonplace convention, the main "choice." If ISAs are a known choice along with loans, then students must make a true decision among multiple, viable options and not simply go with the too well-named "default" option of loans that too often lead to ruinous financial default.

Partnership in Practice:

- Increase the availability of income sharing agreements as one option for student financing.
- Price student loans based on their expected risk and return, for the benefit of the students and the lenders (most often American taxpayers, given the extensive use of federally backed student loans).
- Students: don't take on a loan—an expense—that traps you in debt (plus interest) for an educational venture that will not generate enough additional income to offset that interest-increased expense.
- Students: do the math before committing to the degree program.

Of course, if you don't like these action items or have better ideas, we invite you to email us at info@partnershipeconomics.com with your thoughts.

Arbitrary Arbitration

Recent years have seen a significant increase in the prevalence of forced binding arbitration. "Forced" means that a company requires employees and/or customers, in order to be employees and/or customers of that company, to submit to arbitration as the one and only means to resolve any dispute—*before there is a dispute and regardless of the nature of the dispute.* "Binding" means the results of the arbitration are final and cannot be appealed.

As the terminology makes clear, forced binding arbitration is not something that economic partners freely engage in for mutual benefit. Forced binding arbitration "agreements" are anti-partnership—clearly not mutually beneficial but benefiting one party (the more powerful one) at the direct expense of the other (the less powerful one). These commonly take the form of employers forcing employees to "agree" to binding arbitration instead of legal action as a condition of employment and vendors forcing their own customers to "agree" to waive legal rights, including the ability to participate in a class action lawsuit. There is nothing in this practice that even resembles partnership. At best it's a strategy to mitigate the risks of corporate malfeasance and litigation; for others it's a bald power play to further increase the corporation's power over their employees and customers.

To be clear, we're not suggesting that arbitration is inherently bad, and we have professional experience as a court-approved mediator and arbitrator. Arbitration can be a helpful option when it is in fact an option and when it is the option chosen by all parties involved as beneficial for a particular dispute. The problem is when one party forces arbitration and therefore forcibly removes from other parties all other options for resolving all future disputes. Forced binding arbitration "agreements" are a tragic, and tragically increasing, form of plantation economics.

Google has been on the wrong side of both examples. It made changes to its policies and required account holders—the paying customers who use Google's advertising platform—to take action to opt out of the new default of binding arbitration. Recall our earlier discussion about behavioral economics and the need to establish better norms and defaults—this is the opposite. Google created a new default that is less helpful than the previous one. It put its presumed "partners" in a very challenging dilemma—give up fair representation in disputes, or reject Google's default and risk exclusion from the world's biggest online advertising platform, the lifeline of business generation. The case also illustrates the anti-partnership effects of lack of competition, not coincidentally usually due to anti-competitive behavior. We address antitrust problems in the next chapter.

For a time Google also had forced binding arbitration as part of employment contracts. Eventually employee protests caused that to change. Employees of Google have more leverage than customers—there are many other employment opportunities for talented workers, but few, if any, other companies that are comparable for advertising customers. The concentration of power leads to abusive, rather than partnership, practices, but the example of Google's employees also shows the reality that positive change, in the direction of greater partnership, is possible.

Chase Bank sent a hard copy mailing at the end of June 2019 informing its credit card customers that terms of its customer agreement were changing to include binding arbitration. That was becoming the default, and the only way to opt out was spelled out in the fine print—send a hard copy mailing (no form provided; it has to be entirely created by the customer) with several specific pieces of information. This is a double offense against the partnership practice of making it easier to choose better defaults—this created a worse default and made it harder to change.

The term *agreement* is stretched here beyond recognition. Chase customers did not agree to these terms at all—the terms were imposed on them without any prior agreement whatsoever. They literally just showed up in the mail one day—here's what we (Chase) are agreeing you to. Disagreement could only be expressed through a deliberately inconvenient process. If such maneuvers are legal, that should be addressed by government, but even without government regulation companies with enlightened self-interest should know that working against the best interests of your employees and customers is not a winning strategy.

Here are some direct quotes from the "agreement" Chase forced upon its customers. See if this "fine print" is fine with you.

> Binding Arbitration: What It Means
> Unless you timely reject the agreement to arbitrate, disputes with us may be resolved by arbitration. With arbitration, you cannot go to court, have a jury trial or initiate participation in a class action for your dispute(s) with us. In arbitration, disputes are resolved by an arbitrator, not a judge or jury, and procedures are simpler and more limited than rules applicable in court.

Who picks the arbitrator? What accountability do arbitrators have that makes them preferable to judges or juries? Why not keep all the options open, even including arbitration as an option, rather than forcefully removing options? Doesn't the U.S. Constitution say, in part of the Seventh Amendment, "In all suits at common law, where the value in controversy shall exceed twenty dollars, the right of trial by jury shall be preserved and no fact tried by a jury shall be otherwise reexamined by any court of the United States"? Citizens should not have to take any action to preserve rights, such as the right of trial by jury, that our Constitution says "shall be preserved"! Constitutionally, these rights should be "on" by default, not require an opt-in.

The undesirability of binding arbitration is made obvious as the fine print continues.

> If you are covered by the Military Lending Act, (i) then you are not bound by the Arbitration Agreement below, and (ii) notwithstanding anything to the contrary in this agreement, to the extent required by the Military Lending Act, nothing in this agreement will be deemed a waiver of the right to legal recourse under any otherwise applicable provision of state or federal law.

If military personnel have legislation protecting them from forced arbitration, then clearly it is not in people's best interest. Waiving rights to legal recourse should not be forced upon military personnel—it should not be forced upon anyone. Legislation thus already recognizes the need for protection from forced binding arbitration; that protection simply needs to be expanded to all citizens.

In addition to military personnel, another group has successfully gained protection from forced binding arbitration agreements—motor vehicle dealers. The 2002 Motor Vehicle Franchise Contract Arbitration Fairness Act makes such "agreements" unenforceable unless *all* parties truly agree to arbitration, *after* a specific dispute arises. The justification of this law was to remedy the disparity in bargaining power between vehicle manufacturers and vehicle dealers. We applaud this protection from pre-dispute forced arbitration, yet we lament that it is so narrow. If vehicle dealers, a business group of considerable power, can be seen as needing protection from such abuses of power, how much more do individuals need that protection from powerful businesses?

Ironically, and in a real show of non-partnership, vehicle dealers commonly use forced binding arbitration "agreements" in the contracts they make with vehicle purchasers. The benefit they sought (and won) for themselves they deny to their very own customers. The abuse they sought (and won) protection from they now impose on others. Many used car dealers have earned a bad reputation, but it turns out that we're all getting used by car dealers.

We call for companies to stop forcing binding arbitration because doing so is best for their stakeholders, which means it is ultimately best for the companies, too. Remember from the relentless rules that we are they, and we gain/lose when we all gain/lose (RR4&5). Companies that try to gain at the expense of their employees and/or customers will eventually find that they have a shortage of valuable employees and/or customers. In fact, reading the current business data and surveys it appears the majority of companies *are* finding a shortage of valuable employees *and* customers. (Ostensibly the blame is currently on millennials who aren't loyal to their employers and are too burdened with college debt to be good consumers and buy everything they see advertised. But that just isn't the core reason.) Why not pursue partnership and the mutual benefits of treating your employees and customers well?

Gerald L. Sauer is an accomplished civil trial attorney based in Los Angeles. In his recent article "Arbitration is A Flawed Forum That Needs Repair"[176] he reasonably points to significant flaws in the practice of arbitration that have emerged since the passing of well-intended Federal Arbitration Act of 1925. These flaws are primarily the result of the *business* of arbitration, including how arbitrators are typically selected and paid by the corporate defendant, and how arbitrators don't need to explain their often one-sentence decisions in favor of the corporation. He also points to several examples of states passing legislation to protect workers from forced arbitration clauses.

Sauer, not looking to abolish but restore arbitration, thoughtfully concludes his article with actionable recommendations for state and federal legislators,

---

176. Sauer, "Arbitration Needs Repair."

Legislation at the state and federal levels could also help improve arbitration outcomes, while leaving mandatory arbitration in place. Such laws might require that every arbitral decision include a reasoned, published opinion; that the legal basis for the decision be subject to outside review and judicial appeal if erroneous; and that awards be commensurate with prevailing court awards for similar cases. Such laws would remove the unchecked discretion that now plagues the system and help level the playing field for all parties.

Arbitration isn't bad. It's actually a good vehicle for reducing court dockets and ensuring timely resolution of disputes. The existing system, however, is broken and efforts to outlaw forced arbitration at the state and federal levels prove that it's time to finally fix it.

Congress has taken meaningful first steps to address the abuses of forced arbitration. In September 2019 the House passed and forwarded to the Senate for approval the Forced Arbitration Injustice Repeal (FAIR) Act. The purposes of the FAIR Act are to 1) prohibit predispute arbitration agreement that force arbitration of future employment, consumer, antitrust, or civil rights disputes; and 2) prohibit agreements and practices that interfere with the right of individuals, works, and small businesses to participate in a joint, class, or collective action related to an employment, consumer, antitrust, or civil rights dispute. Do your part—there's no such thing as passive partnership. Go to the National Consumer Law Center website and fill out a simple online form that will notify your senators of your desire to end forced arbitration.

Companies can and should dump forced binding arbitration because it's both the right thing to do and best for their long-term business interests. However, even the promise of competitive advantage—from more satisfied employees and customers—sometimes isn't enough to prompt companies to make positive change for themselves. Sometimes external governance is needed. Government isn't the solution to everything, nor is it the problem with everything, and the next chapter addresses specific ways the government can help facilitate Partnership Economics.

Partnership in Practice:

- Listen to stakeholder complaints. Listening is not an admission of guilt. (Yes. Reread that as often as you need.)

- Listening is a partnership opportunity to address a complaint and make a convert to the corporation. Listening may reveal a truth the corporation isn't getting from anyone else.
- Replace forced arbitration clauses with voluntary mediation clauses.
- Include voluntary arbitration as a prerequisite to litigation in the corporation's terms and conditions (in the event listening and mediation fail).
- Go to https://nclc.salsalabs.org/ArbitrationTakeActionPageforWebsite/index.html and fill out the simple online form to notify your senators that you want to end forced arbitration.

Of course, if you don't like these action items or have better ideas, we invite you to email us at info@partnershipeconomics.com with your thoughts.

A Reader's Response

Each section of this Part 3 ends with our invitation to you to respond with your thoughts, like the invitation immediately above. We mean it—we truly want to know how you'd engage and address the re-living of capitalism. What might your response look like?

Below is an example of one reader's response, provided by a friend who is an attorney turned full-time securities arbitrator. We asked him to consider our arguments about moving from plantation economics to Partnership Economics, and what that move might look like in his profession and industry. Graciously, he agreed to give it thought and responded with the six paragraphs below. We use what he wrote verbatim with his permission and his approval to redact some of the history and procedural details to save space without losing meaning. This is an active professional's real-time view and response from the trenches. We appreciate his thoughtful attention to the issue and his absolutely doable suggestions for improvement.

> Arbitration is supposed to be a less formal, simpler, faster, and cheaper means of resolving disputes than litigation in court. It is founded on an agreement of the parties to use the process to resolve a specified dispute. . . . Arbitration originated among Middle Ages merchants who wanted to stay away from the king's laws and courts so they could resolve disputes among themselves, based on their general practices as businessmen. . . . Properly configured, it is a fair way of avoiding the attorney fees and other expenses of going to court. . . . It can be *binding*, which

means there is no appeal to a higher authority. Even so, however, arbitrators' decisions can be challenged in court on limited grounds set out in state and federal arbitration laws. These grounds are mostly based on some impropriety in conduct of the arbitration....

If arbitrations are not binding, they can become just one more time-consuming expense before the expenses of [taking] the dispute to court. In the present commercial setting, more and more companies are requiring *mandatory* pre-disputes agreements to arbitrate disputes as a condition of doing any business with the company, whether contracting to provide goods or services or simply purchasing the company's products. Mandatory means that parties wanting to do business with the company (and the company itself) surrender their right to go to court if disputes arise. Even this is not necessarily an unfair requirement, *provided* that the arbitration itself will be a reasonably inexpensive, fair and unbiased process.

The American Arbitration Association (AAA) has available a process that is fair and unbiased, where the AAA specifies the rules and handles administrative matters such as lists of approved arbitrators. Unfortunately, not all companies specify AAA arbitration, and require instead some other arbitration service, many of which are for-profit firms that understand where their bread is buttered and do not provide a fair procedure. To require mandatory, pre-dispute arbitration, companies should be required to provide either a choice of a proven, unbiased arbitration service or to specify such a service. Individual businesses, except for the very largest, probably could not justify the cost of creating and maintaining such a system themselves.

However, an industry group could do so, as the securities industry does under the auspices of its federal regulatory authority. Each brokerage firm pays its common expenses to fund the system, and each firm and each employee stockbroker must agree in advance to resolve any disputes among themselves or with customers in the industry arbitration forum. Each customer, upon opening a securities account with a firm, must sign a similar agreement. Arbitration is mandatory and binding.

...

This system is expensive, but the great majority of its costs are borne by the firms, not the individual customers. *That should be the rule for any company/industry that wants to require mandatory, binding arbitration: the company/industry foots the bill, other than a relatively small "co-pay" for the customer. If the company/industry doesn't want to pay the costs of a fair system that meets due-process requirements, then mandatory binding arbitrations should be disallowed* (emphasis added). And upfront sacrifice of any other rights than the right to litigate in court is never justified.

To be a fair process, there must be pre-arranged procedures that, at a minimum, should provide rules for:

1. Choosing neutral un-biased arbitrators;
2. Exchange of documents before hearing;
3. Presentation of evidence to the arbitrators, in a face-to-face (even if on an internet-based platform) opportunity to be heard; and
4. Opportunity to present and question your own and other witnesses.

And overall reasonable expenses for the persons bringing a claim.

Chapter 13

The Rubber Meets the Road —Government

"We, the people, are the boss, and we will get the kind of political leadership, be it good or bad, that we demand and deserve."
—President John F. Kennedy

Short and Sweet or Less is More

"If you can't explain it simply, you don't understand it well enough."
—Albert Einstein

IF DEALING WITH MONEY and religion isn't provocative enough, we'll throw in some politics too. Not politics in a narrow, partisan sense, but politics in the sense of policies that affect the *polis*, the affairs of the "city" of citizens. We don't errantly expect corporate entities to govern themselves and broader economics in the best interests of the overall public without any public oversight, so we necessarily have to deal with public policy via government. We hearken back to Adam Smith's view that governments are "to promote the happiness of those who live under them. This is their sole use and end."

Happily, our first recommendation on policy is to keep it brief. This does not mean that less regulation is always better but that necessary regulation should be stated in brief form to make it as understandable, actionable, and enforceable as possible. Regulation that is not concise and clear is actually counterproductive. Simple rules are easy to interpret, implement, and enforce, bringing consistent and manageable standards to all involved. The more complex rules are, the more resource-intensive they are to comply with, creating a burden for smaller firms and therefore an advantage for firms that are already the largest and most advantaged.

It is not out of ignorance that Facebook executives are saying they would be okay with, or even welcome, regulation as they face scrutiny.[177] They have no love for regulation in and of itself, but they know they are better equipped to handle regulation than any competitor or potential competitor, so any burden created by regulation would be proportionally more burdensome on their competitors or new entrants. This kind of "regulation" would only further Facebook's existing advantages and create a barrier to entry for new challengers.

Some will argue that simple policies will have unintended consequences; they are like blunt instruments where more nuance is needed. We do not disagree that simple policies may have unintended consequences, some of which may be undesirable. We submit, however, that the unintended consequences of long, dense, and complex policies are even worse. Better to have a simple policy that holds all players in a given field to the same standard in a relatively non-burdensome way than convoluted policies that big players can afford to manipulate while smaller players bear a disproportionate burden. In this way, simple policies would have the consequence of far less regulatory burden. We view simplicity as the more profitable and sustainable route for all stakeholders, in keeping with our Partnership Ethic.

For example, in a simple sense, beginning in 2018 America's federal corporate tax rate is 21 percent.[178] A printed version of the Internal Revenue Code, though, has 5,296 pages. But wait, there's more. According to the IRS.gov website, "Treasury regulations (26 C.F.R.)—commonly referred to as federal tax regulations—pick up where the Internal Revenue Code (IRC) leaves off by providing the official interpretation of the IRC by the U.S. Department of the Treasury."[179] A printed version of the Treasury regulations has 14,260 pages.

Massive companies can pay an army of lawyers, accountants, and lobbyists to scour all of those 19,000 pages and find (or create) ways (loopholes) to lower their taxes, and the expense they pay that army is less than what they save in taxes. When we say they can, we mean they *do*. In 2018, 379 of

177. *Los Angeles Times*, "Must Have Regulation."
178. Deloitte, "Corporate Tax Rates 2020."
179. IRS, "Tax Code, Regulations and Official Guidance."

America's Fortune 500 companies were profitable, and together they paid an effective federal income tax rate of 11.3 percent.[180] Ninety-one corporations paid federal income tax of *0 percent or less* on their U.S. income, including names like Amazon, Chevron, FedEx, General Motors, Halliburton, IBM, Netflix, Nvidia, Salesforce, and Starbucks. These ninety-one corporations collectively made $101 billion in profit and *received payment* from *the IRS of $6 billion!*

A small business cannot pay an army of tax experts, so it simply pays the 21 percent headline rate. The upshot is that small businesses, with fewer resources, contribute a higher effective tax rate of 21 percent to public revenue while the largest businesses, with the most resources, contribute much less.

This imbalance places an undue burden on smaller businesses, not to mention individual taxpayers, to meet America's revenue needs, while creating an unfair advantage for those entities already most advantaged. It also diverts large amounts of time, energy, and money away from innovative and productive endeavors that add value to the economy (RR3) into tax management schemes that sap value through friction-laden transfers (RR2).

We propose reducing America's federal corporate income tax rate to 16.8 percent (one fifth lower than the current 21 percent) and removing the loopholes—all of them. What if the corporate tax code could fit on a single page? Who says no, other than the armies of tax experts and the companies that employ them at the expense of public revenue?

Call us naive if you have to resort to *ad hominem* attacks. Call this action item extreme if you're fearful.[181] This is basic and actionable, and that is the intent. For those who have more sophisticated approaches that are also actionable, we welcome the dialogue. For those vested interests in the status quo that oppose making taxation both simpler and at a lower rate, we invite that public dialogue too. Truly we would be intrigued to hear from any company a public statement as to why it prefers higher, complex taxes to lower, simpler ones.

---

180. Gardner, Roque, and Wamhoff, "Corporate Tax Avoidance."

181. Or is the current reality—a tax code of over 5,296 pages and official explanation of 14,260 pages—the real extreme?

Yeah, can you believe?
All this and more to get around
10 Commandments.

Partnership in Practice:

- Keep regulation brief.
- Level the corporate income tax playing field by removing all "nuance" (loopholes).
- Set a simple corporate income tax rate, perhaps 16.8 percent, that all for-profit corporate entities actually pay and that meets public revenue needs.
- Debate issues of public concern in public and vote for public servants who stand up for policies that are mutually beneficial for the public and our businesses.

Of course, if you don't like these action items or have better ideas, we invite you to email us at info@partnershipeconomics.com with your thoughts.

Not-Special Interests

To serve the common good, corporate entities—corporations, unions, non-profits—must operate within society's democratically established parameters, not distort the legal landscape to their own advantage. This requires a significant economic component, namely ensuring that money flowing between corporate entities and government does so in ways that sustain benefit for all stakeholders, rather than distorting public resources away from true public benefit in favor of so-called "special interests." To this end, the role of money in politics, both lobbying and campaign finance, must be addressed from a partnership perspective. We acknowledge that this is a complex and deeply embedded problem, needing far more attention than we have space for here. Nevertheless, in this space we seek to at least gain a toehold on one actionable approach to begin the push in a partnership direction.

In the 2015–2016 election cycle, defined by the Federal Election Commission (FEC) as January 1, 2015 to December 31, 2016, fec.gov reports that Political Action Committees (PACs) had receipts of $4.05 billion, compared to $1.54 billion for presidential candidates, $1.64 billion for congressional candidates, and $1.63 billion for party committees from national all the way through local levels.[182] Far more money for elections is coming from outside influences than from any group officially campaigning.

In that same time frame, $6.39 billion was spent on lobbying—just at the federal level.[183] Using the figures above, and including state and local party committees, in 2015–2016 a total of $4.81 billion was spent by candidates and their parties to get elected. Outside groups spent $4.05 billion on elections and $6.39 billion lobbying (federal) officeholders—$10.44 billion of outside influence compared to $4.81 billion of direct campaign and political party influence. When the so-called "special" interests have more than double the monetary influence of the general public, we have to recognize the tail is wagging the dog. In fact, we probably would be more accurate to call the "special" interests the primary influence and recognize the public as effectively relegated to the role of outside influence.

The reason these stats can be known is because there are, for now at least, laws requiring disclosure of lobbying costs;[184] lobbying is "legal" in the strict sense but it must be reported. (We can only speculate about the extent of unreported lobbying, but the fact is that reported lobbying is more than sufficient to raise concern.) And election campaign expenditures must be reported to the FEC, although the originating sources of funds funneled through PACs can be shadowy at best. Flawed and limited though they may be, there are data on the money in politics.

    182. Federal Election Commission, "Statistical Summary."
    183. OpenSecrets, "Lobbying Data Summary."
    184. The Lobbying Disclosure Act of 1995; the Honest Leadership and Open Government Act of 2007.

The availability of such data leads to our action item. Echoing an idea of Luigi Zingales in *A Capitalism for the People*, we advocate taxing the political expenditures of "special" interests. This builds on the reporting requirements already in place, helping its feasibility. It would transfer funds used for narrow interests to use for the public interest; if done at progressive rates, the more a narrow interest spends to influence public resources for itself, the more it would have to pay for public benefit. This approach would result in either 1) less political spending by corporate entities, as the tax functions as a disincentive, or 2) offsetting the flow of public resources to subsidize private interests (a form of taxation without representation) with taxes flowing from the private expenditures for public benefit.

One could argue this would create an incentive to evade the taxes. Noncompliance is always a risk, and it can be reduced by penalties that are sufficiently stiff for both evading the tax and for fraud in reporting the political spending, as is already required. The noncompliance risk can also be reduced, as Zingales insightfully explains, by empowering and rewarding whistleblowers, effectively incentivizing anyone and everyone involved in the vast network of political influence to benefit from reporting evasion and misrepresentation.[185] This flips the incentive structure from people "on the inside" benefiting from being part of corruption to them benefiting more from reporting corrupt lobbying or electioneering. When all involved know that each person they share information with stands to gain from reporting anything underhanded, there is a ripple effect of accountability—all involved weigh the risk of self-dealing *and likely being reported* as greater than the reward of self-dealing expected when everyone turns a blind eye.

Even something this straightforward could be difficult to enact because, as Zingales colorfully puts it, expecting the moneyed political process to restrain itself "would be like expecting turkeys to vote for Thanksgiving." The "special" interests and the politicians that gain for themselves through the current way of things will not voluntarily put their "special" favors on the chopping block. The public must assert ourselves and create change for public benefit. We must decide—and act accordingly—if we want to be a nation of the people, by the people, for the people or a nation of the money, by the money, for the money. And we have no time to lose, because laws and their interpretation by our U.S. Supreme Court are shifting away from people-based partnership.

---

185. Whistleblower policies bring out the best of both individual responsibility and regulation. They appeal to individual responsibility within a regulatory context that creates and protects desirable individual incentives.

Consider this from Justice Anthony Kennedy's 5–4 majority opinion in the 2010 Supreme Court case *Citizens United v. Federal Election Commission*:[186]

> The fact that speakers may have influence over or access to elected officials does not mean that these officials are corrupt. . . . Ingratiation and access, in any event, are not corruption.

We are forced to differ. In a democratic republic, such as America claims to be, elected officials are to be influenced by and accessible to the electorate; they are elected to represent the electorate. If "public servant" is to be more than a euphemism, those elected by the public must serve the public. Influence over, access to, and ingratiation with "public servants" by not-public (i.e., "special") interests *are* corruption. That is the very definition of corruption of public service, and a standard that was well-supported by Supreme Court precedent prior to this case, guarding against such influence and ingratiation *as well as the appearance of* such influence and ingratiation. The *Citizens United v. FEC* decision did not create the influence of money in American politics (which has a very long history), but to buttress this corruption with the Court's authority does not bode well for mutually beneficial partnership between the public and our public servants.

Wouldn't Milton Friedman blush at the assertion that influence over elected officials is not corruption—even he affirmed that leaders of corporate interests have a responsibility of "conforming to their basic rules of the society, both those embodied in law and those embodied in ethical custom." Now, shockingly, they have been given the green light by the Supreme Court to influence the rules of society. Making the rules is not the same as following them!

Receiving far less media attention than *Citizens United v. FEC*, but equally disturbing, is the 2015 U.S. Supreme Court case *Williams-Yulee v. Florida Bar*.[187] From Chief Justice John Robert's 5–4 majority opinion:

> The State may conclude that judges, charged with exercising strict neutrality and independence, cannot supplicate campaign donors without diminishing public confidence in judicial integrity. Simply put, the public may lack confidence in a judge's ability to administer justice without fear or favor if he comes to office by asking for favors. This Court's precedents have recognized the "vital state interest" in safeguarding "public confidence in the fairness and integrity of the nation's elected judges." . . .

186. Supreme Court, *Citizens United*.
187. Supreme Court, *Williams-Yulee*.

> A State's interest in preserving public confidence in the integrity of its judiciary extends beyond its interest in preventing the appearance of corruption in legislative and executive elections, because a judge's role differs from that of a politician. . . . Unlike a politician, who is expected to be appropriately responsive to the preferences of supporters, a judge in deciding cases may not follow the preferences of his supporters or provide any special consideration to his campaign donors.

We appreciate the concern for integrity and the appearance of integrity for the judiciary, but we are appalled at the fiction that such values are not valued for the legislative and executive branches of government, too! Defending the integrity of and public confidence in judges while asserting that politicians are expected to be responsive to supporters—rather than their constituents—and may provide "special" consideration to campaign donors indicates the Court is on the march toward abdicating its enforcer role in democracy's system of checks and balances. It is not merely turning a blind eye to corruption in the other branches—it is, tragically, endorsing it. At least the lower court judges are still held to the expected standard, but only by the slimmest of margins. Four justices voted that judges can have as little integrity and appearance of integrity, related to the influence of money, as the majority already assigns to legislators and executives. One vote stands in the way of judicial elections also being fully subject to moneyed influence rather than the electorate.

If seeing these direct quotes from America's Supreme Court ticks you off, we understand. Let such troubling words from our highest bench free us to ardently resist becoming a nation of the money, by the money, for the money, while reclaiming the mutually beneficial partnership of the people, by the people, for the people.

Partnership in Practice:

- Protect and enhance reporting requirements on "special" interest spending on politics—elections and lobbying—the more data, the better.
- Implement a tax on "special" interest political spending, that increases as the political expenditure increases.
- Make whistleblowing for public benefit more lucrative than corrupt self-dealing.
- Expect integrity, including in relation to moneyed influence, from all branches of government.

- As the voting public, vote for public servants who serve the public in the above ways.

Love it? Hate it? Have a suggestion? Want to join forces? Email us at info@partnershipeconomics.com to be part of the conversation.

Partnership Rules Apply to Rule-Makers, Too

Edelman Intelligence, a global insight and analytics consultancy, conducts an annual trust and credibility survey. Its twentieth survey, conducted in October and November 2019, analyzed the replies of over 34,000 survey respondents in twenty-eight markets from across the world. The report from that survey, titled "2020 Trust Barometer," measures the public's trust in the major institutions of government, business, non-government organizations (NGOs), and media.[188]

Lisa Osborn Ross, addressing the perceptions around government in the executive summary of the report, opens with, "The outlook for trust in government is alarmingly bleak. . . . Government leaders are among the least trusted people. And on the two central drivers of people's trust—competence and ethics—government lags far behind the other institutions."[189]

Ross seems measured in her words. Three pages earlier in the report a cartesian graph comparing the four major institutions starkly illustrates how far and away government is perceived as incompetent and unethical.[190] Another chart of the executive summary, comparing public trust in eight categories of roles, shows government leaders are next to last, behind religious leaders but ahead of the very wealthy.[191] If you're employed in the government sector, especially if you're an elected official or at the executive level, this is a truth trying to set you free.

With this painful truth in view, don't despair but be encouraged that there is a path to restoring the public's trust in the important work of government. The start of that path is, first, recognizing that partnership rules absolutely apply to rule-makers, same as anyone else, and then embracing and practicing the Partnership Ethic.

We know the path to regaining the public's trust and moving toward a partnership model will be hard, especially for those in government who need to garner the cooperation of co-workers and those who need to reverse

---

188. Edelman, "2020 Trust Barometer."
189. Edelman, "2020 Trust Barometer," 11.
190. Edelman, "2020 Trust Barometer," 8.
191. Edelman, "2020 Trust Barometer," 6.

the tsunami of partisan enemyship. So we offer the following as a practical ethic and way to frame the approach: "Make rules for yourself no better than the rules you make for others." Stated in the alternative: "Make rules for others no worse than the rules you make for yourself." A few examples? Sure.[192] And we'll limit ourselves to just a few big-ticket examples where the U.S. Congress has shown a decidedly non-partnership posture in voting benefits for themselves that are denied to the general public who, remember, pay for those benefits.

The annual base salary for a member of Congress is presently $174,000, five times the median per capita income of the Americans who voted them into office. Some senior members are paid considerably more. Perhaps as a member of Congress you feel that's reasonable. Okay. Now remember that as a member of Congress you've set the rules that you and your cohorts average less than 150 congressional sessions on the docket, compared to a standard workload of about 250 business days per year. How much mutuality is there when you as our representatives make five times more, while being allowed to account for 40 percent less time? Is it still reasonable? Sure, presumably you spend the other 60 percent of a full working schedule at your district office. Are you spending that 60 percent working for your constituents, or for yourself and being re-elected?

Until 2012 members of Congress were, shockingly, not prohibited from insider trading. Although Congress did pass the Stop Trading on Congressional Knowledge Act in 2012, the following year it gutted the primary disclosure component. While arguably making it more difficult to trade on insider information, you as a member of Congress don't have to publicly disclose your trades and potential insider knowledge, so how can we—your constituents—possibly verify and come to trust? Why is an otherwise criminal act so loosely unfettered for you and other members of Congress? In asserting to hold the public trust, shouldn't you and other members of Congress hold yourself to at least as high a standard as the public you presumably serve and legislate for, rather than a lower standard?

As of this writing in early 2020, the average Social Security recipient will net around $15,000 annually and the average public servant pensioner will average around $26,000 annually. Meanwhile, a retired member of Congress who has served only twenty years will average $59,000 annually in pension benefits. Further, you and other members of Congress receive comprehensive gold star health care subsidized by the public while denying much of the same service to the same public. Discrepancies like these simply

---

192. Cranley, "Perks Members of Congress Get." See also Williams, "10 Perks Congress Has That You Don't."

and thoroughly undercut the notion of partnership with and therefore trust in our government leaders.

We find it worth repeating. If you're employed in the government sector, especially if you're an elected official or at the executive level: "Make rules for yourself no better than the rules you make for others." Stated in the alternative: "Make rules for others no worse than the rules you make for yourself."

Of course, in a democracy, government employees and elected officials are only part of the story. *All* of us citizens have a part to play, too. We must engage, as partners, such that the government does in fact represent us well, including economically. Mutual partnership brings responsibility to all of us.

We offer a three-part bare-bones litmus test for considering whether another person has earned a presumption of trustworthiness, a test certainly applicable to our elected officials. Is the other person (e.g., elected official): 1) transparent; 2) does he or she typically make good decisions; and, 3) is he or she empathic, if not compassionate, toward me and my needs? If the other person checks those three boxes we are willing to take the risk with that person and, proceed into a relationship or partnership that presumes trust. We think you'll find this test helpful for your own use.

Partnership in Practice:

- Do not initiate or support laws that benefit special interests over the interest of your constituents or the electorate.

- Teach and retrain special interests by being transparent in your dealings, especially when saying "no" because their schemes don't benefit your constituents or the electorate.

- Be transparent in your work location and your activities or expect your constituents to start questioning what you're hiding or why you're hiding from them.

- Build trust with your constituents by making decisions that benefit them (at a minimum are neutral and do not harm) and let them know of those decisions.

- Be genuinely empathetic toward your constituents or risk that their emerging desire for partnership with their elected official will soon eject you from office.

Of course, if you don't like these action items or have better ideas, we invite you to email us at info@partnershipeconomics.com with your thoughts.

Clear, Consistent, Broad Fiduciary Standard

www.stus.com

From a popular investing website in 2018: "The controversial rule requiring advisers to act in their clients' best interests when it comes to managing retirement accounts is officially dead."[193]

Read that again, and ask yourself, "Why is such a rule controversial?"

Strangely and sadly, we live in an environment where requiring financial advisers to act in their clients' best financial interests is controversial. Worse, we live in an environment where the "controversy" about such a rule resulted in that rule being killed.

Fiduciary perhaps is not a common word for many of us; maybe that is part of the problem. From the Latin *fiduciarius,* related to *fide* (faith, trust, loyalty), its essential meaning pertains to something that is entrusted, loyally held in good faith. You may be familiar with the U.S. Marine Corps motto *Semper Fidelis* (always faithful), which summarizes that organization's core values. Let's trust that motto never becomes controversial or a value that is killed.

Someone who acts as a fiduciary, by definition, is entrusted—they hold in trust what ultimately belongs to someone else, loyally and in good faith seeking the owner's benefit. Through the lens of Partnership Economics, mutual benefit happens when someone trusts a fiduciary with their

---

193. Malito, "The Fiduciary Rule is Officially Dead."

resources and that fiduciary receives a fair payment for managing those resources in a trustworthy, good-faith manner that loyally adds value to the owner.

Despite the 2018 proclaimed death of the U.S. Department of Labor's fiduciary rule, proponents continue trying to breathe life into it.[194] As of 2020, the definition of who exactly is a fiduciary and what standards exactly they would be held to, remain (sadly) controversial yet (promisingly) do continue to garner attention.[195] We prefer simplicity because truths are essentially simple, so we'll state it simply: "Advisers should advise in the best interest of the advisee." Surely a partnership duty of good faith, rather than "legal" acceptance of self-dealing, can come to accompany what should be common sense.

Partnership in Practice:

- Legislators: Don't let common sense rules succumb to duplicitously manufactured controversy. Create rules that facilitate mutual benefit, such as requiring financial advisers to act in their clients' best interests so clients will continue to trust and pay advisers.
- Citizens: Vote for public servants who serve the public in the above ways.
- Financial advisers: Act in your clients' best interests and be transparent about your fees and commissions. Welcome rules that require other financial advisers to do the same.
- Clients: Ask your financial adviser how he/she is compensated, specifically what fees and commissions transfer money from you to him/her. If he/she is unwilling to share that information, find a new financial adviser.

Of course, if you don't like these action items or have better ideas, we invite you to email us at info@partnershipeconomics.com with your thoughts.

---

194. Investopedia, "Everything You Need to Know."
195. Department of Labor, "Improving Investment Advice."

Predatory Lending—When Medicine Becomes Poison[196]

A young father had trouble paying his bills and turned to his Baptist congregation for help. The church gave freely with no questions asked. But when he returned a few months later, and got help with budgeting, it became clear that there was no way for the family to make ends meet. As the church discovered, when the father's monthly income had first fallen short of expenses he turned to a payday loan for help. After securing a loan of $700, every two weeks $200 was automatically deducted from his checking account, making it impossible for the family to keep up with their monthly expenses. After several months, he still owed the original principal and the same amount of fees and interest as the day he walked away with the loan. By the time the church paid the balance in full, that $700 cost over $3,300 in less than five months.

This true story is all too common for many financially vulnerable families. An estimated twelve million Americans take out a payday loan every year. In recent years, the small-dollar lending business has ballooned into a multi-billion-dollar industry made possible through a systematic and deliberate dismantling or avoidance of traditional state usury laws. The result is an industry built not on expensive loans given to risky borrowers, but on the creation of previously illegal loan products designed to act as debt traps for working Americans desperately trying to make ends meet. A loan thought to be an answered prayer, instead becomes a debt trap.[197]

The Old Testament, Hammurabi, Plato, Aristotle, Dante, and Adam Smith all condemn usury. Throughout most of U.S. history, there was a common understanding of usury as immoral and unjust because of the financial burden it places on the borrower. All original states had strict usury limits of less than 8 percent. In the early 1900s, many states adopted a 36 percent rate cap for small loans. Thirty years ago, the storefront payday lender was essentially nonexistent; the current industry began only in the early 1990s. As of this writing, fifteen states and the District of Columbia prohibit or tightly restrict the practice. In the thirty-five states that allow payday lending, the storefronts are ubiquitous. The industry trade association claims over 20,600 are in operation today. The laws and loopholes that allow payday lending vary by state, but the product, practices, core business model, and devastating results are substantially the same.

---

196. Reeves, "Day-to-Day and On a Loan." (This section originated as an article written by Stephen Reeves, Esq., who graciously permitted its edited use here.)

197. A similar image, of offering medicine that ends up being poison, can be traced at least as far back as church leader Ambrose in the fourth century.

Payday loans are high-cost, small-dollar loans offered with no credit check required. The name "payday loan" comes from the term for repayment—typically two weeks or until the individual's next payday. Borrowers need only have a bank account and show a pay stub or other proof of regular income to qualify. Lenders give no consideration to the ability of an individual to repay the loan within the original term given their other obligations and without the need to reborrow. As a condition of the loan, the lender is given direct access to a bank account via a post-dated check or through electronic automated clearing house authorization.

The typical interest rate and fee charges for a two-week loan range from $15–$25 per $100 borrowed. Those charges represent an annual percentage rate (APR) of 391 percent to 700 percent and can often climb even higher. Some states have no limit to the interest rate or fees that can be charged. At the end of the loan term, the borrower must either pay the entire lump sum, principal plus all interest and fees in one balloon payment or that amount will be automatically deducted from their bank account. As an alternative, the borrower can pay only the fee and interest and "roll over" the loan for another two weeks, like the father above. At this point, despite having paid the hefty interest and fee, the borrower will still owe the entire principal plus another round of fees and interest. Lenders rarely accept partial payment beyond interest and fees, which ensures that the principal owed is never reduced.

While marketed as a short-term solution for emergency expenses, neither is typically the case. According to borrower surveys, 69 percent of loans are used for routine, recurring expenses, and the two-week loans often result in five months of debt or longer. A loan of $350 will commonly cost a borrower $800 or more to repay—frequently three to four times what was borrowed. When borrowers can repay under the initial loan terms, the resulting hole in their budget creates the need for another loan. In fact, according to an analysis of fifteen million transactions by the Consumer Financial Protection Bureau, 80 percent of all payday loans are renewed, rolled over, or taken out within fourteen days of a previous loan being paid off. That same analysis showed that 75 percent of all fees generated from payday loans come from the 48 percent of borrowers who have taken out eleven or more loans a year.

The more the borrower fails, the more money the lender makes. What has been referred to by many as a "cycle of debt" is not an unfortunate accident, it is intentional, and it is the most profitable scenario for the lender. Do not forget; prior to the late 1900s this kind of business model was substantially limited to organized crime, except collections were made in cash or, literally, blood.

These lending practices have both personal and systemic consequences. Oftentimes borrowers turn to payday loans feeling it a responsible option to solve their own problem. Loans are quick and anonymous. In many ways it is easier than turning to family, friends, a charity or a credit union, or pawning a possession. However, once trapped in debt, the shame can be consuming. Pastors and others who frequently counsel borrowers testify to the collateral damage these loans cause to relationships and marriages when the emotional impact of never-ending debt hits home. To get out of these loans borrowers often turn for help to those they could have asked in the first place. In addition, payday loans are far more frequent in communities of color. These practices prey upon and exacerbate the persistent racial wealth gap.

Established by the Dodd-Frank Financial Reform Act of 2010, Congress gave the Consumer Financial Protection Bureau the authority and mandate to pass regulations on payday lenders across the country. After years of research and a promising proposal in 2017, the bureau under new leadership moved to repeal the proposed rule before it could take effect. We think it not unreasonable to deduce that decision-makers in President Donald Trump's administration were persuaded by and capitulated to the payday lending lobby to protect the industry's interests, rather than the interests and safety of the governed. Sadly, here's a glaring example of dismantling protections in favor of establishing laws that secure and protect plantation system economics.

There have always been and always will be people desperate for money (Deuteronomy 15:11), and the blessing they provide is the opportunity to practice sharing God's provisions. Torah community legislation confirms lending money is a good response to someone in financial need (Leviticus 25:35–38; Deuteronomy 15:1–11). But on no account should another's misfortune be turned into an opportunity for personal gain (Leviticus 25:37; Deuteronomy 23:19). Where burdensome debt was created, the sabbatical and jubilee years required the full release of debts as part of God's larger social welfare legislation. Luke Bretherton has aptly written, "To be a lender and a borrower is to be situated within economic relations of interdependence, cooperation and mutual responsibility that reflect the God-given pattern of life set out in Scripture. To lend and borrow is to be drawn into real relationships that demand we have to negotiate a common life in which my flourishing is dependent on the flourishing of others."[198] Done properly, lending and borrowing requires a Partnership Ethic.

---

198. Bretherton, "Neither Borrower nor Lender," 33.

No one naively imagines predatory lenders will read this section and simply abandon their soul-scorching business practices. The question is, what to do about those who continue to exploit the desperation of others for one-sided profit?

Partnership in Practice:

- Everyone: reject participating in or supporting the plantation system economic practice of predatory lending.
- Media: turn public opinion against payday lending and embarrass the industry out of existence, as you did for dueling in nineteenth-century America.
- Faith communities: develop creative ways to help those caught in debt traps. See examples at cbf.net/rescueloans and lendjustly.com.
- Elected officials: reverse the laws that permit this aspect of plantation system economics in your jurisdiction. Give your constituents your strength in removing this evil, not the industry your strength in supporting this evil.
- Investors: earn a reasonable return on your cash reserves and advance Partnership Ethics by directly competing against predatory lenders and offering customers micro-loans that carry affordable, simple interest rates.

Of course, if you don't like these action items or have better ideas, we invite you to email us at info@partnershipeconomics.com with your thoughts.

Tax Modifications

Your old road is rapidly aging
Please get out of the new one if you can't lend your hand
For the times, they are a-changin'

—Bob Dylan

For our readers who aren't ultra-wealthy multimillionaires or billionaires, raise your hand if you're fine with being slapped with another tax. No takers? We'll confess, we're not raising our hands either. But just because 90 percent of us feel the real pain of paying our taxes doesn't mean that all

Americans do, or that our Congress and President—whoever is in office when you read this—should continue to avoid meaningful tax reform based on thoughtfully balanced values and ethics. Consider the perspectives and recent message from people who have raised their hands—a few of the richest one-tenth of the richest 1 percent of Americans.

At the time of this writing and coinciding with the ramp-up to the 2020 Presidential election season, insightful and courageous members of at least eleven of America's wealthiest families penned an open letter calling on a wealth tax of them and those similarly situated—the richest one-tenth of the richest 1 percent of Americans.[199] The letter is addressed to all the Presidential candidates and, given its public webpage publication, addressed collaterally to the nation, including members of Congress.

Before we turn to their letter, let's briefly summarize America's current wealth disparity. Over the past thirty years (from late 1980s to late 2010s) America's wealthiest 1 percent grew richer by $21 trillion while the poorest 50 percent grew poorer by $900 billion. Beyond the obviousness of these numbers moving in opposite directions, those are big numbers and difficult to put into perspective. Maybe it's easier to form a mental picture of the wealth gap between the top 1 percent and the poorest 50 percent by saying it grew twenty-three-fold, or 2,300 percent. That is an astounding increase by any measure, and now an astonishing differentiation between the top 1 percent and half of the United States population.

Their letter's argument opens with the twin premises: "America has a moral, ethical and economic responsibility to tax our wealth more," and "Instituting a wealth tax is in the interest of the republic." Underlying these premises is a partnership perspective. Then, to remind those who have forgotten, the letter points out that America already imposes a wealth tax on the millions of middle-income Americans who pay property taxes on their house and/or car(s). For at least the past 100 years, local governments have fined, placed liens, and foreclosed on owners in arrears on their property taxes. Given that clear and longstanding example of taxing wealth, it's beyond reasonable debate whether a wealth tax can be imposed and enforced on the top 1 percent of wealth. Of course it can.

Further, to argue a tax on ultra-wealthy assets is impractical to implement or enforce, or that the assets can't be accurately valued, is similarly disingenuous. As the letter's authors note, "But such assets are frequently valued-upon resale, donation, bankruptcy, divorce, or death." Indeed, for the ultra-wealthy or those in their service to argue against a wealth tax simply validates René Descartes's observation of four centuries ago: "A man is

---

199. Pay it Forward, "It's Time to Tax Us More."

incapable of comprehending any argument that interferes with his revenue [or wealth]."²⁰⁰

We turn to just one example of the implementation and benefit of a wealth tax. The letter references a proposal by Senator Elizabeth Warren that suggests a tax of 2 percent on assets above a $50 million exemption, 3 percent on assets over $1 billion. Those are tall and comfortable thresholds of wealth by any measure. This proposal would affect perhaps just 75,000 families in the United States but generate nearly $3 trillion in tax revenue over ten years.

Senator Warren's proposal is straightforward and eminently practical. So much so that it's being validated by the insightful and courageous representatives of those whose wealth it seeks to tax. And fear not, those of you concerned about a wealth tax being a burden on the ultra-wealthy. They anticipate your concern by noting, "Others have put far more on the line for America. . . . We'll be fine—taking on this tax is the least we can do to strengthen the country we love."

One of the gravest attacks on efforts to level the economic playing field, such as Senator Warren's wealth tax proposal, is the fallacious accusation that anything other than the current bare-knuckle corporate ethic is a slippery slope—if not cliff dive—into socialism (logically, as you likely know, that perspective is termed a false dilemma). As revealed in a recent *Chief Executive* magazine interview, Bernie Marcus, the ninety-year-old co-founder and a retired chairman of Home Depot, seems to imagine socialism threatening the U.S. economy from every direction.²⁰¹

The interview references Marcus co-founding Job Creators Network (JCN) in 2011. JCN has played key roles in generating support and political pressure for the tax cuts passed by the Trump Administration in 2017, supporting the Trump Administration's broad dismantling of laws that regulate corporate America, and vigorously opposing a $15/hour minimum wage. In addition to opposing a wealth tax on billionaires, Marcus opposes the Business Roundtable's revised statement on the purposes of a corporation (referenced in Part 2, chapter 9), declaring it "just a defense mechanism against people like Elizabeth Warren who are running for president. If she's elected, you can say goodbye to the corporate world. She's saying, 'Adios, capitalism' and 'Hello, socialism.'" Marcus continued, "If you are the CEO of a company and you stand by and let this thing happen right in front of your eyes and don't fight back in some way, you're a coward."

---

200. Quoted in San Diego County Bar Association, "Descartes and Mortgage/Foreclosure."

201. Buss, "Bernie Marcus."

Perhaps your authors should not be surprised by Marcus's efficient use of a string of logical fallacies in defense of plantation system economics: the scare tactic ("goodbye to the corporate world"), the *ad hominem* attack (against Warren), the false dilemma ("Adios capitalism, and Hello socialism"), fear mongering ("if you let this happen"), and bullying ("you're a coward"). But we are. Perhaps plantation system economics is all Marcus knows and understands, and since the status quo is working for him he assumes it works for everyone. Take a moment and compare the language and posture Marcus uses in this article with the language and posture Friedman uses in his 1970 *New York Times* article. We'd be interested to know what parallels you draw.

Consider an analogy: early in his career Paul was a construction superintendent with one of the nation's largest new home builders during a long boom cycle. Every workday was long, hectic, pressured, and wearing on everyone. Often he'd have to stop and empathetically listen as well as he was capable to an employee or contractor as they spooled out the litany of reasons why they couldn't maintain that week's busy production schedule. As they calmed down and he confirmed they actually had everything they needed to do the work, except perhaps the will, he'd speak to their willpower by instructing, "Now, ain't nothing to it but to do it." Not necessarily smiling, but soon enough they'd be back on track.

We offer what appears at first blush to be a seemingly simplistic analogy because, in reality, it's substantially the same issue. Implementing and enforcing a wealth tax such as endorsed by that letter is truly no more complicated than a construction superintendent helping the crews recapture the will to contribute their part to the greater whole, which in turn benefits all of us with more work. The challenges of scale and hardened wills can be overcome by a Congress and President with the courage to place a wealth tax on those who can easily (and many, willingly) afford the expense. Perhaps, and not unreasonably, the ultra-wealthy among us who actively practice a Partnership Ethic that measurably benefits others (e.g., MacKenzie Scott [formerly Bezos], Warren Buffett, Bill and Melinda Gates) may receive wealth tax deductions, similar to income tax deductions already in place for donations to nonprofit organizations. For the ultra-wealthy signatories of that letter, they acknowledge paying a wealth tax is the least they can do to strengthen the country they love.

What about you who are among the one-tenth of 1 percent and are less enthusiastic about having your wealth taxed? After a courageous Congress and President has legislated an enforceable wealth tax, there is no reason you too can't come to see a wealth tax as the least you can do for a society that has enabled you to accumulate astounding wealth. Who knows, with some spiritual introspection you may even come to recognize that your hoarding of extreme wealth supports plantation economics, and you may find new ways to be creative and generate mutual benefit with your assets.

Partnership in Practice:

- Enact a rationally related, stepped wealth tax on ultra-large hoards of personal wealth, of the kind proposed by Senator Warren.
- Apply those wealth tax monies to the limited purpose of advancing the economic trajectory of others (e.g., education and skills training, small business creation and support, no-interest business loans, etc.).
- Enact a wealth tax on ultra-large hoards of corporation wealth, of the kind proposed immediately above, applied to corporate reserves beyond three, five, and seven years' operating expenses.

Of course, if you don't like these action items or have better ideas, we invite you to email us at info@partnershipeconomics.com with your thoughts.

We Have Antitrust Laws—Enforce Them!

"Don't be evil."

—Google's former motto[202]

There are many benefits to antitrust laws, and also periods in America's history when they have been implemented well, with good results to show for it. In fact, there are plenty of these regulations still technically in effect but simply not strongly enforced. Zingales emphasizes competition as essential for good value creation, and that is an obvious economic benefit to establishing (and enforcing) anti-competitive regulations. However, he argues (and Tim Wu addresses this also) that the strongest reason for antitrust is political—concentration of economic power invariably leads to accumulation of political power, and that political power undermines democracy itself, as well as distorting the competitive landscape. Firms become rewarded

---

202. Almost since its inception "Don't be evil" was an ethic and summary of Google's corporate code of conduct. That quietly ended after its reorganization under Alphabet. Ross LaJeunesse, Google's former head of International Relations, views the stepping back from this motto and touchstone as a failure in favor of working with governments that have poor human rights records. See, e.g., https://medium.com/@rossformaine/i-was-googles-head-of-international-relations-here-s-why-i-left-49313d23065.

for political savvy more than economic competitiveness. Partnership has a stake in both aspects—it is broad enough to encompass both economic and political dynamics and demands that power not be concentrated in distorted ways but shared for mutual benefit.

The political dangers of anti-competitive practices are not merely theoretical, nor are they relegated to history. Facebook, perhaps the most visible American company (as of June 2020, Facebook's family of platforms has 3.14 billion users per month, including 2.47 billion *daily*)[203] has made the issue very prominent here and now. As potential competitors to Facebook have arisen, it has acquired them, adopted their unique features in ways that undermined their competitive advantages, or prevented them from being discovered on or used with its ever-expanding platforms to stifle their growth. In these multiple ways Facebook has been very effective at reducing and removing competition as it consolidates massive size and resulting power. To be sure, Facebook is hardly alone in making political protection part of its business strategy (see "Not-Special Interests" above). We highlight it here because it is such a prominent example.

As Facebook has grown, including in its anti-competitive practices, political concerns have become linked to its market clout. These political concerns have three aspects. The first is typical of concentrated power—using that power to exert undue influence and undermine the free exchange of political viewpoints. Influence over ideas, including political ideas, is a particular risk in the case of Facebook because its business is "social media"—distributing communications among many social participants. Even for companies not in the business of communications or social interactions, the more concentrated their power, the more they are able to exert undue influence on entities in those fields. Facebook just happens to have concentrated power within that industry itself.

The specifics of particular claims of political bias can be contentious and difficult to prove, but some facts are obvious and undeniable. Facebook cannot show all content equally, any more than a newspaper could put all content at the top of the first page. Inevitably some content receives greater prominence and some lesser, and Facebook decides, through programming and algorithms designed by its employees, how content is displayed. Also inevitably, some content on social media is political in nature. Connect these basic facts and we have to recognize that Facebook is in the business of deciding how prominently political content is displayed on its platforms.

---

203. Facebook, the company, owns not only the Facebook platform but also Instagram, Messenger, and WhatsApp. User numbers are typically shared by Facebook in its quarterly earnings report. See, e.g., https://investor.fb.com/investor-events/event-details/2020/Facebook-Q2-2020-Earnings-/default.aspx.

So, too, are newspapers, magazines, book publishers, television channels, radio stations, websites, blogs, podcasts, and every other content provider or distributor—but size matters.

Facebook receives more critical attention for claims of political bias not because it is the only business where such bias could exist, but because such bias would have outsized impact *in a business with such concentrated power*. If a citizen isn't satisfied with the political content in a newspaper, they can easily choose a different newspaper. If a citizen isn't satisfied with the political content on a radio station, there are many others. Choice among digital options abounds . . . except for the digital world of social media. If a citizen isn't satisfied with the political content on Facebook, there isn't another Facebook, or comparable social media, to switch to.[204]

Claims of political bias against Facebook generally have come from the right of America's political spectrum—thus far. What should be of concern to every American citizen is the fact that an economic entity not accountable to frequent elections could exert so much influence, whether through censoring or favoring, over such a large portion of the population due to concentration of power. When 52 percent of U.S. adults get their news from one company, as Pew Research Center found in July 2019,[205] the risk of undue political influence is undeniably great.

The second political concern due to Facebook's concentrated economic power is more unique to its line of business. Beyond the risk of Facebook itself exerting undue political influence, there is the risk of others exerting undue political influence *through* Facebook. This is an added wrinkle from the nature of social media. By its very nature, social media facilitates interactions, and therefore influence, among many people. Or, we would be more accurate to say, among many accounts used by people. The indirect nature of social media interactions—accounts on a digital platform rather than people in direct contact—allows people to present themselves however they wish through an account or multiple accounts. Social media creates the

---

204. Twitter's platform is not comparable to the functionality of Facebook's platforms in the way that *The Wall Street Journal* and *The New York Times* have products with comparable functions, but for the sake of argument, if you want to view it as a broadly comparable to Facebook, as of June 2020 Twitter had 186 million users per day. While in many comparisons that would be a lot of people, it is only 7.5 percent of Facebook's daily user count, so even if its functionality were comparable to Facebook's, Twitter's social reach is not comparable. LinkedIn also has at best only broadly comparable functionality to Facebook, and active user data is conspicuous by its absence in Microsoft's (which owns LinkedIn) earnings reports, where monthly active users of several other Microsoft products are accounted for.

205. Shearer and Grieco, "Americans are Wary."

possibility of interactions and influence without revealing oneself or one's agenda; without transparency.

This is not just a potential or theoretical risk—it is an actuality that Facebook has acknowledged (despite earlier statements to the contrary, and after considerable outcry and investigation). Following the 2016 U.S. elections, claims of Russian influence through Facebook could not be ignored. A January 2017 report by the U.S. Director of National Intelligence[206] plainly showed, multiple times, the use of social media by Russian parties in relation to the U.S. elections. In April 2017, Facebook released a whitepaper titled "Information Operations and Facebook."[207] This includes a page on what it calls a "case study" of the 2016 election. According to Facebook's whitepaper, "One aspect of this included malicious actors leveraging conventional and social media to share information stolen from other sources, such as email accounts, with the intent of harming the reputation of specific political targets." Facebook then goes on to say that the reach of content from "malicious actors" was "marginal compared to the overall volume of civic content shared during the U.S. election." A footnote indicates that this "marginal" reach was measured as "less than one-tenth of a percent of the total reach of civic content on Facebook" from September to December 2016. Back in the main text, Facebook concludes, "While we acknowledge the ongoing challenge of monitoring and guarding against information operations, the reach of known operations during the U.S. election of 2016 was statistically very small compared to overall engagement on political issues."

Consider us not comforted. Without detailed transparency on how such things as "malicious actors," "civic content," "known operations," and "overall engagement on political issues" are determined/defined and what they do and don't consist of, the company's conclusion of downplaying the significance involved does not carry much weight. Very notable by its absence is any indication that the quantity of malicious activity is small compared to civic content or political engagement *in the United States* or *about the United States*. Three times Facebook's whitepaper states that the volume of information operations was "small," and the comparisons are to

- "the overall volume of civic content shared during the U.S. election"
- "overall engagement on political issues"
- "the total reach of civic content on Facebook"

206. Director of National Intelligence, "Assessing Russian Activities."
207. Weedon, Nuland, and Stamos, "Information Operations and Facebook."

For a platform with billions of users to compare overall volume/engagement and total reach of civic/political content to any one set of focused operations of course is going to result in a small percentage.

Let's do some back-of-the-envelope calculations, taking Facebook's statements at face value. Facebook had 1.79 billion monthly active users in the fall of 2016.[208] One-tenth of a percent of 1.79 billion monthly active users is 1,790,000 monthly active users. Facebook does not make it easy to know what they categorize as "civic content" or "engagement on political issues," much less what portion of their users are reached in these ways. One wonders why. Since we have no choice but to estimate, consider the frequency with which you encountered political content on Facebook in the heated political context of the fall of 2016. Different readers will have different experiences, but we are far from alone in recalling that it was hard to spend any time on Facebook then and *not* encounter political content. You can make your own estimate easily enough, but let's suppose an entire third of the 1,790,000 monthly active users somehow managed to not encounter civic content/political engagement during those months. That would mean 1,193,333 people were subject to malicious political intent in that time. There are nine U.S. states (including Washington, D.C.) with fewer people than that.

Even Facebook's own statements, taken at face value and estimating where necessary, belie Facebook's self-serving conclusion that the impact of malicious users through its platform was small. In fact, the very way that Facebook presented the information makes exactly the point it wishes to avoid—when power becomes so concentrated, even problems that are "relatively" small in percentage terms are large in absolute terms. One-tenth of a percent of the reach of "civic content" on Facebook for four months sounds small in percentage terms, but that translates to a *lot* of actual people affected.

The problem is only small in relation to Facebook's massive size—as citizens we must assess the magnitude of the problem first (millions of people maliciously influenced), *then* view the size of the company in relation to the problem. Rather than taking Facebook's size as the starting point and claiming a problem is small in relation to that, we must take the problem as the starting point. If a company can say with a straight face, as Facebook has, that malicious influence on millions of people is *marginal*, then let us not conclude that all those people are insignificant but that the company is overly big. Imagine if something on Facebook maliciously affected every single person in, say, Delaware; would Facebook dare claim that was marginal? Any entity that—as part of its own defense—can literally marginalize

208. Facebook, "Facebook Q3 2016 Earnings."

that many people has exceeded reasonable scale and poses major political and economic risks. The ability to say that malice at that scale is a "marginal" problem is itself problematic. This is the curse of bigness.

Facebook is only bigger now than it was in 2016, with 3.14 billion monthly active people on its family of products as of June 2020.[209] And understandings of how to exploit its relatively new technology will only increase with time. Yes, following the fall 2016 election scrutiny, Facebook has said it is investing in better security measures. Nevertheless, in May of 2019 it uncovered an Israel-based firm that was using Facebook's platforms to spread political disinformation in countries around the world. The group's Facebook pages had 2,800,000 followers. Before we congratulate Facebook for discovering and then stopping the malicious efforts, we should consider what it means for such efforts to affect 2,800,000 people (more than sixteen U.S. states' populations) *before* they come to Facebook's attention. As long as groups with an agenda can influence millions of people and barely make it to the margins of Facebook's attention, Facebook, or any entity that big, will remain a vehicle for undue political influence.

So, in addition to the typical risk of undue political influence firms with concentrated power tend to exert, platforms with concentrated user bases have the additional risk of being (ab)used by others to exert undue political influence.

The third political concern related to Facebook's concentrated power is, like the first, typical of any overly large and powerful entity. As scrutiny has increased, so has Facebook's spending on lobbying.[210] Enraging, isn't it? Rather than respond to customer concerns by improving the company, this indicates a response of undermining customer concerns by seeking government protection for the company. Strategy that is based on government protection contrary to the will of the people is not good for democratic government, the people as citizens, the people as customers/clients/consumers, or even ultimately for the company pursuing that strategy.

The less a company responds to customers, the less value it offers, making deliberate unresponsiveness ultimately a self-defeating strategy. There is also considerable opportunity cost—the time, effort, and money spent on political protection are resources diverted from strategies to actually improve the company. In a truly free market, companies compete to best serve customers' interests and dedicate all resources toward continual improvement in response to customers. Business continually strengthens and customers continually have better choices. Correspondingly, government is

---

209. Facebook, "Facebook Q2 2020 Earnings."
210. OpenSecrets, "Annual Lobbying by Facebook."

responsive to citizens rather than companies, giving citizens better political representation.

In short, when government and business are responsive to the people, government, business, and people are all better off. When government and business are responsive to each other, each loses legitimacy, and people are doubly diminished. Partnership Economics advocates the former—seeking mutual benefit for all involved, sustaining value for all stakeholders.

For all of these political reasons as well as the economic ones, we advocate for stronger antitrust enforcement. Legislation already exists,[211] but enforcement has been inconsistent or lax. Antitrust is not an end unto itself, not something to be done for its own sake, but it is an effective means toward the end of enhancing competition. For this reason, we specifically advocate for antitrust enforcement that is focused on preserving or increasing the competition in an industry. This means that mergers that would give the merged entity too concentrated a position should be blocked. It also means that firms already holding too concentrated a position should be broken up. To those who might immediately react against the "interventionist" approach of breaking up existing firms, there are prominent examples from various eras in America's history (Standard Oil, Bell/AT&T, Microsoft) that show such breakups can be beneficial in the long term not only for the broader economy but also *for the firms in question.*

To those who might despair that such action against the will of such powerful companies is unrealistic, again, the above examples are instructive. Those were extremely powerful companies, yet action was successfully taken to reduce their concentrated power, for the protection of the citizenry and the government. Everything seems impossible until it happens, and what we are advocating for here is something that has happened before. It is not impossible and can happen again; where there's a will, there's a way. And it just so happens that on this topic there is not only *a* will but an intriguingly wide range of wills.

We should not overlook or take for granted that calls for antitrust with mammoth tech companies are being voiced by politicians as ideologically different as Ted Cruz and Elizabeth Warren! In April 2019, Cruz, a proud-to-be-right Texas Republican, said, "Applying the antitrust laws is complicated, but by any standard measure, the big tech companies are larger and more powerful than the Standard Oil was when it was broken up. They're larger and more powerful than AT&T when it was broken up, and if we have

---

211. The Sherman Antitrust Act, the Clayton Act, and the Federal Trade Commission Act. See, e.g., https://www.justice.gov/atr/antitrust-laws-and-you.

tech companies using their monopoly to censor political speech, I think that raises real antitrust issues."[212]

In March 2019, Warren, a proud-to-be-left Massachusetts Democrat, published an article titled "Here's How We Can Break up Big Tech."[213] The title is clear enough. She summarizes her reasoning in some early lines: "Today's big tech companies have too much power—too much power over our economy, our society, and our democracy. They've bulldozed competition, used our private information for profit, and tilted the playing field against everyone else. And in the process, they have hurt small businesses and stifled innovation. . . . And I want to make sure that the next generation of great American tech companies can flourish. To do that, we need to stop this generation of big tech companies from throwing around their political power to shape the rules in their favor and throwing around their economic power to snuff out or buy up every potential competitor."

Cruz and Warren have different emphases in the concerns they express about the concentrated power these companies wield, but it is no small feat to be recognized as threatening across such a broad sweep of the American political spectrum. When Ted Cruz and Elizabeth Warren agree on something, possibility abounds. Their calls from opposite ends of the political spectrum represent the multiple—all compelling—reasons to more rigorously enforce antitrust measures, as well as opportunity to take meaningful action with broad-based political support.

As we've said in previous sections, specifics are difficult, but without specifics, claims of complexity can prevent any action at all from being taken. Better to debate the specifics than ignore them completely. Also as we've noted previously, much more could be said on topics so far-reaching; for now we begin with but one actionable start. We welcome conversation and debate at info@partnershipeconomics.com so that additional specific guidelines, which are the only kind that are actionable, can be formulated and refined.

As a start, we take the position that breaking up Facebook is an action that can and should be pursued. (Full disclosure: Aaron and Paul are Facebook shareholders at the time of writing.) The concentrated power of Facebook is obvious, as are the economic and political risks of its concentrated power. Given that part of Facebook's concentration of power came through acquisitions of other social networking companies, forcing divestiture of those companies is a natural remedy. Having Facebook, Instagram, and WhatsApp as separate companies would increase competition, increase

---

212. Freiburger, "Ted Cruz Offers Three Solutions to Big Tech Censorship."
213. Warren, "Here's How We Can Break Up Big Tech."

customer choice, and decrease undue political influence. Although there could be a bumpy transition period for those companies as they return to independence, and prediction of company performance is always speculative, there are strong precedents indicating that the companies themselves could also end up being more efficient and valuable post-breakup. For shareholders as well as stakeholders more broadly and society as a whole, there is reason to expect mutual benefit from partnering to disperse Facebook's concentrated power. This would also set a precedent for dispersing other overly concentrated powers that currently exist and would discourage companies, at least for a time, from pursuing such concentration of power.

Partnership in Practice:

- Celebrate and build bipartisan support for rigorous antitrust enforcement and encouragement of constructive competition, increasing the freedom of all market participants.
- Enforce antitrust laws already on the books.
- Advocate against mergers and acquisitions that would further concentrate power for already-concentrated companies.
- Advocate for breaking up companies that have excessively concentrated power, beginning with Facebook.
- As the voting public, vote for public servants who serve the public in the above ways.

Of course, if you don't like these action items or have better ideas, we invite you to email us at info@partnershipeconomics.com with your thoughts.

Public-Private "Partnerships"—Field of Schemes

A glaring, and all too common, anti-partnership phenomenon in our society is the (mis)use of public funds to build sports facilities that are not then owned by the public for public benefit. These facilities have both costs and benefits, and in simple terms, the majority of the costs are borne by the public in the form of taxes and subsidies while the majority of benefits go to private interests, either wealthy individuals or companies. This corrupt transfer does not seek the benefit of all involved but seeks the benefit of a few at the expense of the general public—typical plantation economics and exactly the opposite of partnership principles. How can such a detrimental exchange be made? Public servants failing to serve the public and instead serving special interests. No one can serve two masters . . .

Americans by and large love sports and their sports teams, a fact sports facility developers leverage to convince Americans to make bad deals under threat of relocating a beloved team. Ironically, this team spirit is used to the detriment of the biggest team of all—the public. In the name of supporting, say, the Atlanta Falcons, arrangements are made that are not good for the Atlanta public. Unfortunately, the sports teams are not usually team players with their own patrons.

Our national love of professional sports may make this topic hard to see in its full, destructive force. The fun and even escapist nature of professional sports may make this topic seem trivial—it's just a game, right? What's the big deal? Watching professional sports may be a diversion from real issues, or seem to be a harmless joy in life, but it is worth looking beneath the surface and becoming uncomfortable with the scope and severity of funding abuses in order to pursue better partnership.

Exposing and articulating these abuses has been done extensively since 1998 by Neil deMause and Joanna Cagan. Their book *Field of Schemes: How the Great Stadium Swindle Turns Public Money into Private Profit*, and website, fieldofschemes.com, detail an astonishing array of sports swindles. The fact that they have so many examples eliminates any doubt that this is a massive offense to Partnership Economics, conveniently hiding behind our beloved pastimes. The fact that the swindles show no sign of slowing down despite decades of condemnatory reporting makes clear the need to increase awareness and implement meaningful action.

As just one of too many examples, consider the Atlanta Falcons and their push to get public funding for a new stadium despite the Georgia Dome remaining a quality venue for some of the nation's premier sports events. A 2013 proposal involved $200 million in taxpayer-funded stadium bonds.[214] Those bonds were promptly opposed in court.[215] Aaron recalls living in Atlanta when the new stadium was being proposed. Even sports talk radio personalities were opposed. They commented on air about how that amount of money would be better spent on things like roads and water/sewer infrastructure, which were literally crumbling all over Atlanta.[216] People whose job was to be Atlanta sports nuts, on sports fan airtime, openly

---

214. deMause, "Falcons Could Accept."

215. deMause, "Georgia Supreme Court."

216. For instance, Aaron's entire apartment neighborhood was warned for several days not to drink tap water due to contamination concerns from broken water mains.

preferred funding projects with greater public benefit than the new stadium, but the public-bilking stadium funding happened anyway.

Three years later, the headline cost to the public was up to almost $700 million—3.5 times the cost that was so high it was resisted in court and by sports talk radio.[217] This is an unfortunately common tactic in the sports stadium swindle. Once the project has started, no one wants to stop it—so schemers routinely start with a "low" number for public financing buy-in and then balloon it once things are under way and all but impossible to stop. And that's just the headline numbers; hidden costs, such as public-funded construction around a new stadium (parking, bridges, etc.), tax rebates, and the insane opportunity cost of collecting no property tax from these large, valuable, private-business-owned-and-operated properties, drive the true cost far higher.

Not until July 2018 did all of that expense deliver a roof that was reliably functional and free of leaks in its "state of the art," retractable (major cost driver) way. Fans could then pay for seat licenses that would let them pay for tickets to see games and stay dry in the stadium they paid for.

These public-private (non)partnerships happen with minor league teams too. Even the minor leagues are pros at milking money away from their public "partners." It doesn't matter what sport, or even the level of that sport—this disease is pervasive across the professional sports landscape.

As this book was being written, America's pastime (baseball) was providing an example as ridiculous as any. Tampa Bay Rays owner Stuart Sternberg promoted the idea of his baseball team splitting time between the Tampa Bay-St. Petersburg area and ... Montreal. Yes, playing "home" games in two different countries. Not only that, but they would get new stadiums in *both* locations. The funding of stadiums is so problematic anyway; asking the public to take that on for only half the supposedly benefit-providing games is audacious even in this twilight zone of sports swindles. Besides the absurdity of the idea in its own right, the Rays have a lease with St. Petersburg that runs until 2028. They have no contractual basis to make any location change for nine years, yet they are proposing new stadiums in different countries.

The mayor of St. Petersburg, Rick Kriseman, had this to say about it all: "The Rays cannot explore playing any Major League Baseball games in Montreal or anywhere for that matter prior to 2028, without reaching a formal memorandum of understanding with the city of St. Petersburg. Ultimately, such a decision is up to me. And I have no intention of bringing

---

217. deMause, "Why are Georgia Taxpayers?"

this latest idea to our city council to consider. In fact, I believe this is getting a bit silly."[218] Bravo for a public servant standing up for the public!

The remedy? On one level, public servants must live up to that title and in fact serve the public. When ambitious developers (we speak generously here) seek permission and/or funds for sports facilities, or really any major development project, public servants cannot betray the public trust and simply give away public money. They must negotiate on behalf of the public and seek arrangements that are in the public's best interest. In basic terms, they must align the public's costs and benefits—to the extent the public covers the costs of a project, the public should also receive the profits it generates. If the developer declines to share ongoing profits with the public, then the charade is exposed and the public servants should not cover any costs. Negotiate as if the public funds were one's own and don't make a deal for others that you would never agree to yourself. If, as a public servant, you don't feel you're a strong enough negotiator, hire one of the many lawyers or lobbyists pounding on your door. That could actually be public funds well spent.

If or when public servants fail to serve the public well in such negotiations, then the public must assert itself directly, over and above the failing representative(s). Matters of public funding can generate a lot of publicity. Ballot measures allowing the public to directly decide on development proposals are one option. Publicity campaigns that pressure public servants into heeding the public will are another. Elections in the midst of development proposals present the opportunity to make candidates commit to the public interest in negotiations, and elections after public-abusing proposals are accepted are the opportunity to remove those who failed to serve the public.

Partnership in Practice:

- See beyond the sentimentality of sports and demand square, mutually beneficial deals from the business of sports.
- Refuse to impose costs on the public except in proportion to ownership the public receives in all future revenue streams generated by a publicly funded project.
- As the voting public, vote for public servants who serve the public in the above ways.

Of course, if you don't like these action items or have better ideas, we invite you to email us at info@partnershipeconomics.com with your thoughts.

218. Passan, "Rays to Explore."

Chapter 14

The Rubber Meets the Road
—Professions

Classical Professions

IN AN INTERVIEW PUBLISHED while she served as Chief Justice of the State of Georgia Supreme Court, Justice Carol Hunstein emphasized her call for lawyers to return to the practice of law as a profession and to their roles as trusted professionals. Underscoring her concern for the need of the legal profession to return to its roots, she quoted the ancient axiom, "The practice of law is one of three great professions: theology for preservation of the spirit, medicine for preservation of the body, and law for preservation of civilization."[219]

What anchors and sits at the core of each of these three professions? They are linked and properly called "great" because these are the original caring professions. Traditionally, clergy, lawyers, and sometimes physicians are honored by being called "counselors" because they care for others by providing advice and assistance in accordance with their respective training. As counselors they are expected to act with honesty and integrity. Members of these professions, as well as other professions, affirm or swear an oath to honor their calling and those they serve. A familiar definition of honor speaks to honesty or integrity in one's beliefs and action (e.g., a sense of principled uprightness of character; personal integrity).

---

219. Molander, "Beyond All Odds," 10.

What happened so that many of us aren't even aware of that ancient axiom? In large part, the present corporate business ethic has washed away our predecessors' perspective of the fiduciary care and duty of professionals. As a result, modern culture thinks and acts as if highly skilled professionals should simply run businesses like everyone else. Our thinking is reinforced by every doctor who doesn't spend enough time with a patient to learn him or her as a person, or the law firm advertisement suggesting a big win, or the congregant arguing "the church needs to run like a business." Yes, of course all these professionals need financial resources at the end of the day to stay open, but how much profit and at what expense to their calling as caring professionals?

Back to Justice Hunstein and her interview: she further said, "We [attorneys] have to protect our clients, but we must do what is right—not just win at any cost. Law is a profession, not a competition."[220] She's right to lament the overreach of the corporate ethic, especially as it's turned aspects of the legal profession into the strong arm enforcer of plantation system economics. Likewise, her counterparts in hospitals and houses of worship across the country are right to lament their failures. Are these the only professions that care for others that could use an overhaul? Hardly. Don't we rely on our financial or investment managers, insurance agents, and accountants, just to name a few additional professions, to care for us at least as much as we rely on our doctors, lawyers, and clergy? Not only is it past time to put this ancient axion back into the national dialogue and ethic, it is time to courageously expand and apply it to every profession and professional that purports to care for or have a fiduciary duty to their clients.

Now that we've lamented, how do we turn a corner and help steer professional relationships back to their roots? Better yet, how can professionals and professional relationships shift to a Partnership Ethic? We offer a strong start with the following two easy-to-apply action steps. Easy, but challenging simply because they will require courage to implement.

First, the business disclaimer and marketplace expectation of caveat emptor ("let the buyer beware") simply can't apply to professionals. It's one thing to apply that standard through the centuries to lower-risk products like wagon wheels and entertainment devices, but the concept should never have leached into the professions. Professional organizations by and large do a good gatekeeping job of quality control. But after taking the oath, it's primarily up to the professional as a self-regulated person to be and remain the trusted caretaker and fiduciary that the professionals' association purports its members to be. Far beyond what a law or regulation may require

---

220. Molander, "Beyond All Odds," 10.

at minimum, the source and strength for the professional ethic must flow profusely from the heart, head, and spirit of the individual professional, which then feeds the commitment to love their clients and *de facto* economic partners as they love themselves.

Next, there is no law that prohibits professionals from limiting their income goals. Does a doctor or lawyer *want* to earn seven figures a year and keep it all? Sure, probably. Does a doctor or lawyer *need* to earn seven figures and keep it? No. Neither does anyone *need* to earn seven figures or more a year and keep it. (Alternatively, should clergy and teachers and public safety workers and foster parents and the millions of others in all walks of life who care for us be fairly paid at least twice what they are on average paid now? Of course, and that'll be a topic for a later time.)

Professionals and the services they provide become more elusive as their rates increase, not just for the average wage earner but for everyone. Our collective and common experience is that people unnecessarily suffer illness because they can't afford to visit a doctor and sit in jails because they can't afford a lawyer. Every person needs the services of a professional at one time or another, and the pro bono work donated by the thousands of professionals who try to fill the unmet needs simply isn't enough.

Permit a real-time example. While writing this section, Paul unexpectedly had to have a root canal. Maybe this is God's way of providing us an object lesson. The endodontist charged just under $2,000 for the maybe ninety minutes in the dental chair needed to repair the tooth. The other option was to pull the tooth and move on, a nonstarter because that would just cause later additional issues. Paul doesn't have dental insurance, so in addition to the physical pain, this unexpected expense is financially painful. We trust professionals like this with the health of our teeth in crisis, but we don't like paying what amounts to $1,300 per hour for their service any more than they like paying $600–$900 per hour for a lawyer. We suspect they don't have to charge this much for this service, no matter how badly it is needed. For some, choosing to receive such expensive service is financially painful but can be done; how many others have missing teeth because they simply can't afford an endodontist?

Professionals don't need to be leashed with price controls or wage caps. Nevertheless, as a group and as supported by our respective professional associations, we can take a leading role in shifting toward Partnership Economics by recognizing and stepping back into our roles as caretakers, and partnering with those who benefit from our services at *affordable* rates. And all can partner with professionals by fairly, appreciatively, and timely compensating them for their beneficial services, as well as referring more business to them when their services and prices provide mutual benefit.

Partnership in Practice:

- Students: find, learn, and practice your school's honor code for the ethics training it's trying to teach you. You'll reduce the risk of having your future license revoked.
- Professionals: find, reaffirm, and live into that oath you took to uphold your profession's ethics or code of conduct.
- Industry influencers: motivate your industry leaders to stop treating clients, employees, and vendors as the equivalent of FBUs.
- Professionals: stop putting your desires above the needs of your client. Seek ways to meet the needs of both you and your client before turning to your desires.
- Clients: hire professionals with a reputation for being caring partners and treat them well.

Of course, if you don't like these action items or have better ideas, we invite you to email us at info@partnershipeconomics.com with your thoughts.

Financial Professions—Truly Mutual Funds

The Office of the Comptroller of the Currency (OCC) is the administrator of America's federal banking system. The OCC's mission "is to ensure that national banks and federal savings associations operate in a safe and sound manner, provide fair access to financial services, treat customers fairly, and comply with applicable laws and regulations."[221] What might the OCC do when a bank's leadership falls short of being the financial professionals they profess to be?

Consider just the 2016 fake account scandal of the multinational financial services company Wells Fargo, for example. (Full disclosure: Paul is a long-time Wells Fargo customer.) Founded in 1852, Wells Fargo is the world's fourth largest bank by market capitalization and the fourth largest bank in the United States by total assets. But it appears that kind of global domination wasn't enough for Wells Fargo leadership.

In September 2016, after the revelation that bank employees created 1.5 million fake deposit accounts and over 500,000 fake credit card accounts—all in customer names without their permission—the OCC, joined by other agencies, penalized the company with $185 million in fines. The

---

221. Comptroller, "31st Comptroller."

fake accounts stemmed from overzealous sales practices in an effort to hit lofty performance targets. Then CEO John Stumpf was fired, had $41 million in compensation clawed back, and in a class action suit the company agreed to pay $142 million to the affected parties including customers. No less than seven smaller scandals ensnared the company for the next eighteen months, including the Federal Reserve announcing it would restrict the bank's growth, "responding to widespread consumer abuses and compliance breakdowns."[222]

In January 2020 the OCC announced that Stumpf, a thirty-four-year career employee of Wells Fargo until his resignation in October 2016, will pay a settlement of $17.5 million for his connection in the fake accounts scandal, and he is now barred from working in the banking industry. Further, seven former executives, including the bank's chief administrative officer, chief risk officer, chief auditor, general counsel, and executive audit director, have been charged with civil penalties totaling more than $40 million for their individual misconduct in the scandal. This is the first time the regulator has charged individuals for a bank's wrongdoing. Well, at least it's a start.

"The root cause of the sales practices misconduct problem was the Community Bank's [the division where the scandal erupted] business model, which imposed intentionally unreasonable sales goals and unreasonable pressure on its employees to meet those goals and fostered an atmosphere that perpetuated improper and illegal conduct," the OCC said in a notice. Speaking to the wake and echoes of Gordon Gekko proclaiming "Greed is good!" the OCC also noted, "Community Bank management intimidated and badgered employees to meet unattainable sales goals year after year, . . . subjecting employees to hazing-like abuse, and threatening to terminate and actually terminating employees for failure to meet the goals."[223]

For perspective, understand these practices were in place at Wells Fargo for at least several years before being exposed in 2015, still in the shadow of the painful years of the Great Recession. The Great Recession, you'll remember, was itself precipitated by not dissimilar financial industry abuses, which required the extraordinary rescue of the industry by the federal government and painfully financed by us taxpayers.

Will the OCC penalties prevent future abuses at Wells Fargo? We could hope, and it could easily take a few years to determine if Wells Fargo has effectively repented. Will the OCC penalties prevent similar abuses at other financial institutions? We could hope, although more likely those with

222. Wolff-Mann, "Wells Fargo Scandals."
223. Hrushka, "OCC Bans Ex-Wells Fargo CEO."

ethics that foster similarly abusive behaviors will just laugh at not being caught and stay their course.

Wells Fargo's current CEO Charlie Scharf said in a statement following the OCC's notice, "At the time of the sales practices issues, the Company did not have in place the appropriate people, structure, processes, controls, or culture to prevent the inappropriate conduct."[224] We understand the need for Scharf to issue a defense cloaked as an apology. But wait a minute. Isn't this the same organization with the resources to grow to be the world's fourth largest bank by market capitalization and the fourth largest bank in the United States by total assets? Why, yes, it is. As this crisis reveals, it's past time for the bank to redirect some of its astounding resources to grow toward purposes other than market domination.

This example of Wells Fargo, selected simply as the current financial services debacle unfolding as we began writing this section, is an object lesson of how an organization ought not to behave. What is the least expensive—virtually free, and most effective corrective—and virtually guaranteed measure Wells Fargo could readily implement to avoid future debacles? Could other financial institutions likewise implement this measure to avoid being the next wrong kind of object lesson? Consider the last element on Scharf's list of inadequacies: "culture."

The ethics of an organization's leadership meaningfully influences, if not drives, the organization's culture. What might happen if a new ethic among financial professionals led them to choose to elevate themselves to being one of the great professions? Our financial professionals are at least as involved and influential in our lives as our doctors and clergy, so financial professionals are certainly positioned to make that choice. What might happen if financial professionals chose to create and engage a unified ethic with the goal of caring; that as one of the great professions they will care for their customers and markets? With a caring ethic in place among our financial professionals, we are confident that at a minimum Main Street would experience more stability and Wall Street would experience less volatility.

Might financial professionals disenfranchise shareholders by having a unified ethic that includes caring for the organization's stakeholders, particularly customers and even the OCC? Of course not. The question, as popular as it is, frames the logical fallacy of a false dilemma. Instead, a leadership that possesses a character-based mode of caring can instill a goal-based mode and rules-based mode that supports a unified ethic of a caring culture. Through the lens of a unified ethic that supports a caring culture, we can see upstream of Scharf's defenses to find that controls,

---

224. Hrushka, "OCC Bans Ex-Wells Fargo CEO."

processes, and structure, to the extent they are needed, can be meaningfully leaner and more effective than that needed to support the current ethic. And the organization's people—the organization's caring people—will not only ensure compliance but will likely enjoy doing so.

What does a caring ethic cost? Literally, nothing; and financial professionals gain the whole world rather than having regulators like the OCC restrict growth. Talk about an attractive path to the market domination Wells Fargo and similar financial institutions are chasing, how could the right path be made any easier?

Partnership in Practice:

- Everyone: work to awaken, if not force, financial professionals to accept their sector's responsibility as a caring profession.
- Financial professionals: reject the Gordon Gecko and Bernie Madoff ethic of "Greed is good!" in exchange for an ethic of caring for your clients.
- Financial services leaders: initiate and enforce (as rigorously as you do monthly reporting) a unified ethic with the ultimate goal of caring and an ideal set that advances that goal.
- We're all consumers: make clear to your financial professionals (whatever their roles and view of themselves) that you expect them to care for you by putting your needs before their desires, or switch to professionals that care and respond.

Of course, if you don't like these action items or have better ideas, we invite you to email us at info@partnershipeconomics.com with your thoughts.

Trusted Trustees? Beginning the World Anew

"How do I know he's lying? His lips are moving."
—unfortunately, a common "joke"

Turning to the roles and responsibilities of trustees, we were tempted to simply draw on the common law principles of agency to craft a definition of a trusted trustee, then move on. In various earlier sections we provided guidelines for fiduciary duty as a baseline responsibility in a Partnership Ethic, and here contemplated a construct of a trusted trustee as a bookend.

Such a construct would be both aspirational and attainable, and a construct to which we might aim and by which we might measure ourselves.

We stepped back from that temptation, however, after discerning that the high road to becoming a trusted trustee begins with the ethics of truthful speech and that old ethic should be our focus for now. Why the ethics of truthful speech? Well, that's the narrow gate to exploring and connecting to that high road.

In their modern classic *Kingdom Ethics*, Christian ethicists Gushee and Stassen point "attention to the moral issues associated with truth telling and its negations, such as lying, promise breaking, and deceit."[225] They observe, rightly, "Many forces—economic, political, moral, familial, and more—are undermining moral traditions that taught practices of truth telling and promise keeping, and we believe this is a major threat to the health of society, its interactions, and its members."[226]

We all know anecdotally about the pervasiveness of lying in our society because it's our lived experience. By way of empirical data, a 2002 study by UMass Amherst psychologist and researcher Robert S. Feldman found that 60 percent of the 121 pairs of undergraduate students observed lied at least once during a ten-minute conversation, telling an average of two to three lies. "It's so easy to lie," Feldman said. "We teach our children that honesty is the best policy, but we also tell them it's polite to pretend they like a birthday gift they've been given. Kids get a very mixed message regarding the practical aspects of lying, and it has an impact on how they behave as adults."[227]

What might it look like to pivot from our current societal agreement that accommodates lying, promise breaking, and deceit (with the implied "so long as you're not caught") to a transforming initiative of truthful speech, which is consistent and not situationally pliable? Here's how Jesus said a covenant of truthfulness and responsibility might look: "Again, you have heard that it was said to those of ancient times, 'You shall not swear falsely, but carry out the vows you have made to the Lord.' But I say to you, Do not swear at all . . . Let your word be 'Yes, Yes' or 'No, No'; anything more than this comes from the evil one" (Matthew 5:33–37). This pivot—this transforming initiative—moves us from a practice of choosing and changing our words as we try to navigate a situation, to a covenant of living truth wherein who we are gets reflected in our truthful speech.

---

225. Gushee and Stassen, *Kingdom Ethics*, 288.
226. Gushee and Stassen, *Kingdom Ethics*, 289.
227. UMass, "Most People Lie."

We have also come to discern that to be a disciple is to inherently be a trustee. In the most general sense of the word, a disciple is someone who is disciplined by and seeks to faithfully live the doctrine of another. In being a disciple, he or she has accepted the responsibility of protecting and advancing that doctrine with the example of their very life. Disciples do not merely accept the responsibility of watching or managing the property of another like a trustee, disciples go further by embracing and personifying their responsibility of being disciplined by that doctrine. How much more trusted can a person be, than to embody and protect that which is entrusted to them with his or her very life?

The various faith traditions typically understand truth as being rooted in and flowing from God. In the Judeo-Christian traditions, the moral issue of truthful speech is captured in the Ten Commandments (Exodus 20:16; Deuteronomy 5:20) with, "You shall not bear false witness against your neighbor." Gushee and Stassen observe, "phrases describing God as 'the God of truth' (Ps 31:5; Is 65:16, Rev 15:3) point to God's reliability, fidelity, and trustworthiness. It is not just that God speaks truth but that *God is true*; this is God is characterized by fidelity and is reliable in keeping divine commitments" (emphasis in original).[228] Christians view Jesus as the embodiment of truth in both speech and action (e.g., John 1:14; 14:6), and the Holy Spirit as "the Spirit of truth" (e.g., John 14:17; 15:26; 16:13).

The truthfulness and trustworthiness of God in the form of the Spirit of truth flow to and empower disciples to move from merely trying to know and do under their own power, to being the embodiment of truth and trust. This, we have discerned, is the narrow gateway and high road to being a trusted trustee.

How do you recognize or become a trusted trustee? Gushee and Stassen connect to two moral themes in their exploration of truthful speech, themes we see can be adopted as a two-prong litmus test. "First, the truth is not simply something that is believed or spoken, but instead is a character quality, a way of being. . . . Second, one's commitment to the truth is verified by deeds. These deeds, of course, do include the nature of one's characteristic speech—whether we lie and deceive or instead speak the truth (Ps 5:9; Prv 8:7; 12:20; Jer 9:3)."[229] Truthful character evidenced by truthful deeds, these are the fundamental traits of a trusted trustee.

Cultures and societies around the world have sprinted quite far from that cultural and lifesaving guidance, only to become ensnared in the byzantine customs and laws that buttress our continual efforts to deceive each

---

228. Gushee and Stassen, *Kingdom Ethics*, 295.
229. Gushee and Stassen, *Kingdom Ethics*, 296–97.

other. We are confident that the number of laws a society has on the books are in direct proportion to the untrustworthiness of its people. The corrective, the transforming initiative, toward being a trusted trustee no matter our profession, is to change our minds and lives such that truth is one of our character qualities, and that quality is evident by our words and deeds.

Businesses, and we can't think of any exceptions, can't exist without a basis in trust. Beyond the professions and roles discussed elsewhere in this book, which all fail when trust is breached, we offer here a few common practices required to be trusted trustees.

Partnership in Practice:

- Pitch or spin if you must, but never stray materially from the accuracy of the underlying facts.
- Perform to your best abilities every task entrusted to you, recognizing it will likely one day be exposed and examined.
- Explain clearly and transparently to the other person the work you're performing on the task they've entrusted to you, and dutifully complete what you've represented; this is especially true when working for those without the technical expertise to verify your work.
- Insurers and warranty providers: make coverage clear and stop making your insured fight to receive the coverage you represented you'd provide.
- The goal of every human in every relationship (including the relationships of economic exchanges) should be that of being a trusted trustee.

A list of examples could go on for miles. What examples from your experiences would you add? Of course, if you don't like these action items or have better ideas, we invite you to email us at info@partnershipeconomics.com with your thoughts.

Meet the Press

"Things that are perceived as real are real in their consequences."

—Jo Anne Earp

Having just introduced an ethic of truth-telling and a recognition that we all have the responsibility to be trusted trustees, we turn a spotlight on media professionals and the media outlets that support them (here, together designated "Media"). We don't do this to tee up criticism; rather, for the extreme opposite reason. First, everyone is aware of the extraordinary influence Media wields. Because of this extraordinary influence there is a profound need for the Media to recognize and live into their responsibilities—as professionals and as the trusted trustees of the products they produce and disseminate. Second, it may be acceptable to apply the principle of caveat emptor to tangible products a buyer can reasonably examine and verify, but that's not a standard that can be applied to news and information, products a consumer can't easily examine and verify.

America has a difficult *intellectual* relationship with its First Amendment's right of free speech clause. This difficulty springs in large part from the evolving ways the U.S. Supreme Court (U.S. S.Ct.) has wrestled with and written about this right. Americans ourselves similarly have a difficult *cultural* relationship with our right of free speech. This difficulty springs in large part from misinformation, misunderstanding, and missed ethics. We propose that a way to step back from these difficulties begins with correctly recalling and then living into a famous First Amendment line from the landmark U.S. S.Ct. decision of *Schenck v. United States*, 249 U.S. 47 (1919).

Writing for a unanimous Court about how the government must analyze whether certain speech can be judged seditious, Justice Oliver Wendell Holmes Jr., observed by way of analogy how speech that is false and dangerous is not protected speech: "The most stringent protection of free speech would not protect a man in *falsely* shouting fire in a theatre and causing a panic" (emphasis added).[230] This sentence is dictum—meaning not to be regarded for establishing the law of the case at hand or setting legal precedent, but which of course *can* be instructive, quoted, and followed.[231]

As we write this section, the whole world is responding to the spread of COVID-19, which is already among the greatest public health and economic crises since 1918. Uncertainty grips much that was previously taken for granted. How do we know about this novel coronavirus and its origins, that its spread is labeled a pandemic, of its prevalence rate, the names of those who have died of it, the comorbidities that increase risk of dying if infected, how to minimize the spread, how to protect ourselves going forward, and countless additional questions? The information any of us have

---

230. *Schenck v. United States*, 249 U.S. 47, 52.

231. Regarding its procedural history, *Schenck* was later partially overruled by *Brandenburg v. Ohio* (395 U.S. 444)(1969) with a revised framework directed to how our government must analyze speech that may be considered criminal. Despite the later *Brandenburg* revision, limited to government actors analyzing potentially criminal speech, one hundred years later Holmes's single-sentence free speech ethic and analogy remains logically sound and eminently practical.

is gained primarily through the Media. Our perceptions and our reactions, individually and as nations, are in response to the information we have through the Media and our level of trust in that information.

Under such conditions, anyone *falsely* shouting a COVID alarm (equivalent to *falsely* shouting fire in a crowded theater) causes a panic—large or small depending on the size of his or her audience. And this yield results both ways. To *falsely* shout there is COVID when there is not, or to *falsely* shout there is not COVID when there is, violates the elegant guardrail ethic Justice Holmes provides for free speech. Sadly, people of all stripes and positions have falsely shouted COVID-19 misinformation. Given the risks and lives at stake, at every level our need for trust in the Media and the services it provides is literally a matter of life and death.

Caveat emptor can't reasonably be the standard the Media hides behind to shield itself and the information it dispenses. Neither can we as consumers of information be so open minded that our brains leak out. Consumers have a responsibility to guard ourselves from the 24/7 tsunami of information from the Media, and protect ourselves from the 24/7 malevolent peddlers of misinformation. We have simple defenses to guard and protect ourselves from, and even further stop transmitting, the disease (dis-ease) of misinformation.

For starters a handful of those defenses include: unceasingly identifying and distinguishing facts from opinions; never holding opinions as facts; limiting your information sources to reputable Media that publicly hold to a trustworthy ethic (such as the Society of Professional Journalists' code of ethics comprising an ethical frame of: seek truth and report it; minimize harm; act independently; and, be accountable and transparent)[232]; make it a practice to never repeat or forward information until you've cleared it through your own trustworthy ethic, such as the one provided by the Society of Professional Journalists; and recognize that an increasing percentage of Media are not reporting news but theatrically spinning and bashing opinion, so know which you're viewing and why.

What might a Media Partnership Ethic look like? LinkedIn, the business networking and services platform that is a subsidiary of Microsoft, is one of countless Media outlets. While writing this section we received an unusual email blast from LinkedIn's Chief Business Officer Dan Shapero regarding its reporting of the COVID-19 crisis. The most relevant paragraph of that email reads:

> We're also moving quickly to share reliable information and resources. As a leadership team at LinkedIn, we have made using

---

232. Society of Professional Journalists, "Code of Ethics."

facts one of our first principles in our decision making. Recognizing there is a lot of noise out there, our global editorial team is curating trusted, real time news and facts on COVID-19, including insights on the impact to the economy, how organizations are responding, and policy changes being made by the World Health Organization.[233]

We found this LinkedIn email distinctive in that a media outlet had reached out to its users to transparently communicate its ethics and how it intends to be trusted with the information it curates, creates, and disseminates. We hope it follows through successfully. Below are practical partnership steps all Media can implement to become trusted Media trustees, not just in times of crisis, but every story every day.

Partnership in Practice:

- Media should move quickly to share reliable information and resources, and be transparent in reporting.
- Media should eliminate the term "investigative journalism" to mean a niche in the landscape in favor of that being its fearless standard for all reporting.
- Media must make facts—not opinion—a primary factor in what is reported and used to curate trusted, real-time news.
- Editorials and opinions should be clearly labeled as such, like graphic warnings on tobacco products, and never passed off as news or facts.
- Media must never falsely report any information for any reason or price, such as influence from an advertiser or sponsor.
- All of us (including social media platform providers): waste no time becoming discerning consumers of information, guarding and protecting ourselves, and preventing the spread of misinformation.

Of course, if you don't like these action items or have better ideas, we invite you to email us at info@partnershipeconomics.com with your thoughts.

---

233. LinkedIn email received March 16, 2020.

CHAPTER 15

The Rubber Meets the Road—Culture

"Culture eats strategy for breakfast."
—Peter Drucker

Eating Strategy for Breakfast

FOR OUR PRESENT PURPOSES a good description of "culture" is: "The set of predominating attitudes and behavior that characterize a group or organization" (thefreedictionary.com/culture). We all understand culture. Or do we, especially in the context of business?

Warren Buffett is credited with saying, "Culture, more than rule books, determines how an organization behaves." Peter Drucker was among the best-known and most influential management thinkers of the twentieth century; shortly before he died, *BusinessWeek* named him "the man who invented management." Drucker famously observed, "Culture eats strategy for breakfast."[234] These extraordinary leaders clearly understand the dominating influence of culture on an organization. Any kind and nature of organization. Examples are helpful, so let's contrast two.

Earlier we introduced the crisis that erupted at Wells Fargo in 2016. Recall the statement from current CEO Charlie Scharf, "At the time of the sales practices issues, the Company did not have in place the appropriate people, structure, processes, controls, or culture to prevent the inappropriate

---

234. Buffett, "Berkshire Hathaway Letters"; for Drucker, the Management Centre, "Culture."

conduct." Just as we were earlier obligated to push back on this apology we push back again, this time from the perspective of culture.

Wells Fargo is currently the world's fourth largest bank by market capitalization and holds the same ranking in the United States as measured by total assets. With empathy for Mr. Scharf's spin and efforts to restore the bank's reputation, Wells Fargo has all the structure, processes, and controls it needs and proves it by its rankings. The focus should be, and what Mr. Scharf is understandably minimizing by conflating with other factors, is the fact that the Company's *people* created and supported a *culture* that intentionally ignored its rule books. In Drucker language, the Company culture ate the Company strategy. We are not about pounding on Wells Fargo; indeed, one day we'd be honored to be able to write about a marvelous cultural reversal and recovery. Meanwhile, the crisis Wells Fargo created for itself is just one clear object lesson illustrating how the wrong culture can harm if not destroy shareholders and stakeholders alike.

Let's turn to Southwest Airlines for a contrasting object lesson about people and their culture. In a 2018 *Forbes* interview, Southwest CFO Tammy Romo was asked, "What about Southwest's culture do you feel supports this [high] level of employee retention?" No workplace is perfect all the time, but her response is timeless and available to be applied to every organization:

> Our people and our culture are by far two of our key strengths at Southwest Airlines. We have a very caring culture. . . . It's one of the key reasons we've been recognized for 24 straight years as one of *Fortune* magazine's Most Admired Companies. As employees, we celebrate one another *and* we take time to appreciate each other. . . . Each individual that joins Southwest makes a difference, whether it's flying the planes or booking the accounting entries. . . . It takes all of us working together as a team to accomplish our vision to be the world's most loved, most flown, and most profitable airline. This instills ownership and pride because we all have such a meaningful purpose.[235]

Let's quickly connect three dots in Romo's quote: "caring culture" connects to "most loved" connects to "most profitable." This is mutuality; this is a Partnership Ethic. Frankly, the mystery is why more corporations don't seem capable of connecting those same dots.

Southwest's Co-founder and Chairman Emeritus Herb Kelleher has said, "The business of business is people." This kind of Partnership Ethic set the groundwork for the cultural DNA that is Southwest. As of this writing

---

235. Thomson, "Company Culture Soars."

Warren Buffett owns 10.2 percent of Southwest; he's clearly a fan of the culture. In Drucker language, Southwest's culture supports its strategy.

Kristen Robertson, CEO of Brio Leadership and a company culture consultant, has studied and consulted with Southwest. After attending a half-day event that showcased Southwest's methods of strengthening, reinforcing, and maintaining its strongly positive culture, she took away five lessons.[236] With credit to Ms. Robertson we present those as actionable lessons here, which are low-cost, profitable, and sustainable—like the airline itself.

Partnership in Practice:

- Evolve your culture—establish a culture task force, or department like Southwest, whose mission is to retain focus on the culture that serves it so well.
- Equip your leaders—recognize, train, and celebrate leaders at all levels of the organization's hierarchy, not just the C-suite.
- Empower and appreciate your employees—give each the freedom to do their job well and actively appreciate each when the job is well done.
- Model your culture—executives and managers lead the way with their exemplary behavior, and coach or dismiss the associates who fall short of the cultural expectations.
- Nurture your culture—design space, marketing, and reward systems around values that enforce and support your culture.

Of course, if you don't like these action items or have better ideas, we invite you to email us at info@partnershipeconomics.com with your thoughts.

---

236. Robertson, "5 Culture Lessons."

We Are They!

"No one else is your problem."
—Fr. Richard Rohr, OFM

There is no way around it, We = They.

They've made a mess of it, haven't they? Those corporations, those politicians, and all those people taking advantage of all of us. We could spend days recounting the people and things that need fixing; couldn't you? So where do we start, you know, start fixing all those corporations, those politicians, and those people making a mess of everything?

We start by defining the current problem, mostly because we were schooled that a problem well defined is half solved. Also, we remember Einstein is quoted as saying, "If you can't explain it simply, you don't understand it well enough." Pulling those two tools from our toolbox we present the starting point, problem, and solution for the needed cultural shift as simply: "We are they!" (RR4).

All shareholders own the corporation, do we not? Are we responsible shareholders, aware of what we own and engaged in the oversight of where we put our money? Yes, it is impossible for boards and executives of S&P 500 companies to hear the small voice of a single investor over the booming and bellowing voices of institutional or hedge fund managers. But corporations are not entirely deaf, and we are not at all powerless. Indeed, it is impossible for corporations to be deaf to public criticism or scrutiny. Especially to the public outcry of thousands of those previously small voices rising up and speaking as one, and any other concerted and sustained action that might cause investors to pull away and stock value to decline. Declining stock value negatively impacts executive and board compensation, so a declining stock value quickly gets attention. If we attend to our roles of being diligent shareholders then we, the accumulated small voices, will be in a position to flex our power. Our power to break the systemically harmful practice of us serving corporations and replace it with the transformatively beneficial practice of corporations partnering with us—their owners.

Pity the politicians? Not at all. They too are us! Done properly, politicians are authentic and intelligent people with our collective interests at heart and hand, whom we entrust with the responsibility of making good decisions for the benefit of our common good. We voted for them, put them into office, our tax dollars pay their salaries, and we should be pleased to pay them well for work well done. By way of reasonable comparison, we own our politicians as we own the corporations in which we have stock. Not unlike corporate executives, few if any politicians are willing to hear that message and will likely try to dismiss it as quaint idealism, but it is a truth fundamental to both capitalism and democracy. If we would simply attend to our responsibilities of being diligent voters and citizens, voting into public office those who are trustworthy and voting or storming out of public office those who are not, then we properly do our part to clean up the mess.

We look forward to Partnership Economics being sufficiently realized that our earlier story of two farmer-brothers who caught each other sneaking bags of grain into each other's barns (Part 2, chapter 9) will not be aspirational, but a standard operating procedure. Meanwhile, here and now, how do we all start the cultural transformation toward becoming those brothers for each other throughout the economic landscape?

First, we have to recognize that in today's business world and in most exchanges we do not get what we deserve but what we negotiate. Many, if not most of us, are significantly under-compensated for our labor. So many, if not most of us, need to become more effective negotiators and self-promoters (not fakers) of real skills. Second, we must recognize that every party in every exchange has important basic and psychological needs (e.g., at least the first four sets of Maslow's hierarchy of needs from food to self-esteem) and those needs should never be sacrificed for another party's mere wants or goals (e.g., an executive denying sustainable wages in order to support their own lavish lifestyle). Third, each of us must be a trustworthy person. Remember our earlier litmus test for trustworthiness: 1) being transparent; 2) typically making good decisions; and, 3) being empathic, if not compassionate, toward others and their needs. Ask yourself and gauge honestly: how well do you measure up to each of those three elements?

Partnership in Practice:

- Shareholders: vote the proxies (don't ignore those notices), and attend the meetings and calls if possible.
- Shareholders: know the corporation beyond its stock value returns; talk to your financial manager or directly to the corporation if you do not like the corporation's ethics, or practices, or if you see abuses. If circumstances and conscience drive you, sell your shares and loudly encourage others to do the same.
- Stakeholders: complain but offer options, alternatives, and constructive suggestions. Raise public relations hell if needed.
- Voters: vote! Exercise your right to vote to the fullest; at every level of government your voice should be heard loudly and clearly.
- Voters: know who you are voting for and know what they are doing on behalf of your community and the greater good. Thank your public servants for work well done.
- Consumers: stop doing business with people who take advantage of you or others. Give your business and refer others to those businesses and professionals who demonstrate—not just talk—a Partnership Ethic.
- All of us: be trustworthy, keep trustworthiness top of mind, then find and partner with others working to do the same.

Of course, if you don't like these action items or have better ideas, we invite you to email us at info@partnershipeconomics.com with your thoughts.

Enough—the Household Version

Bruce Springsteen holds up an unexpected mirror to an aspect of behavioral economics with four lines of lyrics from his song "Badlands":

> Poor man wanna be rich
> Rich man wanna be king
> And a king ain't satisfied
> 'Til he rules everything

With that kind of insight and poetic framing, no wonder we call him the Boss. There is wisdom to mine in those lyrics, but for now we use them to help you explore "what's enough for my household?"

There are general, societal perceptions around wealth. In a September 2018 YouGov survey of a thousand Americans, the public opinion tipping point for being considered rich was when 56 percent agreed an annual income of $90,000–$100,000 clearly qualified a single person as being rich. The financial firm Charles Schwab asked the same number of Americans a related question about wealth for its 2018 Modern Wealth Index, and its respondents averaged in with the opinion that a net worth of $2.4 million was needed to be considered wealthy.[237] Opinions and emotions around income and wealth vary, of course, but these responses reflect consistent perceptions from a variety of reliable financial reporting sources.

Perceptions are instructive, primarily because perceptions are real in their consequences. Matthew Smith, the author of the YouGov survey, observed, "What is perhaps more interesting here [than the actual numbers] is that, although people become less likely to consider themselves poor the more money they make, they don't really become much more likely to consider themselves rich." The YouGov survey supports Smith's observation around a sliding-scale perception of the annual income needed to be considered rich. Beginning with 60 percent of those with an annual income of less than $20,000 and who think that an annual income of $90,000 is rich, perceptions slide down to 45 percent of those with an annual income of $40,000–$60,000, and slide down again to 19 percent of those with an annual income of $90,000–$150,000 and who think the same.[238]

The YouGov and other data support Smith's observation that, in sum, the richer we are the higher we set the bar for what we consider rich. The result is that we never feel we are ever rich enough. This behavioral flaw is why our world has unsustainable sayings and goals such as, "you're never too rich or too thin" and "I'll be rich when I get the next million (or billion)." Robert Reeves, of the Brookings Institute, has described this flaw as the "Me? I'm not rich!" problem. It describes the phenomenon whereby most people tend to believe they are not rich, and the point where others become rich is the next earning level immediately above where they themselves are

---

237. For reasons that are explained further in this section, we note an invested portfolio of $2.4M that yields a conservative 4 percent return generates $96,000/yr. without encroaching on the principal.

238. Clement of Alexandria, who made the first attempt at a systematic treatment of faith and wealth late in the second century, observed then that the rich tend to be too lenient with themselves in determining their own sufficiency. See Gonzalez, *Faith and Wealth*, 112–18.

The Rubber Meets the Road—Culture

perched. So, we never stop striving or envying others, and we are never satisfied.[239] Now that you see and understand this tendency toward a sliding-scale perception, you can see and understand how this tendency is critical to supporting and sustaining plantation systems, and why it is encouraged.

We anticipate some might errantly dismiss perceptions as merely subjective. That is errant because things perceived as real are real in their consequences. But we will oblige the doubters and turn for a look at other numbers. At the time of this writing the most current benchmarks regarding national average poverty thresholds are from the 2019 Census Bureau, and benchmarks regarding national average minimum incomes levels to qualify as middle and upper income are from a 2016 Pew Research Center analysis. The table below shows those poverty thresholds and minimum income levels for household sizes from one to five persons. As a cultural point of reference, these data are from the years toward the end of what just finished as America's longest running bull market (2009–2020).

Household Size	1	2	3	4	5
Poverty Threshold[240]	$13,300	$17,120	$19,998	$26,370	$31,800
Minimum Middle Income[241]	$26,093	$36,902	$45,195	$52,187	$58,347
Minimum Upper Income	$78,281	$110,706	$135,586	$156,561	$175,041

How does your household income bracket compare to others? Why do we even invite the comparison? Not so that you are embarrassed, nor to give you a reason to be prideful, nor to create pressure to increase your income. In fact, we have altruistic motives. We want to help you objectively determine whether your household has enough income and whether it may be time you stop striving for more. To that end we have introduced our concept of the enough-ratio. For some we also want to help you realize that if you're capable of making excess money (that does not involve others suffering in order for you to gain), then it is past time for you to start applying a Partnership Ethic to your current income and future increases.

---

239. Clement, recognizing this tendency so many centuries ago, recommends we humble our pompous nature and submit ourselves and our possessions to a firm, godly guide. See Gonzalez, *Faith and Wealth*, 112–18.

240. Census Bureau, "Poverty Thresholds." (Note: Census Bureau poverty thresholds as a whole are higher amounts than Health and Human Services (HHS) poverty guidelines. For purposes of comparisons to middle and upper income we selected the higher Census Bureau thresholds.)

241. Kochhar, "Middle Class."

You know your household income, and the chart is right in front of you. Take a look. We understand this can be an emotionally charged exploration, but you need to do it with clear eyes, head, and heart. You do not have to share this information with anyone outside your household, we just want you to be informed so that you can get a clear perspective about "what's enough" for your household. If you have beyond enough then this is your reality check that you can clearly invest more in a Partnership Ethic.

The chart above shows minimum middle income levels average 204 percent of the respective poverty thresholds; minimum upper income levels average 300 percent of the respective middle income levels; and upper income levels average 611 percent of the respective poverty thresholds. You can extrapolate the thresholds and income levels if your household comprises more than five people.

What is enough for your household? We've created and offer you the following enough-ratios as both guidance and a reality check of what is enough for any American household, wherever you are physically or in your career: If your household income is more than ten times (10x) the latest Census Bureau poverty threshold, or twice (2x) the latest Pew Research upper income threshold, then you exceed these enough-ratios and you objectively have more than enough income for your household. You have excess to share and can clearly invest more in a Partnership Ethic. What reasons would you have to strive for and accumulate more, beyond being trapped in a plantation system mentality?

Enough-ratios apply to passive income as well. Above we noted that $2.4M net worth is considered wealthy. A modest 4 percent return on that wealth generates income of $96,000, also in the range considered rich for a single person as noted above, as well as exceeding the threshold for upper income based on the Pew analysis. Even in an environment with interest rates and yields as low as they are as of this writing, 4 percent yields can be sustained with conservative, high-quality investments. The math of (enough income) ÷ (yield percentage that can be sustained perpetually without encroaching on the principal) = (enough principal) can be applied in any situation. For instance, (enough income of $96,000 for an individual) ÷ (4% yield) = $2,400,000. What is enough wealth for the "nest egg" thus depends on the all-important determination of what is enough income for yourself or your household.

In countries other than the United States, these 10x and 2x enough-ratios, pegged to similar benchmarks, will likewise provide guidance and a reality check for what is enough. Of course, if your household is middle or upper income yet spends more than its annual income it will never have enough, and that begs analysis around why your household is over-consuming. A direct answer to your specific situation is beyond the scope of this book, but the following wisdom applies.

The environmentalist and author Bill McKibben writes:

> And—this is for me the second lesson—the most curious of all those lives are the human ones, *because we can destroy, but also because we can decide not to destroy.* The turtle does what she does, and magnificently. She can't not do it, though, any more than the beaver can decide to take a break from building dams or the bee from making honey. But if the bird's special gift is flight, ours is the possibility of restraint. We're the only creature who can decide *not* to do something we're capable of doing. That's our superpower, even if we exercise it too rarely.
>
> So, yes, we can wreck the Earth as we've known it, killing vast numbers of ourselves and wiping out entire swaths of other life—in fact, as we've seen, we're doing that right now. But we can also *not* do that....
>
> We have the tools (nonviolence chief among them) to allow us to stand up to the powerful and the reckless, and we have the fundamental idea of human solidarity that we could take as our guide....
>
> Another name for human solidarity is love, and when I think about our world in its present form, that is what overwhelms me. The human love that works to feed the hungry and clothe the naked, the love that comes together in defense of sea turtles and sea ice and of all else around us that is good. The love that lets each of us see we're not the most important thing on earth, and makes us okay with that. (Emphasis in original.)[242]

Contrast our superpower of restraint with a recent news article (and we are confident more will follow) that speculated Jeff Bezos may become the world's first trillionaire, as if this were an admirable goal and not something more than simply a notch in the belt of "a king that ain't satisfied 'til he rules everything."[243] Rather than knowing his wealth, we suspect most of the world would be much more impressed to know how many families Mr. Bezos permanently lifted out of poverty to at least the middle class without, of course, driving other families into poverty. We are all in an uncomfortably similar position to Mr. Bezos; our numbers are different, but the concept is the same.

Now that you know income levels that are enough and more than enough for a Partnership Ethic, what is yours to do?

242 McKibben, *Falter*, 255–56.
243. Sonnemaker, "Jeff Bezos."

Partnership in Practice:

- Identify your household income bracket from the chart above, and determine your desire for income.
- Restrain and limit your income desire to no more than the enough-ratio benchmarks of 10x poverty thresholds or 2x upper-income levels.
- If your present income already exceeds those enough-ratio benchmarks, recognize and accept that you objectively have excess income.
- With a behavioral reset initiated by an objective understanding of what's enough income (and recognition that many of us actually have enough or even excess), begin using both your resources and short life to meaningfully benefit others beyond yourself and your own household.

Of course, if you don't like these action items or have better ideas, we invite you to email us at info@partnershipeconomics.com with your thoughts.

False Idols and False Rewards

A Greyhound named Mine frequently won every heat she ran, and her owners couldn't be more pleased with her winnings. One spring evening at the Palm Beach Kennel Club she ran her fastest race, winning by a full four lengths and scoring her biggest payout ever.

The next day Mine woke up, ate and played, but refused to run. Nothing the trainers did could motivate this otherwise perfect thoroughbred to run. Eventually an animal psychologist was summoned. After a lengthy discussion that confirmed Mine wasn't injured or mistreated, and was well-fed and cared for, the psychologist asked, "Then why won't you run?" To which she replied, "Whatever for? Do you not know? The rabbit's not real." So it is with us and the false idols we've made of our entertainers, athletes, Fortune 500 CEOs, and politicians. So that no one thinks you're getting a pass, recognize we've also made false idols of ourselves with our culture's deeply rooted myth of rugged individualism.

This is being brought to light as we write this section. The world has been forced to stop racing and watch as the COVID-19 pandemic crisis unmasks so many of our flaws, including the truth that our culture creates and supports far too many false idols. With large-scale gatherings like concerts and sporting events shut down, our entertainers and athletes are effectively silenced. For all the adoration and money heaped on them, none of them are capable of pushing back the pandemic or raising the dead. Likewise, the usual power and wealth of our business leaders is muted against this virus. While some American politicians have shined, others have made things worse by acting like the virus would bow to the false idol of American exceptionalism.

We're not criticizing any group for being halted in the face of a worldwide crisis. We are, however, observing a truth and asking those from above, "If you're privileged enough to be overloaded with widespread popularity, or the levers of power, or extreme wealth, and none of it is of meaningful use in a genuine crisis such as a pandemic, then why should We the People continue to bless you with these resources?"

We're also observing this pandemic collapse hierarchical models at breathtaking speed and accelerate cultural shifts. If one such shift is from "me and mine" to "us and we," that would be an unexpected gift borne by the pandemic—the opportunity to reconfigure our culture in almost real time.

Individually and collectively we can make the choice to stop creating false idols out of our entertainers, athletes, business leaders, and politicians. But if we continue to support them and they continue to accept their roles—it is a two-way relationship after all—then we should measure and hold them accountable by other standards. Instead of measuring them by how much income or attention we give them, or the awards they give each other, we need to reset and measure them differently. We recommend measuring them according to the percentage of their incomes or influence they use to improve the lives of others.

Let's introduce that reset, a starting point for how to guide a cultural transformation that is sustainable—moving from false idols to partnership, with a from-above perspective. In a 2018 study that analyzed data from over 1.7 million people in 164 countries, the researchers presented a bold conclusion: the ideal income for individuals is $95,000 (worldwide average and dollar-valued in 2017) a year for life satisfaction, and $60,000 to $75,000 a year for emotional well-being.[244] (That's for individuals; families with children, of course, will need somewhat more.) After that threshold, more income was actually associated with reduced happiness.

With that $95,000-buys-us-satisfaction amount in mind, let's consider the income of our false idols. More specifically, the extraordinary potential they have for partnership in their great income. Let's assume an annual income of $1M for our average false idol. We understand that's a meagerly low number, particular for our sports and entertainment idols, yet it's far

---

244. Fottrell, "Amount of Money to be Happy."

beyond the $95k that brings satisfaction and it'll make for an easy illustration and math. Let's also assume we're only asking our false idols to consider partnering with their income amounts over $1M.

A mere 10 percent donation[245] on income over $1M means anyone with an annual income of just $2M could donate $100,000, leaving 95 percent ($1.9M) of his or her income to spend on themselves (less taxes). A not unusual year's income of $5M for many cultural idols allows for a donation of $400,000, leaving 92 percent ($4.6M) to spend on themselves (less taxes). If you're spending or stockpiling $1.9M/yr (less taxes) or more on yourself, consider that you've been misled into being selfish and you're wasting resources you could certainly put to more intelligent use. If your number is $4.6M (less taxes) or greater, know for certain that you've been misled and that you're wasting resources you could use to meaningfully partner.

Business leaders, like Fortune 500 CEOs who typically reap outsized rewards from the efforts of everyone in their organization,[246] have the unique leadership opportunity to demonstrate the best of a Partnership Ethic, their humanity, and cultural transformation by limiting their total compensation to no more than a generous enough-ratio of forty times (40x) the hourly rate of their lowest paid employee.[247] For example, a company that pays its lowest hourly employee $8/hr. should limit the CEO's total compensation to $640,000/yr. ($8/hr. x 2000 hrs./yr. x 40). Likewise, it could compensate its CEO as much as $1.6M/yr. if it also pays $20/hr. to its lowest paid employee. This generous 40x enough-ratio addresses a number of systemic issues by elegantly performing a number of functions, including, as a tangible connection between the from-above and from-below, as a corporate compliance metric, as a mechanism to establish income equity—fairness, as a corporate justice statement, as a governor to executive compensation creep, and as a tangible measure of sustainability among competitors.

---

245. Nothing prohibits people with this amount of income from donating greater than 10 percent. Also, we acknowledge the reality of taxes on the amount of non-donated income, which of course affects the ultimate amount that can be spent on one's self.

246. The common misconception that CEOs are in charge of corporations shows just how backward our corporate culture has become. The owners—shareholders—of corporations are (supposed to be) in charge, with the board representing them and the CEO managing the organization according to the owners' interests. Far from being a "privilege" for regular shareholders to so much as be heard by CEOs, CEOs are to be agents of the shareholders—they work for us.

247. We expect 40x may feel high to many readers, but compare that to the actual ratio of many prominent companies (warning: prepare for "sticker shock"—many are over 1,000x): https://aflcio.org/paywatch/company-pay-ratios.

Partnership in Practice:

- Identify your false idols and detach from them. Reclaim and redirect the energy and resources you previously wasted on them to something that creates mutual benefit.
- Identify the collective false idols our cultural crises (e.g., the Great Recession, the COVID-19 pandemic, civil unrest, political polarization, etc.) expose and determine how you're going to respond differently through the lens of a Partnership Ethic.
- To those we idolize: stop serving yourself only; leverage your influence going forward to benefit those who need your help and have no way of directly repaying your kindness, but will generate mutual benefit as part of an enriched society.
- Board directors: waste little time ensuring that your highest executive compensation is no more than the enough-ratio maximum of 40x, and within twelve months adjust compensation throughout the organization as needed for equity—fairness.

Of course, if you don't like these action items or have better ideas, we invite you to email us at info@partnershipeconomics.com with your thoughts.

Too Easily Satisfied vs Transformational

Greek mythology tells of the siren (Σειρήν, *seirēn*), a sea nymph typically found on rock outcroppings in shallow waters and along island shores. Through their seductive singing the siren attracts and lures passing sailors close, only to ground and destroy their ships. It's where the term "siren song" originates, which we use to warn each other not to risk being seduced and destroyed.

Modern capitalism has a siren song. You know the basic plot: an eager young entrepreneur launches a one-trick startup that he or she hopes will catch the attention of some behemoth tech company, which they'll then lure into paying an extraordinarily inflated price to acquire the startup. Once in a great while (enough to be newsworthy) that hopeful plan materializes, but most typically that plan crashes and sinks like so many shipwrecks before.

Rather than entrepreneurs being lured by the siren song of being too easily satisfied by that variation of plantation economics (a limited number of people reaping outsized rewards), we call on entrepreneurs to have the desire, courage, and determination to be transformational. To be a transformational entrepreneur is to be a cultural mind-bender that creates and sustains organizations that follow a partnership model. Clarence Jordan (1912–1969), the founder of Koinonia Farm and originator of the "partnership housing" concept that launched Habitat for Humanity, is a blazing bright example of a transformational entrepreneur from our recent past.

We introduced the term *koinonia* earlier. By way of quick refresher, koinonia is a transliteration of the Greek word κοινωνια, which nicely points to the gestalt of Partnership Economics. Our Greek-English lexicon from seminary translates κοινωνια as "contributory help . . . sharing in . . . spiritual fellowship . . . partnership." Jordan was a farmer, New Testament Greek scholar, and author of several popular books including *Cotton Patch Gospel*, later produced as a popular off-Broadway play. He understood clearly the transformational nature of the word *koinonia* he chose to label the many facets of his life: his understanding of Christ's teachings, his life as an intentional reflection of those teachings, and his partnership-based businesses (including farming, mail order, homebuilding, and publishing).

Most if not all the partnership-based businesses founded by or with Jordan continue to operate profitably at least fifty years later. For example, Habitat for Humanity—the manifestation of Jordan's partnership housing initiative—now works in all fifty states in the U.S., in more than seventy countries, and has helped more than twenty-nine million people into safe and affordable shelter. Habitat is perhaps the leading example of a large-scale partnership-based organization. There is endless room at the table for partnership-based organizations of all sizes.

Who and where are the culturally transformational entrepreneurs lured by the kind of voice and song that lured Clarence Jordan? What are they doing that causes us to point to them as culturally transformational? We offer four contemporary examples, a small but mighty sampling, to learn from and contextualize for your purposes.

John Bogle, the founder and longtime chairman of The Vanguard Group, created the first index fund. First ridiculed as "Bogle's Folly" and now among the world's largest investment houses, the company is owned by the funds managed by the company, and is therefore owned by its customers. This effort by Bogle, to offer safer and lower-cost investing to the masses by tying a passively managed investment fund to stock market indexes like the S&P 500, fosters financial transparency that builds trust and profit sharing that builds growth.

Earlier we told of Dan Price, the co-founder/CEO of Gravity Payments. He is known in the business world for his decision in 2015 to give up millions in personal annual compensation so he could afford to pay a minimum annual wage of $70k, beginning with himself, and without increasing costs to his clients. In 2020 Fast Company honored this transformational entrepreneur's pay policy as one of its "World Changing Ideas." In a response worthy of Clarence Jordan's reputed pith, Dan writes, "I'm honored and humbled by this recognition, but I am also deeply saddened by the fact that taking care of your employees by paying them a decent salary is still considered world changing. When are more so-called 'leaders' going to realize that inequality hurts us all?"[248]

Max De Pree, the longtime CEO of furniture innovator Herman Miller, Inc., shares that tribal storytelling teaches and reinforces everyone's commitment to their values, which include "participative management." To that end, De Pree writes, "We know that the soul and spirit, the gifts, the heart and dignity of each of us combine to give the corporation these same qualities. We who invest our lives in Herman Miller are neither the grist of a corporate mill nor the hired guns of distant, mysterious stockholders."[249]

Sharon Koh is the president/CEO of International Ministries (IM). Shortly before she joined IM, this non-profit pivoted from its more than 100-year practice of paying its field missionaries through centralized fundraising efforts. Now the IM missionaries were required to raise their own salaries through individual fundraising. Even if financially necessary, the cultural chasm created between the field missionaries and the home office by this reversal was quick and profound. Almost immediately after taking the helm, and spotting the inequity of her salary still being paid through centralized fundraising efforts, Sharon voluntarily and silently began fundraising for her salary just like her missionaries. Eventually her salary fundraising came to light, which caused an unexpected healing among the missionaries and transformational closing of the chasm. The IM missionaries witnessed their leader willingly place herself under the same rules and financial burdens as them, and perform as they were expected to perform. Following her example, all of Koh's senior staff have since voluntarily engaged in individual fundraising for their salaries. With Koh's kind of leadership, IM will easily see another 100 years.

Partnership in Practice:

- Follow the entrepreneurial model of Clarence Jordan; become culturally transformational by standing up to and dismantling cultural barriers to partnership—like sexism, racism, and ageism.

---

248. Price, "I Cut My Salary."
249. De Pree, *Leadership is an Art,* 89.

- Like the entrepreneurial example of John Bogle, become culturally transformational by creating business models that build trust and growth.
- Create business models that fulfill actual human *needs* rather than artificially created *desires*.
- Follow the entrepreneurial model of Dan Price; become culturally transformational by using your mind and hands to implement the Partnership Ethic "World Changing Idea" piercing your heart.
- Follow the leadership model of Sharon Koh; have and show compassion for your people by bearing the same burdens you place on them.

Know of additional examples? We invite you to tell us about them at info@partnershipeconomics.com.

Comparative Advantage vs Community Advantage

Charlie Munger, Warren Buffett's business partner for decades, doesn't mince words. Speaking to a group of foundation money managers in 1998, near his conclusion he shared some truths that could set free, if the listeners were willing to listen.

> My controversial argument is an additional consideration weighing against the complex, high-cost investment modalities becoming ever more popular at foundations. Even if, contrary to my suspicions, such modalities should turn out to work pretty well, most of the money-making activity would contain profoundly antisocial effects. This would be so because the activity would exacerbate the current, harmful trend in which ever more of the nation's ethical young brainpower is attracted into lucrative money-management and its attendant modern frictions, as distinguished from work providing much more value to others. Money management does not create the right examples. Early Charlie Munger is a horrible career model for the young, because not enough was delivered to civilization in return for what was wrested from capitalism.[250]

Too much of the "nation's ethical young brainpower" are being lured by thoughts of an elusive or illusive bigger piece of the pie; too few are paying attention to the size of the pie itself. Ultimately this is self-defeating. Simply trading around existing value not only fails to grow the pie—it

---

250. Munger, "Institutional Funds Management."

shrinks the pie because of frictional costs (RR1). When the pie shrinks, all pieces—even the bigger ones—are diminished (RR2). Opposite of Partnership Economics, seeking a bigger piece of a shrinking pie results in mutual loss. Partnership Economics is about seeking a bigger pie, so all involved experience gains.

Bogle adds his strong words to Munger's. After speaking about the relentless rules of humble arithmetic that make comparative advantage (out-trading other money movers) mathematically possible only for a minority, Bogle points to a far more advantageous kind of advantage.

> Yet it is within our power to do exactly that, creating a *community* advantage that provides value to *all* investors. Enriching the returns of all investors as a group ought to be a vital goal for society itself... So long as money-making activity simply shifts returns from the pedestrian to the brilliant, or from the unlucky to the lucky, or from those who naively trust the system to those who work at its margin, of course it has "profoundly anti-social effects." Wouldn't making capitalism work better for all stockowners, increasing their returns while holding risk constant, have, well, "profoundly *social* effects"?[251]

Indeed it would! We are well convinced and hopefully by now have well convinced you too, that making capitalism work better for all *stakeholders,* making the whole of economics more mutually beneficial for all involved (including investors), will have even more profound social effects. As Bogle innovated in both theory and practice from the mutual fund to the mutual company and created immense value for many, we endeavor to innovate in both theory and practice from the mutual company to the mutual economy and unleash an even wider ripple of mutual benefit for all. This is the cultural vision of Partnership Economics. We are inspired by Bogle's goal and respond with: *enriching the economic exchanges of all people as a group ought to be a vital goal for every society.* This is our goal, and we expect you'll see the expansive value in partnering in it.

Partnership in Practice:

- Seek to grow the whole pie—this makes everyone's piece bigger, including yours.
- Incentivize work that creates value more than "work" that merely trades already-created value.

---

251. Bogle, *Don't Count On It,* 41.

- Aim high, be bloody bold and resolute—change the culture of capitalism with a ripple effect of mutually beneficial partnership economic exchanges.

Of course, if you don't like these action items or have better ideas, we invite you to email us at info@partnershipeconomics.com with your thoughts.

No Such Thing as Passive Partners

In Part 1 we unmasked our current form of capitalism by properly identifying and referring to it as "plantation economics." We argued plantation economics is harmful to everyone, even the 1 percent who mistakenly think they're winning by acquiring vast sums of money, and pointed to a better form of capitalism.

In Part 2 we named that better form of capitalism "Partnership Economics" and set its foundation by taking familiar concepts and rearranging them in a novel way to yield a different result. (As an inventor does when meeting the legal standards for patentability of new, novel, and non-obvious.) We also provided a vision for why Partnership Economics is not just a better form, but a strongly attractive, desirable, and doable form for capitalism's next reinvention.

In this Part 3 we have blueprinted an introductory framework of Partnership Economics using the constructs of companies, government, professions, and culture. We have supported and fleshed out this framework with tangible, actionable steps that are scalable and can be implemented everywhere. And to what end? To help guide the next reinvention of capitalism.

Capitalism is constantly reinventing itself, usually in small and subtle steps punctuated every few decades by a major disruption. These major disruptions are liminal time. Liminal time is that transitional or indeterminate period between two states or conditions that is described in various terms and ways. Medical professionals have described it as a feeling of suspension as one slips between life and death. When speaking of deep and exhausting spiritual growth, mystics have described that liminal time as the "dark night of the soul." The economic liminal time from the crash of 1929 and up to about a decade later we call the Great Depression.

From the vantage point of 2020, the global community appears to be entering a liminal time. As the global community navigates this disruptive time, where the entire world is simultaneously suffering from and trying to respond to a powerful economic disruption, we have the opportunity to intentionally and comparatively swiftly reinvent capitalism from plantation economics to Partnership Economics. The relentless rules are relentless as ever and are still holding true, so they remain foundational building blocks during and beyond this economically leveling pandemic.

What does this reinvention look like? It begins with us all participating rather than spectating. We can't sit on the sidelines wishing things were better. There is no such thing as passive partnership. Partnership involves actively working together for results that benefit as many stakeholders as possible. Going forward no investor should ever be passive, and "activist investor" should not be a slur but a duty. In addition to all the Partnership in Practice actionables listed in this Part 3, the following are starter examples of inventive steps, based on this book, you might create and contextualize to your situation.

- For businesses and their leaders: move public corporate earnings reporting from quarterly to at least semi-annually as a first step toward redirecting the focus away from short-term and limited perspectives.

- For governments, elected officials, and civil servants: apply an enough-ratio to military spending. Our nation has more than enough armament to destroy everyone on the planet. Limit military spending to an enough-ratio that never exceeds more than our federal government's spending for environment management (infrastructure building and maintenance, and creation care for our fifty states and territories) or its collective spending for free public education (preK–12 plus two years of junior college) for all its residents.

- For every professional: stop running your profession like a competition. Instead, practice your profession like a ministry that provides physically, financially, spiritually, and socially for both you and your every client.

- For individuals and our collective culture: publicly praise those who use their wealth to financially advance others, beyond their own families. Reward those who do so with the opportunity to make more wealth. Make "making and partnering" the new competitive game of a reinvented capitalism.

Partnership in Practice:

- Select and implement a suggestion or Partnership in Practice action item described in this Part 3. Really—do one. There is no such thing as passive partners.

- Create, contextualize, and implement your own Partnership in Practice action items. Don't worry, you won't run out of possibilities. There is no such thing as passive partners.

When you implement a Partnership in Practice action item or create one of your own, we'd love to hear about it. We invite you to email us at info@partnershipeconomics.com with your thoughts.

Chapter 16

So What? Where Do We Go from Here?

"We but mirror the world. All the tendencies present in the outer world are to be found in the world of our body. If we could change ourselves, the tendencies in the world would also change. As a man changes his own nature, so does the attitude of the world change towards him. This is the divine mystery supreme. A wonderful thing it is and the source of our happiness. We need not wait to see what others do."

—Mahatma Gandhi

Relentless Rules and Partnership Economic Ethic Reminder

1. Frictional costs are in every economic exchange.
2. Therefore merely transferring existing value is a losing proposition.
3. Therefore exchanges must create value greater than frictional costs to produce a true net gain.
4. We are they, and we, altogether, are average.
5. I gain/lose when we gain/lose, and we gain/lose when we all gain/lose.
   - God provides and we partner.
   - To partner is to seek mutual benefit.

- Mutual benefit is created by engaging in exchanges that are profitable for our self *and* the other—pursuing our economic neighbor's interest *and* our self-interest.
- Corporately our purpose is to sustain profitability for all stakeholders.

Because of the relentless rules of economics, the Partnership Economic Ethic is to love your economic neighbor as yourself.

Simple but Not Easy

"You can't always get what you want . . . But if you try sometimes, well, you might find, you get what you need."
—Mick Jagger and Keith Richards

As we near the end of this book we envision you thinking, "I get it. I get the need and vision for Partnership Economics. But can this really be implemented? Really?" We get your concern, even your disbelief. We have been asking ourselves a similar question since before we began writing: "Is it possible for us as individuals, companies, nations, and as a world to pivot in order to save ourselves and each other?"

When COVID-19 burst onto the global stage, a worldwide slowdown occurred. Then we witnessed an increasingly coordinated global response. As challenging as the pandemic is, it has also shown that we are capable of pivoting relatively quickly and on a global scale and implementing necessary changes and innovations (understandably some have been more willing and effective than others). So, yes, the world is capable of pivoting from the continued threat of plantation systems and implementing the remedy of Partnership Economics (understandably some will be more willing and effective than others).

Take as just one example the relatively fast workplace transformation that occurred during the early weeks of the global shutdown. For decades prior to the global shutdown, countless concerns about remote work were said to be impossible to address. In corporate America, for instance, examining and commenting on the issues of employee work-life balance, employee adaptation of technology, and employee engagement have long been cottage industries with little meaningful progress. Then the days surrounding the

So What? Where Do We Go from Here?

global shutdown saw most corporations and government agencies quickly invest the time and expense to move to entirely virtual platforms and remote access for their employees whose physical presence wasn't an absolute requirement.

The immediate results of the workplace transformation include many people able to work from home (WFH) and realize an improved work-life balance (with mixed but majority of positive results as of this writing); older employees learning the technology needed for WFH (and discovering they are quite capable if they do not resist); and managers supervising remotely which creates the breathing room for WFH employees to be self-directed and more efficient (or at least enables the managers to determine which WFH employees are or are not engaged).

While awaiting vaccines, the concepts of physical distancing and wearing face coverings to reduce infections from a virus that spreads through the air are simple, but not easy to implement and maintain. Many have appreciated the evidence-based need to make these behavioral changes for their own self-interest and the interests of others. These behaviors demonstrate mutuality and a Partnership Ethic, and lives are better off for the understanding and discipline in making these behavioral changes. Many also have struggled with making behavioral changes for their own self-interest, let alone the interest of others. As with behavioral economics, ignorance, uncertainty, and confusion are unfortunately strong factors. These factors inhibit us from experiencing mutual benefit and a Partnership Ethic, and lives are worse off because of these behavioral challenges.

You have stories of successes and struggles from your pandemic response experience. The various successes point to our intelligently creating our response to a coronavirus-threatened world. The various struggles point to the truth that our journey to a world relatively unburdened by COVID-19 won't be easy because not everyone will partner; nevertheless, we have to continue the work until we eventually realize the healthy physical world we need. This serves as an object lesson and analogy for our journey to a world relatively unburdened by plantation economics, which likewise won't be easy because not everyone will partner. Ignorance, uncertainty, and confusion are persistent challenges. Nevertheless, we have to continue the work until we eventually realize the healthy economic world we need.

Change is not easy and it's not automatic. No positive change happens automatically—it happens with tremendous effort: intentional, strategic, loving, mutually beneficial effort that is both intense and sustained. If it's not intense enough, it won't make a difference; and if it's not sustained, whatever difference it makes for a moment won't last. Our efforts must be intense enough to effect change and sustained enough for such positive change to take root.

When's the last time any room in your home became cleaner all on its own? When has your health ever improved automatically? When, with no effort, has your knowledge ever increased? The "gravity" of our world is a tendency toward deterioration, not improvement. Simply maintaining anything of quality requires considerable effort; all the more effort is required to create improvement.

The civil rights movement in 1960s America demonstrated at the social level this same truth of the effort required to create positive change. We should not expect the work of improving capitalism, the way in which we conduct economics, to be any easier. We believe it can be done, but merely believing change can happen is not the same as change actually happening. Talking about the change that needs to happen is important, but talk alone won't create change either—especially talk about what other people should do.

At the end of each day, our effort to change how we ourselves do economics—how we handle our individual affairs, how we handle our business, how we handle our profession, how we handle the corporations that we ultimately own, and how we handle our civic responsibilities to vote for politicians and support policies that frame our economic landscape—is change that, in fact, we can make. We can each make change, in our sphere of influence, starting with ourselves, each day. Because of the relentless rule that we are all interconnected economically (RR4), changing how we do business, how we do capitalism, will interconnect with others and lead to change that ripples outward.

What can we, individually and collectively, do to begin the transforming initiative from plantation to Partnership Economics? We begin with the necessary work of changing the heads and hearts that move the hands. Do not be afraid; be bold and bloody resolute!

Not Easy but Worthwhile

"Make no mistake about it: Change is hard, but change is necessary."

—Lori Lightfoot

Imagine you are hiking through a beautifully dense forest. You sit down to rest when, silently, a creature vaguely resembling a human materializes before you. Without it speaking, you understand it wants to show you the difference between hell and heaven. You are stunned but curious, and not feeling threatened you nod your agreement.

You follow the creature with your eyes as it glides toward then around you. Standing and turning around, you see before you an ancient wood door surrounded by a stone doorway, as if these had been there forever. Just a door frame and door, which you can see behind is the path and forest you just traveled. The creature reaches for the doorknob, swings open the door, and beckons you to follow.

Stepping through the doorway you find yourself in a cavernous banquet hall filled with those large round tables common to conference rooms around the world. Sitting at the tables are people of every possible description and background, trying to eat the abundant food heaped in the middle. You quickly notice each person's arms are longer than normal and misproportioned in the oddest way. From shoulder to elbow is half the usual distance, and from elbow to hand is three times the usual distance. The effect is that while everyone can reach the food, their arms do not bend in a way that allows them to bring food to their own mouth. Throughout the banquet hall what looks like and, is in fact, a perpetual food fight, is the result of angry and hungry people screaming and tossing food into the air and trying to catch it with their mouths, but mostly missing. Sporadically food lands in each person's mouth, and occasionally there is an astoundingly obese person who has mastered the ability to catch food in his or her mouth.

Exiting the banquet hall and closing the door behind you both, the creature communicates, "This shows you hell, created by people with free will. Hell is here on earth and you need not look elsewhere for it." Pushing the same door open again, the creature steps through and you follow. You both are back in the same room with the same people and their weird arms. Food is still stacked in the center of each table. The difference in this room is that everyone has learned to reach the food and use their long arms to feed each other. There is no food fight atmosphere, no anger or hunger, and although some have more than others, no one has less than then they can reasonably eat to be filled. The creature turns to you but it does not need to communicate anything because you say it aloud: "This is heaven, here on earth created by people with free will, and I do not need to look elsewhere for it." The creature nods, bows, and disappears along with the door and doorway. In gratitude you resume a better journey with your new mind-set.

We do not need to belabor the analogy. You understand hell is plantation system economics and heaven is Partnership Economics. We do, however, emphasize that this illustration of Partnership Economics meshes with the teachings of Jesus. And with Adam Smith's structure for economics in his books *Theory* and *Wealth*. And with Ayn Rand's philosophy of self-interest and exchange she has John Galt voice in *Atlas Shrugged*. And with the "where do we go from here" vision of Dr. Martin Luther King Jr.

We do not expect moving from our collective and familiar hell to an enlightened heaven will be easy, primarily because it will require most if not all of us to change our mind-sets and do hard work. We might even say with real work and with real ministry. But it will be worthwhile and successful because Partnership Economics is supported by those four luminaries and because it builds on rules of economics that are as relentless as gravity. Those invested in plantation economics may push back on that claim, and the more invested the louder the push-back. We just encourage them to push back intelligently and thoughtfully, or they will undermine their own position and help the rest of us carry the case for Partnership Economics and better capitalism. Better yet, we invite them instead to direct their energy to testing this transformation from plantation to Partnership Economics and proving the results for themselves.

How Does the Story End?

"A journey of a thousand miles begins with one step."

—Lao Tzu

Our economic story is not finished nor static nor predetermined. It is a work in progress, with every day bringing new decisions and interactions and therefore new opportunities as well as challenges. Economics is too important and too far-reaching to leave in the realm of ignorance, uncertainty, and confusion, and it is too powerful to leave in the destructive plantation mode.

Quite apart from any ideology or preference, there are relentless rules of economics, culminating in "we are they" and economic gains or losses happening with inescapable mutuality. Because of these realities that simply *are*, we all stand to gain by partnering economically: intentionally seeking mutual benefit, economically exchanging in ways that advance our individual self-interest *and* the interest of our economic partners. Corporately, because of the same underlying and relentless rules of economics, we all stand to gain by partnering economically: sustaining profitability for all stakeholders.

Re-viewing plantation economics in their destructiveness is necessary—but not sufficient. Re-thinking economics in more constructive ways, namely partnership, is also necessary—but also not sufficient. Economic gains do not come from viewing or thinking but from taking action in light of gainful viewing and thinking—the re-living! Ultimately it is what we do, how we actually live, that tilts our economics toward either plantation or partnership, from individual interactions up to the whole of capitalism.

No matter how severe the shortcomings of plantation economics or how high the potential of Partnership Economics, positive change is anything but automatic. We have to choose, decide, take action.

- Deuteronomy 30:19—"I call heaven and earth to witness against you today, that I have set before you life and death, blessing and curse. Therefore *choose* life, that you and your offspring may live" (emphasis ours).

- Jesus, in Matthew 7:24–27—"Everyone then who hears these words of mine *and does them* will be like a wise person who built a house on the rock. And the rain fell, and the floods came, and the winds blew and beat on that house, but it did not fall, because it had been founded on the rock. And everyone who hears these words of mine *and does not do them* will be like a foolish person who built a house on the sand. And the rain fell, and the floods came, and the winds blew and beat against that house, and it fell, and great was its fall" (emphasis ours).

- Adam Smith, in *Wealth of Nations*—"Nobody but a beggar *chuses* [chooses] to depend chiefly upon the benevolence of his fellow-citizens" (emphasis ours).

- Ayn Rand, in the voice of her alter-ego John Galt—"Now *choose* to perish or to learn that the anti-mind is the anti-life. . . . Man has to be man—by *choice*; he has to hold his life as a value—by *choice*; he has to learn to sustain it—by *choice*; he has to discover the values it requires and practice his virtues—by *choice*" (emphasis ours).

- Martin Luther King Jr., in *Where Do We Go from Here*—"I'm not talking about emotional bosh when I talk about love, I'm talking about a strong, demanding, love. . . . I have *decided* to love. If you are seeking the highest good, I think you can find it through love" (emphasis ours).

And what, exactly, would be most beneficial to choose, decide, act on?

- Jesus—"Love your neighbor as yourself."

- Adam Smith, in *Wealth of Nations*—"He will be more likely to prevail if he can interest their self-love in his favour, and shew [show] them that it is for their own advantage to do for him what he requires of them."

- Ayn Rand, via Galt's speech—"Neither love nor fame nor cash is a value if obtained by fraud. . . . It is only with their mind that I can deal, and only for my own self-interest, when they see that my interest coincides with theirs."
- Martin Luther King Jr., in *Where Do We Go from Here*—"A true alliance is based upon some self-interest of each component group and a common interest into which they merge."

Partnership Economics' great potential and mutual benefit is tied to our willingness to *choose* to act on its painful revelations and transforming initiatives. Plantation economics leads to destruction; Partnership Economics leads to flourishing, profitable life. The choice is *yours and ours* to act on, every day. What's yours to do? Get started; there's nothing to it but to do it. Take the first step.

Better capitalism is found in this: *love your economic neighbor as yourself.*

Recommended Further Reading

As you read and reread *Better Capitalism*, you may find these authors interesting through the lens of Partnership Economics.

Binyamin Appelbaum, *The Economists' Hour: False Prophets, Free Markets, and the Fracture of Society*

Sheila Bair, "Reforming Mortgage Finance," *Business Economics* 43 (October 2008) 13–16

Joel Bakan, *The Corporation: The Pathological Pursuit of Profit and Power* (book and documentary film)

The Bible

John Bogle, *The Battle for the Soul of Capitalism*

John Bogle, *Enough*

Louis Brandeis, *Other People's Money and How the Bankers Use It*

Luke Bretherton, "'Neither a Borrower Nor a Lender Be'?" in *Crunch Time: A Call To Action*

Clayborne Carson, ed., *The Autobiography of Martin Luther King Jr.*

Ed Catmull, *Creativity, Inc.: Overcoming the Unseen Forces that Stand in the Way of True Inspiration*

Chuck Collins and Mary Wright, *The Moral Measure of the Economy*

Russell Conwell, *Acres of Diamonds*

Neil deMause and Joanna Cagan, *Field of Schemes*

Max De Pree, *Leadership is an Art*

Frederick Downing, *Clarence Jordan: A Radical Pilgrimage in Scorn of the Consequences*

Pope Francis, *Fratelli Tutti (Brothers All): On Fraternity and Social Friendship*

Milton Friedman, *Capitalism and Freedom*

Millard Fuller, *Theology of the Hammer*

David Gushee and Glen Stassen, *Kingdom Ethics,* 2d edition

Thich Nhat Hanh, *The Art of Power*

Rebecca Henderson, *Reimagining Capitalism in a World on Fire*

Napoleon Hill, *Think and Grow Rich*

Martin Luther King Jr., *I Have a Dream: Writings & Speeches that Changed the World*

Martin Luther King Jr., *Where Do We Go From Here: Chaos or Community?*

Michael Kirwan, *Political Theology: An Introduction*

Charles Koch, *Good Profit: How Creating Value for Others Built One of the World's Most Successful Companies*

Robert Monks, *Corpocracy*

Robert Monks and Nell Minow, *Corporate Governance*

Netflix video series *Dirty Money*

Michael Porter and Mark Kramer, "Creating Shared Value," *Harvard Business Review* 89, no. 1 (January–February 2011) 2–17

Dan Price, *Worth It*

Ayn Rand, *Atlas Shrugged*

Jeffrey Sachs, *The End of Poverty: Economic Possibilities for Our Time*

Adam Smith, *The Theory of Moral Sentiments (Moral Sentiments)*

Adam Smith, *An Inquiry into the Nature and Causes of the Wealth of Nations (Wealth of Nations)*

Philip Smith and Manfred Max-Neff, *Economics Unmasked: From Power and Greed to Compassion and the Common Good*

Vernon Visick and J. Mark Thomas, eds., *God and Capitalism: A Prophetic Critique of Market Economy*

Tim Wu, *The Curse of Bigness*

Luigi Zingales, *A Capitalism for the People*

Bibliography

Amadeo, Kimberly, and Michael J. Boyle. "The U.S. Debt and How It Got So Big." thebalance.com (July 2020). https://www.thebalance.com/the-u-s-debt-and-how-it-got-so-big-3305778.

Batnick, Michael. "Bogle's Big Mistake." *theirrelevantinvestor.com* (January 2019). https://theirrelevantinvestor.com/2019/01/19/bogles-big-mistake/.

Betz, Hans Dieter. *The Sermon on the Mount*. Hermeneia: A Critical and Historical Commentary on the Bible. Minneapolis: Fortress, 1995.

Bogle, John C. *Don't Count On It!: Reflection on Investment Illusions, Capitalism, "Mutual" Funds, Indexing, Entrepreneurship, Idealism, and Heroes*. Hoboken, NJ: John Wiley & Sons, 2011.

———. *Enough: True Measures of Money, Business & Life*. Hoboken: John Wiley & Sons, 2009.

———. "The Policy Portfolio in an Era of Subdued Returns." June 2003. http://johncbogle.com/speeches/JCB_IASC0603.pdf.

Bretherton, Luke. "'Neither a Borrower nor a Lender Be'? Scripture, Usury and the Call for Responsible Lending." In *Crunch Time: A Call to Action*, edited by Angus Ritchie, 17–34. London: Lulu, 2010.

Bower, Joseph L., and Lynn S. Paine. "The Error at the Heart of Corporate Leadership." *Harvard Business Review* 95, no. 3 (May–June 2017) 50–60.

Buckley, Tim. "A Look Back at the Life of Vanguard's Founder." *vanguardcanada.ca* (January 2019). https://www.vanguardcanada.ca/advisors/v/jack-bogle-a-look-back.htm.

Buffett, Warren. "Berkshire Hathaway Letters to Shareholders." https://www.goodreads.com/work/quotes/25195056.

Bureau of Economic Analysis. "Gross Domestic Product: Fourth Quarter 2008 (Final) Corporate Profits: Fourth Quarter 2008 (Final)." *bea.gov* (March 2009). https://www.bea.gov/news/2009/gross-domestic-product-fourth-quarter-2008-final-and-corporate-profits.

Burton, Jonathan. "Opinion: Jack Bogle Gave Individual Investors The Power to Triumph Over Wall Street." *marketwatch.com* (January 2019). https://www.marketwatch.com/story/bogle-gave-individual-investors-the-power to-triumph-over-wall-street-2019-01 16.

Business Roundtable. "Statement on the Purpose of a Corporation." *opportunity.businessroudtable.org* (August 2019). https://opportunity.businessroundtable.org/ourcommitment/.

Buss, Dale. "Home Depot Co-Founder Bernie Marcus Challenges CEOs to Fight U.S. Flirtation with Socialism." *chiefexecutive.net* (January 2020). https://chiefexecutive.net/home-depot-co-founder-bernie-marcus-challenges-ceos-to-fight-u-s-flirtation-with-socialism/.

Carson, Clayborne, ed. *The Autobiography of Martin Luther King Jr.* New York: Warner, 1998.

Census Bureau. "Poverty Thresholds." *census.gov* (April 2020). https://www.census.gov/data/tables/time-series/demo/income-poverty/historical-poverty-thresholds.html.

———. "Statistical Abstract of the United States: 2008." *census.gov* (2008). http://www.census.gov/prod/2007pubs/08abstract/pop.pdf.

———. "Table 753. Corporations–Selected Financial Items: 1990 to 2008." *census.gov* (2012). http://www.census.gov/compendia/statab/2012/tables/12s0753.pdf.

Chernow, Ron. *Titan: The Life of John D. Rockefeller, Sr.* New York: Random House, 2004.

Claiborne, Shane. *The Irresistible Revolution: Living as an Ordinary Radical.* Grand Rapids: Zondervan, 2006.

Clardy, Alan. "Galt's Gulch: Ayn Rand's Utopian Delusion." *Utopian Studies* vol. 23, issue 1 (2012) 238–62.

Collins, James C. *Good to Great.* New York: HarperCollins, 2001.

Collins, James C., and Jerry I. Porras. *Built to Last: Successful Habits of Visionary Companies.* New York: HarperBusiness, 1994.

Comptroller of the Currency. "31st Comptroller, Joseph M. Otting." occ.treas.gov. https://www.occ.treas.gov/about/who-we-are/comptroller/bio-comptroller-joseph-otting.html.

Cranley, Ellen. "Haircut, Flights, and an Alumni Club: Here Are the Perks Members of Congress Get That the General Public Doesn't." businessinsider.com (January 2019). https://www.businessinsider.com/perks-members-of-congress-get-that-the-general-public-doesnt-2018-12.

Croce, Brian. "Builder 100: The Top 25 Private Companies." https://www.builderonline.com/builder-100/builder-100-the-top-25-private-companies_o.

De Pree, Max. *Leadership is an Art.* New York: Doubleday, 2004.

Deloitte. "Corporate Tax Rates 2020." *www2.deloitte.com.* https://www2.deloitte.com/content/dam/Deloitte/global/Documents/Tax/dttl-tax-corporate-tax-rates.pdf.

deMause, Neil. "Falcons Could Accept $200M Hotel-tax Subsidy as Early as Monday." *fieldofscemes.com* (February 2013). http://www.fieldofschemes.com/2013/02/01/4474/falcons-could-accept-200m-hotel-tax-subsidy-as-early-as-monday/.

———. "Georgia Supreme Court to Hear Appeals of Falcons, Braves Bond Sales." *fieldofschemes.com* (October 2014). http://www.fieldofschemes.com/2014/10/29/8042/georgia-supreme-court-to-hear-appeals-of-falcons-braves-bond-sales/.

———. "Why are Georgia Taxpayers Paying $700M for a New NFL Stadium? *theguardian.com* (September 2017). https://www.theguardian.com/sport/2017/sep/29/why-are-georgia-taxpayers-paying-700m-for-a-new-nfl-stadium.

Denning, Steve. "The Origin of 'The World's Dumbest Idea': Milton Friedman." *Forbes.com* (June 2013). https://www.forbes.com/sites/stevedenning/2013/06/26/the-origin-of-the-worlds-dumbest-idea-milton-friedman/#27949524870e.

Bibliography

———. "The 'Pernicious Nonsense' of Maximizing Shareholder Value." *Forbes.com* (April 2017). https://www.forbes.com/sites/stevedenning/2017/04/27/harvard-business-review-the-pernicious-nonsense-of-maximizing-shareholder-value/#21ad60f371fo.

Department of Labor. "Improving Investment Advice for Workers & Retirees." *dol.gov.* https://www.dol.gov/agencies/ebsa/about-ebsa/our-activities/resource-center/fact-sheets/improving-investment-advice-for-workers-and-retirees.

Director of National Intelligence. "Background to 'Assessing Russian Activities and Intentions in Recent U.S. Elections': The Analytic Process and Cyber Incident Attribution." *dni.gov* (January 2017). https://www.dni.gov/files/documents/ICA_2017_01.pdf.

Economist, The. "America's Public-sector Pension Schemes are Trillions of Dollars Short." *economist.com* (November 2019). https://www.economist.com/finance-and-economics/2019/11/14/americas-public-sector-pension-schemes-are-trillions-of-dollars-short.

———. "Facebook Unveils Details of Its Content-oversight Board." *economist.com* (January 2020). https://www.economist.com/business/2020/01/30/facebook-unveils-details-of-its-content-oversight-board.

Edelman. "2020 Edelman Trust Barometer." *edelman.com* (January 2020). https://www.edelman.com/trustbarometer.

Edly. "Invest in Student Success." *edly.co.* https://www.edly.co/.

Encyclopedia.com. "Atlas Shrugged-Criticism." *encyclopedia.com* (November 2020). https://www.encyclopedia.com/arts/educational-magazines/atlas-shrugged#Introduction.

Facebook. "Facebook Q2 2020 Earnings." *investor.fb.com* (July 2020). https://investor.fb.com/investor-events/?section=pastevents.

———. "Facebook Q3 2016 Earnings." *investor.fb.com* (November 2016). https://investor.fb.com/investor-events/?section=pastevents.

Federal Election Commission. "Statistical Summary of 24-month Campaign Activity of the 2015–2016 Election Cycle." *fec.gov* (March 2017). https://www.fec.gov/updates/statistical-summary-24-month-campaign-activity-2015-2016-election-cycle/.

Fein, Ester B. "Book Notes." *nytimes.com* (November 1991). https://www.nytimes.com/1991/11/20/books/book-notes-059091.html.

Fottrell, Quentin. "Psychologists Say They've Found the Exact Amount of Money You Need to be Happy." *marketwatch.com* (March 2018). https://www.marketwatch.com/story/this-is-exactly-how-much-money-you-need-to-be-truly-happy-earning-more-wont-help-2018-02-14.

Freiburger, Calvin. "Ted Cruz Offers Three Solutions to Big Tech Censorship of Conservative, Pro-life speech." *lifesitenews.com* (April 2019). https://www.lifesitenews.com/news/ted-cruz-offers-three-solutions-to-big-tech-censorship-of-conservative-pro-life-speech.

Friedman, Milton. "The Social Responsibility of Business is to Increase its Profits." *nytimes.com* (September 1970). https://graphics8.nytimes.com/packages/pdf/business/miltonfriedman1970.pdf.

Friedman, Zack. "Student Loan Debt Statistics In 2020: A Record $1.6 Trillion." *forbes.com* (February 2020). https://www.forbes.com/sites/zackfriedman/2020/02/03/student-loan-debt-statistics/#7b84e603281f.

Fuller, Millard. *The Theology of the Hammer.* Macon, GA: Smyth & Helwys, 1994.
Gardner, Matthew, Lorena Roque, and Steve Wamhoff. "Corporate Tax Avoidance in the First Years of the Trump Tax Law." *itep.org* (December 2019). https://itep.org/corporate-tax-avoidance-in-the-first-year-of-the-trump-tax-law/.
Gardner, Tom. "Jack Bogle on Index Funds, Vanguard, and Investing Advice." *The Motley Fool* (January 2019). https://www.nasdaq.com/articles/jack-bogle-index-funds-vanguard-and-investing-advice-2019-01-17.
Gelles, David, and David Yaffe-Bellany. "Shareholder Value is no Longer Everything, Top C.E.O.s Say." *nytimes.com* (April 19, 2019). https://www.nytimes.com/2019/08/19/business/business-roundtable-ceos-corporations.html.
Gonzalez, Justo L. *Faith and Wealth: A History of Early Christian Ideas on the Origin, Significance, and Use of Money.* San Francisco: Harper & Row, 1992.
Gravity Payments. "Dan Price." *gravitypayments.com*. https://gravitypayments.com/dan-price/.
———. "$70K Minimum Wage Initial Results." *gravitypayments.com*. https://gravitypayments.com/thegravityof70k/#infographic-1.
Guelich, Robert A. *The Sermon on the Mount: A Foundation for Understanding.* Waco, TX: Word, 1982.
Gushee, David P., and Glen H. Stassen. *Kingdom Ethics: Following Jesus in Contemporary Context.* 2d ed. Grand Rapids: Eerdmans, 2016.
Habitat for Humanity. "Annual Reports and 990 Forms." *habitat.org*. https://www.habitat.org/about/annual-reports-990s.
Hanna, Jason, and Sarah Moon. "PG&E's Failure to Maintain Transmission Tower Helped Lead to the Deadly Camp Fire, Report Says." *cnn.com* (December 2019). https://www.cnn.com/2019/12/03/us/pge-transmission-lines-camp-fire/index.html.
Hörisch, Felix. "Co-Determining the Future." *fesdc.org* (December 2018). https://www.fesdc.org/news-list/e/co-determining-the-future/#.
———. "The Macro-economic Effect of Codetermination on Income Equality." *mzes.uni-mannheim.de* (2012). https://www.mzes.uni-mannheim.de/publications/wp/wp-147.pdf.
Hrushka, Anna. "OCC Bans Ex-Wells Fargo CEO, Fines Him $17.5M Over Fake Accounts Scandal." *bankingdive.com* (January 2020). https://www.bankingdive.com/news/occ-bans-ex-wells-fargo-ceo-fines-fake-accounts-scandal/570998/.
Investopedia. "Everything You Need to Know About the DOL Fiduciary Rule." *investopedia.com* (December 2019). https://www.investopedia.com/updates/dol-fiduciary-rule/.
IRS. "Tax Code, Regulations and Official Guidance." *irs.gov* (May 2020). https://www.irs.gov/privacy-disclosure/tax-code-regulations-and-official-guidance.
Johnson, Sydney. "Wall Street Wants in on Income-share Agreements." *edsurge.com* (April 2019). https://www.edsurge.com/news/2019-04-05-wall-street-wants-in-on-income-share-agreements.
Kagan, Julia. "What is a Pension Shortfall?" *investopedia.com* (November 2019). https://www.investopedia.com/terms/p/pensionshortfall.asp#:~:text=A%20pension%20shortfall%20means%20that,greatly%20reduce%20the%20fund's%20assets.
Keegan, Paul. "Here's What Really Happened at That Company That Set a $70,000 Minimum Wage." *inc.com* (November 2015). https://www.inc.com/magazine/201511/paul-keegan/does-more-pay-mean-more-growth.html.

Bibliography

King, James. "It's Crazy, Right?" Sermon preached August 4, 2019, at Parkway Baptist Church, Johns Creek, GA.

Kochhar, Rakesh. "The American Middle Class is Stable in Size, But Losing Ground Financially to Upper-income Families." *pewresearch.org* (September 2018). https://www.pewresearch.org/fact-tank/2018/09/06/the-american-middle-class-is-stable-in-size-but-losing-ground-financially-to-upper-income-families.

Latonero, Mark. "Can Facebook's Oversight Board Win People's Trust?" *hbr.org* (January 29, 2020). https://hbr.org/2020/01/can-facebooks-oversight-board-win-peoples-trust?utm_medium=email&utm_source=newsletter_daily&utm_campaign=dailyalert_activesubs&utm_content=signinnudge&referral=00563&deliveryName=DM66537.

Library of Congress. "Books That Shaped America." *loc.gov* (July 2012). https://www.loc.gov/item/prn-12-123/.

Liptak, Adam. "Justices, 5–4, Reject Corporate Spending Limit." *nytimes.com* (January 2010). http://www.nytimes.com/2010/01/22/us/politics/22scotus.html.

Little, Becky. "Details of Brutal First Slave Voyages Discovered." *history.com* (March 2019). https://www.history.com/news/transatlantic-slave-first-ships-details.

Los Angeles Times. "Facebook Needs, Wants, Must Have Regulation, Zuckerberg Says." *latimes.com* (February 2020). https://www.latimes.com/business/technology/story/2020-02-17/facebook-needs-regulation-zuckerberg.

Ludema, Jim, and Amber Johnson. "Gravity Payment's Dan Price On How He Measures Success After His $70k Experiment." *forbes.com* (April 28, 2018). https://www.forbes.com/sites/amberjohnson-jimludema/2018/08/28/gravity-payments-dan-price-on-how-he-measures-success-after-his-70k-experiment/#39af7747174b.

Luz, Ulrich. *Matthew 1–7.* Continental Commentary, vol. 1. Translated by Wilhelm C. Linss. Minneapolis: Fortress, 1989.

Malito, Alessandra. "The Fiduciary Rule is Officially Dead. What its Fate Means to You." *marketwatch.com* (June 2018). https://www.marketwatch.com/story/is-the-fiduciary-rule-dead-or-alive-what-its-fate-means-to-you-2018-03-16.

Management Centre, The. "Cultures eats strategy for breakfast." https://www.managementcentre.co.uk/management-consultancy/culture-eats-strategy-for-breakfast.

McKibben, Bill. *Falter: Has the Human Game Begun to Play Itself Out?* New York: Henry Holt, 2019.

Molander, Beverly. "Beyond All Odds, Chief Justice Carol W. Hunstein." *Attorney at Law Magazine* vol. 1, no.5 (December 2012) 8–10.

Munger, Charles. "Charlie Munger on Institutional Funds Management." *valuewalk.com* (October 1998). https://www.valuewalk.com/wp-content/uploads/2014/06/Charlie_Munger_on_Institutional_Funds_Management.pdf.

Niebuhr, Reinhold. *Moral Man and Immoral Society: A Study in Ethics and Politics.* Louisville: Westminster John Knox, 1932.

Nouwen, Henri. *A Spirituality of Fundraising.* Nashville: Upper Room, 2010.

Oates, Stephen B. *Let The Trumpet Sound: A Life of Martin Luther King Jr.* New York: HarperPerennial, 1992.

OpenSecrets. "Annual Lobbying By Facebook Inc." *opensecrets.org*. https://www.opensecrets.org/federal-lobbying/clients/summary?cycle=2019&id=D000033563.

———. "Lobbying Data Summary." *opensecrets.org*. http://www.opensecrets.org/federal-lobbying/.

Passan, Jeff. "Rays to Explore Splitting Games with Montreal." *espn.com* (June 2019). https://www.espn.com/mlb/story/_/id/27016429/rays-explore-splitting-games-montreal.

Pay it Forward. "An Open Letter to the 2020 Presidential Candidates: It's Time to Tax Us More." *medium.com* (June 2019). (https://medium.com/@letterforawealthtax/an-open-letter-to-the-2020-presidential-candidates-its-time-to-tax-us-more-6eb3a548b2fe.

PG&E Corporation. "2007 Corporate Responsibility Report." *pgecorp.com* (2007). http://www.pgecorp.com/corp_responsibility/reports/2007/business/our-vision.html#:~:text=Our%20Vision%20and%20Values,utility%20in%20the%20United%20States.&text=Our%20vision%20and%20goals%20are,times%20at%20every%20touch%20point.

———. "Company Profile." *pge.com* (2020). https://www.pge.com/en_U.S./about-pge/company-information/profile/profile.page.

Price, Dan. "In 2015 I Cut My Salary and Announced a $70k Minimum Wage at Gravity Payments." https://www.facebook.com/DanPriceSeattle/posts/in-2015-i-cut-my-salary-and-announced-a-$70k-minimum-wage-at-gravity-payments5-ye/1465310090319664/.

Rand, Ayn. *Atlas Shrugged*. New York: Signet, 1992.

Rae, John. *Life of Adam Smith*. London: Macmillan, 1895.

Reeves, Stephen K. "Day-to-Day and On a Loan." *A Matter of Spirit* 123 (Summer 2019) 10–11.

Richards, Brian. "5 Unbelievably Solid Companies." *The Motley Fool* (November 2016). https://www.fool.com/investing/dividends-income/2010/02/27/5-unbelievably-solid-companies.aspx.

Robertson, Kristin. "Southwest Airlines Reveals 5 Culture Lessons." *humansynergistics.com* (May 2018). https://www.humansynergistics.com/blog/culture-university/details/culture-university/2018/05/29/southwest-airlines-reveals-5-culture-lessons.

San Diego County Bar Association. "On René Descartes and Mortgage/Foreclosure Legal Services: Ethics Alert re Participating in Mortgage Modifications." *sdcaba.org* (March 2009). https://www.sdcba.org/?pg=Legal-Ethics_Corner_3_2.

Sandel, Michael J. "What Isn't For Sale?" *theatlantic.com* (April 2012). https://www.theatlantic.com/magazine/archive/2012/04/what-isnt-for-sale/308902.

Sauer, Gerald. "Arbitration is a Flawed Forum That Needs Repair." *law360.com* (February 2020). https://www.law360.com/access-to-justice/articles/1239175/arbitration-is-a-flawed-forum-that-needs-repair?nl_pk=2c24e3b6-72a8-4243-b920-ddf6ce861c14&utm_source=newsletter&utm_medium=email&utm_campaign=access-to-justice.

Shearer, Elisa, and Elizabeth Grieco. "Americans are Wary of the Role Social Media Sites Play in Delivering the News." *journalism.org* (October 2019). https://www.journalism.org/wp-content/uploads/sites/8/2019/09/PJ_2019.09.25_Social-Media-and-News_FINAL.pdf.

Smith, Adam. *The Theory of Moral Sentiments*. Mineola, NY: Dover, 2006.

———. *The Wealth of Nations*. New York: Bantam, 2003.

Society of Professional Journalists. "SPJ Code of Ethics." *spj.org* (September 2014). https://www.spj.org/ethicscode.asp.

Sonnemaker, Tyler. "Jeff Bezos is on track to become a trillionaire by 2026—despite an economy-killing pandemic and losing $38 billion in his recent divorce." *businessinsider.com* (May 14, 2020). https.//www.businessinsider.com/jeff-bezos-on-track-to-become-trillionaire-by-2026-2020-5.

Spencer, Nick. "'Use Worldly Wealth to Gain Friends': Thomas Piketty's Capital and Ideology." *theosthinktank.co.uk* (August 2020) https://www.theosthinktank.co.uk/comment/2020/07/28/use-worldly-wealth-to-gain-friends-thomas-pikettys-capital-and-ideology.

Supreme Court of the United States. *Citizens United v. Federal Election Commission. supremecourt.gov* (January 2010). https://www.supremecourt.gov/opinions/09pdf/08-205.pdf.

———. *Williams-Yulee v. Florida Bar. supremcourt.gov* (April 2015). https://www.supremecourt.gov/opinions/14pdf/13-1499_d18e.pdf.

Thomson, Jeff. "Company Culture Soars at Southwest Airlines." *forbes.com* (December 2018). https://www.forbes.com/sites/jeffthomson/2018/12/18/company-culture-soars-at-southwest-airlines/#28ef7196615f.

Tutu, Desmond M. *No Future Without Forgiveness*. New York: Doubleday, 1999.

University of Massachusetts Amherst. "UMass Amherst Researcher Finds Most People Lie in Everyday Conversation." *umass.edu* (June 2002). https://www.umass.edu/newsoffice/article/umass-amherst-researcher-finds-most-people-lie-everyday-conversation.

Warren, Elizabeth. "Here's How We Can Break Up Big Tech." *medium.com* (March 2019). https://medium.com/@teamwarren/heres-how-we-can-break-up-big-tech-9ad9e0da324c.

Washington, James M., ed. *Martin Luther King Jr., I Have A Dream: Writings & Speeches That Changed The World*. New York: HarperOne, 1992.

Weedon, Jen, William Nuland, and Alex Stamos. "Information Operations and Facebook." (April 2017). https://fbnewsroomus.files.wordpress.com/2017/04/facebook-and-information-operations-v1.pdf.

Williams, Sean. "10 Perks Congress Has That You Don't." *The Motley Fool* (September 2018). https://www.fool.com/investing/general/2013/10/20/10-perks-congress-has-that-you-dont.aspx.

Wolff-Mann, Ethan. "Wells Fargo Scandals: The Complete List." *finance.yahoo.com* (March 2019). https://finance.yahoo.com/news/wells-fargo-scandals-the-complete-timeline-141213414.html.